HUMAN RESOURCE
MANAGEMENT

An Introduction

Trevor Bolton
Anglia Polytechnic University

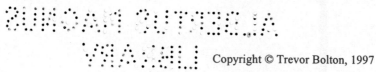

First published 1997

Reprinted 1999

Blackwell Publishers Ltd
108 Cowley Road
Oxford OX4 1JF, UK

Blackwell Publishers Inc
350 Main Street
Malden, Massachusetts 02148, USA

British Library Cataloguing in Publication Data
A CIP catalogue record for this book is available from the British Library

Library of Congress Cataloging in Publication Data
Bolton, Trevor
Human resource management: an ntroduction / Trevor Bolton
p. cm.
Includes bibliographical references and index.
ISBN 0–631–19626–9 (alk. paper)
1. Personnel management. 2. Personnel management—Great Britain.
I. Title.
HF5549.B759 1997
548.3—dc20
96–9236
CIP

Designed by Ian Foulis Associated
Typeset in 10 on 12pt Palatino
by Graphicraft Typesetters Limited, Hong Kong
Printed and bound in Great Britain by MPG Books Ltd, Bodmin, Cornwall

This book is printed on acid-free paper

CONTENTS

LIST OF FIGURES

LIST OF TABLES

PREFACE: HOW TO USE THIS BOOK

It is often said that an organization's most important assets are its people; however, this does not stop many organizations failing miserably to get the best out of their employees. The challenge of having the right people in the right place with the right skills and attitudes, people who are willing and able to work to their best to achieve the objectives of the organization, and all at an affordable cost, is common to all organizations. This book considers a number of the techniques and practices that can be employed by the organization in order to meet that challenge.

The book is written with the actual or aspiring human resource manager in mind, but should also be of value to the general manager and administrator. It should apply equally to those in the private, public and not-for-profit sectors of the economy. It will be especially appropriate for students for whom human resources management, or personnel management, forms a specific part of their study. This might include students on courses leading to the following (or similar) awards:

BA Business Studies / Administration

Other degree courses with an HR element

BTEC HND / C in Business and Finance or Public Administration

DIM and CIM

NVQs 4 and 5 in Management

Institute of Personnel and Development (parts 1 and 2)

IPD Certificate in Personnel Practice (CPP)

Institute of Chartered Secretaries and Administrators

NEBSM

Institute of Administrative Management

Advanced Levels GNVQs

Chartered Institute of Bankers

Each chapter takes a similar approach in that it attempts to give a balanced view of developments of, and current issues surrounding, the key issues in the HR field. By nature the book is wide ranging in its coverage, and although this means that some areas are not covered in great detail, each chapter is supported by an extensive reading list which is designed to direct the student to a variety of texts. These texts fall into three categories: classic works where the development of the subject material is to be found; more general texts which cover the subject in a more accessible way; and a selection of the more topical works which bring the subject up to date in a user-friendly manner.

Chapters are designed to be free-standing, but because of the interrelated nature of the subject matter extensive referencing is given to other chapters. Usually this is detailed at the start of the chapter, although specific references may appear throughout the text.

Each chapter (with the exception of the first and the conclusion) is followed by a short case study with questions designed to be considered either individually or in small groups. The case study applies some of the issues developed in the chapter to real or derived business situations. Following the case study is a section that contains additional questions for consideration. These are designed to be more reflective; and although to a degree they can be answered by reading the chapter, the student will gain more by accessing the references mentioned earlier.

A considerable portion of the text is devoted to matters European. It is my view that the directives and decisions emanating from the various bodies of the European Union form together the greatest challenge to current United Kingdom HR practice. To enable the reader to give the issue of Europe full and balanced consideration, I have devoted one whole chapter to the development, structure and organization of the European Union. It is my experience that relatively few students understand in simple terms the roles and relationships of the major institutions of the European Union, nor understand how European law comes into being and how it is enacted into national law. The chapter covering this vital area is to be found appended at the back of the text. No comparable chapter is included to cover the UK institutions and legal systems – it is assumed that the reader will be familiar with these matters. For those who are not, or are not studying Business Law concurrently with this subject, access and reference to an up-to-date introductory law text will be of considerable value.

In the introductory chapter reference is made to the disciplines which inform HRM – namely, law, social and behavioural science, economics and administrative management. I assume that the reader will have some degree of familiarity with these disciplines. It would be easier, for instance, to fully understand 'reward management' if one already had an appreciation of motivation theory. However, in the chapter covering 'reward' I have given very little attention to motivation, assuming that this will be covered by the reader in other parts of their studies. In a relatively short and focused book such as this it is neither possible, nor desirable, to give full treatment to all of those disciplines informing HRM. To get the best from this book (or indeed any other HRM book), it helps to bring to bear a basic network of understanding, familiarity and appreciation of those supporting disciplines.

In structure the book is designed in part to follow the natural cycle of HRM activity – from planning human resources, to recruitment and selection, training and development, appraisal and reward, welfare, and, finally, redundancy. Throughout the book reference is made to the influence of Europe, but I considered this to be insufficient to do full justice to what many consider to be the most important challenge to United Kingdom HR practice. Chapter 15 (The Influence of Europe: Implications for UK HR Managers) brings together many of the points made in earlier chapters while also setting out some of the significant areas in which new European legislation might be passed. This chapter also tries to introduce issues relating to the challenges for organizations emanating out of the Single European Market – linguistic and cultural challenges, international recruitment, the emergence of the so-called 'international worker' and the methods by which this creation might be rewarded. Chapter 16 looks at HR practice in Germany and Spain, and hopefully the reader will gain some impression of the range of HR systems that exist in Europe. If the reader gets anything from this chapter, then it should be a realization that HR practices in a number of other countries are almost unrecognizable from how we do things in the UK. Chapter 17 looks at training and development in five of our partner countries. This chapter is included to emphasize again the different practices that exist, but also to allow the reader to draw comparisons with chapters 8 and 9, which consider the comparatively unstructured approach that we appear to take to training in the UK. Similar chapters *could* have been prepared covering any of the other topics considered in this book, but training and consideration of national approaches to training do much to illuminate points of comparison and difference between national systems. The logic for the inclusion of chapter 19 is outlined in a preceding paragraph.

Both the male and female pronoun are used throughout the text. However, except when explicitly stated both are equally applicable.

ACKNOWLEDGEMENTS

A number of people have made invaluable contributions to the writing of this book: most significantly my wife Hilary and my daughter Jennifer, without whose support and tolerance the long hours spent at the word-processor would not have been possible. Many of the ideas used have been tested on unwitting students at Anglia Polytechnic University, and their comments and ideas have been very useful. Jackie Stephens of Nottingham Trent University and Christine Renshaw of Cambridge Regional College also provided much-needed constructive criticism and many suggestions for revisions to the manuscript – all ideas were gratefully received. In the latter stages Susan Hughes of Anglia Business School helped clarify my thinking on several important matters. I am also grateful to the editorial staff at Blackwell – Tim Goodfellow and Catriona King for their support and encouragement. Any errors, mistakes or omissions remain, or course, my own.

•CHAPTER•

1

INTRODUCTION

AS A RESULT OF STUDYING THIS CHAPTER YOU SHOULD BE ABLE TO:

- Appreciate the development of the personnel function and the various strands that have contributed to it.

- Consider the weaknesses and criticisms of the traditional personnel function.

- Compare personnel and human resource management as philosophies for the management of employees.

- Examine the main applications of HRM and how they can impact upon business performance.

1. Introduction

Peter Drucker's (1955: 269) classic and often recounted observation, that Personnel saw itself as:

> partly a file clerk's job, partly a housekeeping job, partly a social worker's job and partly 'fire fighting' to head off union trouble or to settle it

touched a nerve among personnel people and neatly summed up what for many was the uncertain, reactive and low-esteem status of the function. Writing thirty years later Tyson and Fell (1986: 8) noted:

> There have been periodic crises among personnel practitioners, a cause of comment among management writers, where the value of personnel management as a specialism has been questioned. The main charge is that personnel specialists have failed to live up to their own claims as 'professionals'. They have been unable to solve problems of managing people, and have failed to gain the necessary authority for success in the role.

More recently still Rob Kuijpers (1995), Chief Executive of DHL, in an article entitled 'Why Time is Running Out for HR, Unless . . .', offered four main criticisms of the HR function: that it did not contribute to the business, that HR did not know what it was like at the 'battle front', that HR could not think strategically, and lastly, that HR had little to show for its work.

Such criticisms and comments are not new, and have added, and continue to add, to the debate about the developing contribution the function can make to organizational success. However, the function has not reached its current position entirely by accident, nor by careful pre-planning. Personnel is without doubt a product of its history, and it is impossible to fully understand current issues and controversies without some appreciation of how, and from where, the function has developed.

2. The Historical Context in the UK

Many would trace the personnel function back to the middle years of the last century, and the introduction by some benevolent employers of company housing, rudimentary company health care and company schools for families. This was overseen and managed by what were known as welfare workers. Their role, acting as an intermediary between the employer and worker, was to ensure a suitable and ongoing supply of labour to keep the 'wheels of industry turning'. Additionally many Quaker-owned businesses tried to demonstrate that the search for profit was not necessarily at the expense of the individual worker. Indeed, for a number of organizations the provision of 'welfare' was fundamental to their existence, for it allowed the development of the spiritual, moral and religious dimensions of the employee and his or her family.

The need for professionalism in the management of organizations became increasingly apparent as the nineteenth century progressed and as organizations became larger and more complex. On the human side, the legalization of trade unions in 1871 established the need to put in place systems for negotiation, and the management of relations with the representatives of labour.

The British government's concern about the labour force of the country was never greater than when it was recruiting soldiers for the Crimea and Boer wars. Many of the young men who wished to enlist were found to have significant health and medical problems rendering them unsuitable to fight. This caused a great outcry about the state of the nation's youth – it made the front pages of most national newspapers – and there were calls for the government to act positively to do something to improve the situation, for fear that Britain could not defend her empire.

The increasingly active role taken by labour and its representatives, and the government's recognition of its social responsibility towards the workforce, led to the passing of the National Insurance Act in 1911. For the first time a national insurance scheme made (minimal) provision for workers during times of unemployment and sickness. In 1916 the British government established a Ministry of Labour, which of course became the Department of Employment and has now been absorbed into the Department for Education and Employment. Having a Ministry of Labour meant that the 'macro' workforce issues could be properly represented in and considered by government. Such issues would concern training, women in the workplace, health and safety, the rights of trade unions and many more.

The post-war consensus – that a fundamental responsibility of government was to maintain full employment – together with the 1944

Education Act and the establishment of the National Health Service in 1948, both of which aimed to produce a workforce for Britain that was educated and healthy, set the scene for the next thirty years, before an enemy worse than unemployment was identified in the mid 1970s: namely, inflation. With this came a retreat by government in setting policies and priorities for the workforce. The National Training Levy was scrapped and with it most of the National Training Boards who had done so much to develop a national training strategy for the workforce. With the exception of trade union reform the government tried to back away from interfering in the relationship between employers and employees, claiming to prefer instead to let both parties act in what they perceived to be their own best interests, rather than following the dictate of government. This was a path followed by very few of our European partners – most governments continued (and still do) to work closely with employers and unions to produce strategic policies for the development of their workforce. In this way governments worked to try to ensure that the skill base of their workforce was high and suitable for the requirements of new and developing industries.

The post-war years saw the passing of more legislation relating to employment than at any other time in British history. This legislation related to almost all parts of the relationship between the employer and employee, including health and safety, equal opportunities, equal pay, redundancy, employment protection, the rights and responsibilities of trade unions, to name but a few. Between 1970 and 1990 alone over twenty pieces of legislation concerning employment-related matters passed into law. Clearly the law governing the relationship between employer and employee is a complex matter.

During this time the United Kingdom also entered into a number of international agreements, many of which also had implications for employment. The most significant of these was the decision to join the European Economic Community in 1973. (See chapters 15, 16, 17.)

The personnel function, then, has developed out of a number of traditions (see Tyson and Fell 1986), not all of which are mutually compatible:

a. The welfare tradition

The welfare tradition is predicated on the notion that much of the work of personnel staff is conducted away from the concerns of the business. That is, that personnel managers operating in the welfare area did not align themselves with the management of the organization, but saw their prime responsibility to be to employees. Today the welfare side of the personnel function would include occupational health and employee counselling services.

b. The industrial relations tradition

This developed out of the legalization of the trade unions in the last century, and came to prominence in the 1960s and 1970s as the power and influence of the unions reached its peak. Here the personnel manager was able to act as a mediator, conciliator and sometimes arbitrator between the two sides in any dispute. It was noted and regarded with some suspicion, the close working relationship that some personnel managers were able to maintain with some trade unions officials, even during and after quite acrimonious disputes, leading some to voice the concern that Personnel straddled an uneasy divide, between management and workforce.

c.   The control of labour tradition

As the number of staff employed by organizations has increased, those employed possess a wider range of skills, and the methods and places where and by which work is performed have also increased, the need for a bureaucracy to control, monitor and support this workplace activity has also grown. Personnel procedures have had to be developed to monitor work, record time-keeping, absence, sickness, holidays and many other aspects of workplace life.

d.   The professional tradition

Particularly since the Second World War the Institute of Personnel Management (now known as the Institute of Personnel and Development) has tried to make a profession out of the work of the personnel manager. To this end it has established and developed a body of knowledge from which it has written programmes of learning and set examinations, allowing successful students the opportunity to become 'qualified personnel managers'. Although many employers value the IPD qualification, it is still beyond doubt that many successful personnel managers are not specifically qualified, and lack of qualification has rarely been seen as a barrier to practice.

The body of knowledge that makes up Personnel is drawn from at least four disciplines and ideally needs to be located in the context of an appreciation of the wider business environment, issues and concerns (see figure 1.1).

Figure 1.1 illustrates the range of skills and knowledge required

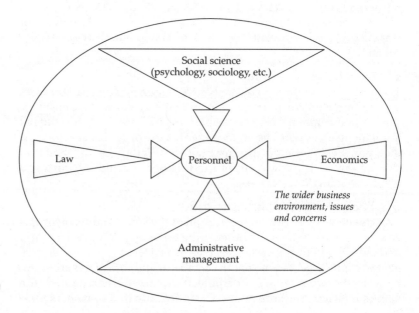

Figure 1.1
The disciplines informing personnel

of the personnel manager. These include the need to be able to apply principles of *behavioural science* to the benefit of organizational systems such as rewards, communications and appraisal. The manager will also need to be well versed in *employment law* and how it relates to employment, equal opportunities, dismissal and workplace discipline. Additionally the manager will need to be a competent *administrator* and leader, using the most appropriate systems to ensure the monitoring and compliance with organizational policies relating to absence, annual leave, sickness and staff utilization. A knowledge of *economics* will also assist with manpower planning, predicting changes in the demand for and supply of labour, and the flows of labour through the organization. The application of this knowledge must be seen in the context of the wider business environment and the major issues and concerns impacting upon the organization. And finally, the personnel manager must be proactive, addressing not only current problems but identifying future opportunities and challenges and putting into place systems, policies and procedures to take the organization forward.

Arguably, it is the baggage of the past that has inhibited Personnel from taking as full and active a part in the strategic-level operation of the organization as many would wish.

3. Personnel Management – A Contradiction in Terms?

The four traditions which have contributed to Personnel raise a number of interesting questions about its role and functions. Most notably, 'to whom is Personnel responsible?' The welfare tradition identifies Personnel firmly with its 'clients', i.e. the workforce, while the industrial relations tradition sees Personnel as occupying some central position, somewhere between management and unions, or stranded on the middle ground, as some have said. This is not a comfortable position to occupy and led to Personnel being regarded with suspicion by both sides of industry.

The tradition of Personnel as an integral part of the central management function is a weak one, and given the predispositions and constraints discussed above, one that was unlikely to develop further. The question posed in the title of this section 'Personnel Management – A Contradiction in Terms?', is not a flippant one. How can the personnel function wish to be regarded as a serious player at the top table when it is far from certain that Personnel's aims and objectives are congruent with the rest of the senior management team?

The answer to this question lies in part in the reappraisal of the underlying philosophy of personnel that occurred in the late 1970s and early 1980s, and the emergence of what is now called 'human resource management'.

4. Human Resource Management

Human resource management (HRM) as a body of management thought developed in the late 1970s and early 1980s, and can be linked to the coming together of a number of factors: a reassertion of the right of management to manage, industrial restructuring, recession, changes in international competition, and in Britain, the emergence of a government (in 1979) committed to reappraising the relationship between labour and capital. These changes have gone hand in hand with the statement and restatement, that successful organizations are those that are best able to harness the power of their human resources to achieve extraordinary things (see Deal and Kennedy 1988, Peters and Waterman 1982, Moss Kanter 1984, and Peters 1988, to name but a few).

This position of change and statement of the central importance of the human resource, led organizations to seek new ways in which to pursue objectives that put people at the front of that change, while at the same time not allowing it to become entirely Personnel driven.

As managers 'regained control' of their organizations, due in no small measure to the barrage of legislation in the early 1980s restricting the power of trade unions, managers took the opportunity to reduce costs (causing widespread job loss), restructure organizations (flattening hierarchies) and introduce systems of greater accountability and control. The newly flattened hierarchies, the thinned out supervisory levels, the new emphasis on quality and the customer, on accountability and control, all gave rise to the need for a new approach to the management of people. The new approach would have a number of features not enjoyed by the 'personnel' model. It would need to encourage flexibility, adaptability, greater commitment and the willingness to take on greater responsibility and learn new skills. It would need to encompass reward systems that were biased in favour of the individual and which recognized individual contribution rather than being comprised of monolithic systems rewarding all equally for their unequal contributions. The new philosophy that emerged was 'human resource management', and while no widely agreed definition exists for this new beast, Storey (1992) has identified a number of major differences between the new HRM model and the personnel model. Some of the significant differences are summarized in table 1.1.

So, both philosophically and practically, personnel management and HRM are very different. Personnel lays a greater emphasis on standardization, proceduralization, rules and regulations. HRM is concerned to promote flexibility, responsibility, and shared goals and objectives, and aims to reward according to individual performance.

So what is the new philosophy of management that HRM embraces? Molander and Winterton (1995: 15) claim that:

> Their interests are clearly managerial. The liberalism of the 1950s and 1960s has been replaced by a new profit-orientated pragmatism which will lead the organization to adopt those HR policies and behaviours which contribute most successfully to profitability.

5. Human Resource Management Issues

Human resource management is not something that can be left to the professionals (that is, to the HR manager). To be effective it must permeate the whole organization, be 'owned' by all managers and

Dimension	Personnel model	HRM model
Contract of employment	Careful delineation of written contracts	Aims to go 'beyond contract'
Rules	Importance of devising clear rules	'Can-do' outlook, impatience with rules
Nature of relations	Pluralist	Unitary
Conflict	Institutionalized	De-emphasized
Key relationships	Labour–management	Business–customer
Corporate plan	Marginal to	Integrated
Pay	Job evaluation, multiple fixed grades	Performance-related, few if any grades
Conditions	Separately negotiated	Harmonization
Labour–management	Collective bargaining contracts	Towards individual contracts
Training and development	Controlled access to courses	Learning organizations

Table 1.1
Some significant
differences between
personnel and HRM

Source: after Storey 1992.

influence the attitudes, performance and motivation of all employees. It must operate in a number of ways in the organization and must be felt in all places. Significantly, and unlike personnel management, it needs to be integrated into the strategic level of organizations to be fully successful. So, HRM is an activity for strategic managers, line managers and for HR professionals. Its applications can be seen in a number of areas:

Strategic planning   It is difficult to imagine that any business decision of any real significance can be taken without due reference to the human resource implications. Many decisions will have implications for training, staff deployment, manpower planning and reward. Harrison (1995: 35) defines the strategic-level contribution of HRM as:

> the overall and coherent long-term planning and shorter term management, control and monitoring of an organization's human resources so as to gain from them maximum added value and to best position them to achieve the organization's corporate goals and mission.

Planning human resources   If employees are central to the success of the organization, then how the actual and potential workforce must develop in order to meet current and future challenges is of vital importance. The future demand for labour, the supply of labour within the economy and the speed and methods by which labour will flow through the organization will need to be taken into account. This will involve HR professionals working closely with colleagues in line management and with strategic planners.

Recruitment and selection   Working with strategists and line managers, HR specialists will need to develop recruitment and selection policies and practices that are congruent with the wider and long-term aims of the organization. That is, those employed now should not be employed with only the short term in mind. In times of rapid product obsolescence, changing and developing technologies and new and emerging patterns of work, leadership and reward, technical profi-ciency alone will never be a sufficient criterion for employment. Allied to technical proficiency must be appropriate attitudes and a willing-ness to accept change as the normal state of being. The requirement is for recruitment and selection policies that are both far-sighted and owned and implemented by line managers.

Rewards management   HR managers will need to keep themselves apprised of reward systems new and emerging, data and statistics con-cerning pay and its management, and trends in conditions of service. All such information will be needed by the HR managers to enable them to make a contribution to the strategic-level debate concerning how the organization should achieve its goals through its people. Reward management policies are not cast in stone, and not only do they tend to corrupt over time, they will also need fine-tuning and ultimately replacing as the objectives and policies of the organization change.

Training   The development and use of analytical appraisal methods as well as the undertaking of regular reviews of departmental progress, performance and challenges should allow the line manager to identify the training needs of his subordinates. The HR specialist will have an input into the form and framework within which this training needs identification will take place, and will contribute to the formulation of the corporate training plan. This will take account of short-, medium-and long-term corporate objectives, and may well involve some rationing of training resources as they are allocated to priority areas. However, care should be taken for the HR specialist not to become a rationer of the training effort. Individuals and their managers should 'own' their training needs, and be encouraged – and indeed expected – to take proactive steps to address them, rather than patiently waiting for their turn in the training budget queue.

To summarize, a passage from Molander and Winterton (1995: 15):

> It is hoped that the reader will have gathered that human resource management is a cooperative, strategic and hard-headed activity staffed by managers committed to the financial success of the organization. The role of honest broker, adopted in the past by personnel managers anxious to see themselves as poised between manager and worker, interpreting the one to the other, has long gone. So has the image of the personnel officer as the good fairy, primarily protecting the interests of the non-managerial employee.

6. Conclusion

This text draws much from the HRM philosophy. It allies 'personnel' firmly with management in terms of its loyalty, disposition and orientation. The techniques and ideas described and discussed in this book are similar to those that appear in many traditional personnel texts, except that in all cases the attempt is made to apply to them the principles of HRM. Many recent HRM texts fail to give adequate consideration to the operational side of the discipline, and how HRM manifests itself in the day-to-day activities of practitioners. This book gives little consideration to philosophical or strategic notions of HRM, preferring instead to look at its applications to practical HR issues and problems – for instance, employee resourcing (recruitment and selection), employee development (training, and development) – and to consider some of the issues relating to control, such as law and discipline, as well as appraisal and reward.

Throughout the book reference is made to the influence of Europe and particularly the European Union – indeed several chapters are devoted to it. This book, then, sets the discipline of Human Resources Management in the context of the problems and issues facing practitioners, and gives due attention to some of the significant challenges that are current within the environment. It is the view of the author that Europe is preeminent among those challenges, and it is hoped that the four chapters dedicated to Europe will give some flavour not only of how the European Union is continuing to provide challenges for practitioners, but also of the connotations for the free movement of labour of the Single European Market, and of how practice is conducted in some of our partner countries. From each of these human resource managers must learn and adapt their policies and practices to allow effective competition with not only the best in Europe, but increasingly the best in the world. These are challenges that cannot be shirked, if HRM is to live up to the top billing that it has given itself.

QUESTIONS FOR FURTHER CONSIDERATION

1. What are the major factors that lead to the reappraisal of personnel management?

2. What is human resource management, and what are the principal differences between it and personnel management?

3. Consider the personnel function in your own organization (or one with which you are familiar). What is it called, and does it follow the personnel or HR philosophy? Refer to table 1.1 for guidance.

4. Consider the personnel or HR function in relation to the following statement:

   There has grown a whole level of administration where the activity of managers is so remote from risk bearing action that it is not possible to assess their work by showing any directly related adjustment to revenue, profit or costs as a consequence of their behaviour. (Tyson and Fell 1986)

5. Many employers who espouse the HRM philosophy would argue that the contract of employment is a legal necessity rather than an operational document. That is, they would expect the employee to show greater commitment and accept more responsibility above and beyond their contractual duties. How far can organizations expect employees to go 'beyond contract' in order to fulfil their jobs?

•REFERENCES•

Connock S (1991)
HR VISION: MANAGING A QUALITY WORKFORCE
London, Institute of Personnel Management.

Deal T & Kennedy A (1988)
CORPORATE CULTURE: THE RITES AND RITUALS OF CORPORATE LIFE
London, Penguin.

Drucker P (1955)
THE PRACTICE OF MANAGEMENT
London, Harper & Row.

Farnham D (1984)
PERSONNEL IN CONTEXT
London, Institute of Personnel Management.

Gilder G (1986)
THE SPIRIT OF ENTERPRISE
London, Penguin.

Goss D (1994)
PRINCIPLES OF HUMAN RESOURCE MANAGEMENT
London, Routledge.

Harrison R (1995)
HUMAN RESOURCE MANAGEMENT: ISSUES AND STRATEGIES
Wokingham, Surrey, Addison-Wesley.

Kuijpers R (1995)
Why Time is Running Out for HR, Unless . . .
People Management, May.

Molander C & Winterton J (1995)
MANAGING HUMAN RESOURCES
London, Routledge.

Moss Kanter, R (1984)
THE CHANGE MASTERS
London, Allen and Unwin.

Pascale R & Athos A (1981)
THE ART OF JAPANESE MANAGEMENT
London, Penguin.

Peters T (1988)
THRIVING ON CHAOS: HANDBOOK FOR A MANAGERIAL REVOLUTION
London, Macmillan.

Peters T & Waterman R (1982)
IN SEARCH OF EXCELLENCE
New York, Harper & Row.

Storey J (1989)
NEW PERSPECTIVES ON HUMAN RESOURCE MANAGEMENT
London, Routledge.

Storey J (1992)
DEVELOPMENTS IN THE MANAGEMENT OF HUMAN RESOURCES
Oxford, Blackwell.

Storey J (1995)
HUMAN RESOURCE MANAGEMENT: A CRITICAL TEXT
London, Routledge.

Tyson S & Fell A (1986)
EVALUATING THE PERSONNEL FUNCTION
London, Hutchinson.

·CHAPTER·

2

PLANNING HUMAN RESOURCES

AS A RESULT OF STUDYING THIS CHAPTER YOU SHOULD BE ABLE TO:

- Consider the importance of manpower planning for organizations.

- Identify the main components of the manpower plan and the problems inherent in estimating future manpower requirements.

- Show an appreciation of the major criticisms of manpower planning as a business tool.

- Consider the problems facing human resource practitioners in contributing to corporate strategy formulation.

- Assess the significance of human resource planning as an alternative to manpower planning.

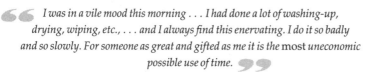

I was in a vile mood this morning . . . I had done a lot of washing-up, drying, wiping, etc., . . . and I always find this enervating. I do it so badly and so slowly. For someone as great and gifted as me it is the most *uneconomic possible use of time.*

Alan Clark, *Diaries*

1. Introduction

The Institute of Personnel Management (IPM – of late, the Institute of Personnel and Development) (IPD 1975: 12) have defined manpower planning as:

> The systematic and continuous process of analysing an organization's human resource needs under changing conditions and developing personnel policies appropriate to the longer term effectiveness of the organization. It is an integral part of corporate planning and budgeting procedures since human resource costs and forecasts both affect and are affected by longer term corporate plans.

However Livy (1988: 20) offers a somewhat broader definition and lays greater emphasis on the wider labour market and states that additionally:

> an organization must consider . . . the external environment (competition from other employers in product and labour markets;

the external supply of labour; wage trends; and government policies affecting employment).

He expands the definition to include the internal labour market (1988: 20), stating that:

> forecasts of likely wastage (labour turnover) *and* . . . forecasts of manpower flow through hierarchical levels in the organization according to promotion and development policies (including assessments of qualitative changes in manpower stock). [my italics]

It can more simply be defined as 'having the right people, with the right skills, in the right place, at the right time, and at the right price'.

Manpower planning is a dynamic area of human resource management in that it attempts to analyse current manpower strengths and weaknesses, to consider future manpower needs and project how those needs should be met from both inside and outside the organization. It must consider at least two labour markets – that which exists within the organization (i.e. current employees), and that which exists outside the organization (i.e. the wider, or external, labour market). It needs to take account of predicted changes in the organization's activities as well as changing methods of working. Not surprisingly, it is considered to be an imperfect science and has in the past been the subject of much criticism. Whatever its imperfections, it is inconceivable that large employers can afford to ignore manpower planning.

In September 1995 the world of football was thrown into turmoil by a decision of the European Court. The Court decided that for football clubs to demand a transfer fee for players who had reached the end of their contracts was illegal. The decision arose out of a five-year battle by Belgian footballer Jean-Marc Bosman, whose club, RFC Liège, refused to let him transfer to another club at the end of his contract. The Court decision, which applies across the whole of the European Union, has implications for many smaller clubs, who depend upon spotting and developing young or raw talent to provide revenue from transfer income to fund day-to-day activities. The new law will allow players to negotiate their own transfers, and on their own terms, and may result in far higher salaries being paid to the best players. In the longer term it may also drastically cut the number of full-time professional footballers in the lower divisions as clubs recruit for their own current needs, rather than also trying to develop young players for the future.

2. Lessons From Neo-classical Microeconomics

Consideration of the supply of labour has traditionally been the preserve of the labour economist. However, to attempt to construct a manpower plan without considering both the demand and supply sides of the equation would be foolhardy indeed; and so the human resource practitioner must have knowledge of the forces that affect labour.

Traditional theories of labour supply are derived from neoclassical economics which developed models (principally that of 'perfect' competition) that state that as individuals we act rationally in our decision-making. That is, we know what is in our own best interests and therefore act accordingly. One implication of this is that workers will make decisions between work and leisure time, i.e., the cost to the worker of working overtime is reduced leisure time, and as leisure time is reduced its perceived value will increase. To compensate for the loss of this high-value time the employer will be required to pay enhanced rates for additional hours of work.

Employers can also be considered to be rational economic maximizers. That is, they will employ that combination of fixed (land and capital) and variable (labour) factors of production that will maximize their revenue in relation to their costs. This is often called the 'least-cost combination' of factors of production. It should be noted, however, that the demand for labour is a derived demand – workers themselves are not in demand but are instead required for the skills and abilities that they bring with them. So, for example, a plumber is not in demand for himself but for the skills of plumbing that he is able to perform.

The model of the competitive labour market is similar to other models of perfect competition and like those models is built on a number of assumptions. These would include the following (for a fuller explanation the reader should refer to an appropriate economics text, such as Beardshaw – see chapter end for full reference):

a. There are a number of buyers (employers) and sellers (workers) of labour, each so small that they are unable to influence the market price of labour.

b. All buyers and sellers must have perfect information with regard to the market, so, for instance, workers would know of all job vacancies and the pay on offer, while employers would know of the wages offered by other employers.

c. Labour is perfectly mobile, both occupationally and geographically, and there are no restrictions on either hiring or firing labour.

d. All workers and all jobs are homogeneous (i.e. workers all possess the same skills, all employers require those same skills).

e. There are no restrictions on either entry into, nor exit from, the market.

f. The only cost of hiring labour is the wage rate – there are no other costs of either recruitment or redundancy.

Given these conditions there can be only one single wage rate, beyond the influence of any single buyer or seller. If different wage rates were offered by different employers then the perfect knowledge condition would mean that many employees would put themselves forward for the position, competing the price down. This is illustrated in figure 2.1, which plots the relationship between the demand for labour and the price of labour.

The relationship is depicted as a horizontal straight line representing the fact that all labour will be employed at the wage rate (W). The decision as to how much labour will be employed will be determined by both short- and long-term considerations. In the short term (which is

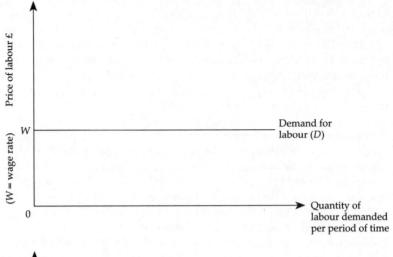

Figure 2.1
The demand for labour
under conditions of
perfect competition

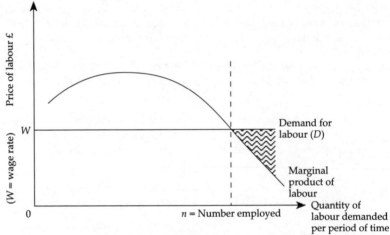

Figure 2.2
Diminishing marginal
productivity of labour

defined as the time period during which fixed factors of production, i.e.
capital, cannot be increased) employment levels will be determined by
the law of diminishing marginal returns, which states that as successive
units of a variable factor of production (i.e. labour) are added to fixed
factors of production (i.e. capital) then output will rise to a point and
then diminish. This indicates that up to a point the addition of more
units of labour (i.e. workers) to capital (i.e. a factory) will increase the
output of the factory. Beyond that point the capital is insufficient to support the additional labour (e.g. there are not enough machines for
everybody to work), and so output per worker will gradually diminish,
and eventually overall output will fall as the additional workers get in
the way of the productive ones. At this point output will diminish. This
is illustrated in figure 2.2.

    Neo-classical economics tells us that employers will take on
workers up to the point where the marginal cost of employing an additional worker is equal to the marginal revenue product of that labour.
(Marginal revenue product is the value of the output of each additional

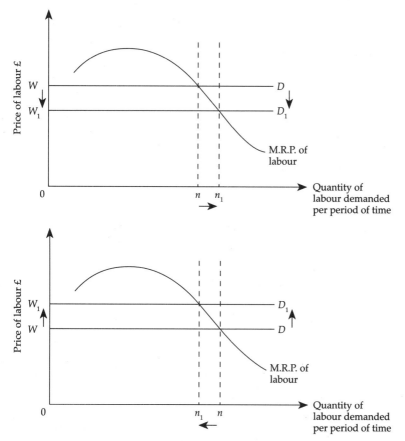

Figure 2.3
Employment and falling wage rate

Figure 2.4
Employment and rising wage rate

worker employed). This is illustrated in figure 2.2 by the dotted vertical line marked n. To the right of this point (the shaded area) the two lines diverge, indicating that the cost of employing labour remains constant (marginal cost) while the marginal revenue product of that labour has fallen below the cost of employment.

In the longer term organizations are able to vary the amount of capital (machinery) and land also. This may involve the use of new technologies and the replacement of labour with capital.

3. Criticisms of Neo-classical Theories

One of the predictions of neo-classical theory is that there is an inverse relationship between the number of workers employed and the price of labour (the wage rate). So, if the price of labour falls the demand for labour will rise and vice versa. See figures 2.3 and 2.4. This is quickly refuted by the evidence of labour market statistics (see table 2.1).

The table indicates that during the period 1987–93 unemployment first fell and then grew, while pay continued to increase for those in jobs. This was not an exceptional period. This illustrates the point that there is little real correlation between the wage rate and the level of employment.

Year	Unemployment (000s)	Average earning index (1988 = 100)
1987	2,807	93.5
1988	2,275	100.0
1989	1,784	110.3
1990	1,623	121.2
1991	2,287	130.5
1992	2,770	137.8
1993	2,900	140.1

Table 2.1
Unemployment and
average earnings
1987–1993

Source: *Barclays Economic Review*, second quarter, 1994.

The tendency of the wage rate to drift upwards also questions another prediction of the neo-classicists: that there exists a market clearing wage rate at which no unemployment would exist. All the evidence suggests that the labour market is too inflexible to allow this to happen. The existence of widespread and persistent unemployment does not appear to have the effect of driving down wage rates. This apparent rigidity in the labour market has received much attention. The argument goes that if in times of surplus the price of oranges will fall to the market clearing price why not the price of labour? The answers to this puzzle call into question many of the assumptions that the neo-classicists make about the labour market. These reasons include:

a. Labour is not particularly mobile, neither geographically nor occupationally, leading to a regional imbalance in employment and shortages of skills even in times of recession.

b. The provision of highly skilled or technical personnel has a long lead time. This places curbs on the speed of possible employee replacement.

c. Protective employment legislation and the desire to hang on to staff even in times of economic downturn has the effect of making labour a 'semi-fixed' factor of production, reducing the scope and flexibility for organizations to change their employee numbers.

d. To consider employees as merely factors of production is to ignore the possible impact of policies designed to motivate and reward staff for individual performance. Neo-classical economics does not consider employees as individuals, but as homogeneous.

Many organizations are monopoly employers for certain groups of workers. For instance, the Army is almost the only employer of soldiers. To talk of a 'market' for soldiers under these circumstances would seem absurd. At the other end of the spectrum some individuals offer skills for which they hold the monopoly. These would include the most popular entertainers, who are able to demand a wage rate that reflects the uniqueness of their talents.

Restrictions apply to entering some labour markets. These include teaching, airline pilots and accountancy. All (at least in some aspects of their work) require specialist qualifications which are usually acquired over time. These barriers to entry can affect both the supply of labour and the wage rate.

Trade unions and employers associations act to influence the market price of labour through the use of their collective power. This has led to the development of institutional theories of labour markets which claim that the labour market is dominated not by individual workers and employers acting in their own perceived best interests but by collective action by workers and employers acting to formulate preferences that reflect some collective position. This of course does include trade union industrial action, but has a more general manifestation in the way that all workers will judge their own rates of pay in comparison with the pay of other groups and individuals around them. Thus a notion of 'fairness' is developed in which workers are less concerned about their absolute levels of pay but more about their comparative rate.

Government also has a major influence over pay: both as a significant direct employer, and via the influence it is able to exert over levels of pay of staff that it does not directly employ but ultimately picks up the tab for – for example, teachers, local government staff, NHS trust staff, etc.

The government also sets benefit levels for those without work, and so influences the level of pay below which it is not worthwhile for the individual to seek work.

4. Lessons for the Human Resource Practitioner

Much of this discussion of the economics of the labour market will appear abstract to the HR manager. However, all HR managers involved in recruitment will need to consider the following influences on the supply of labour and the possible consequences for wage rates:

a. Changing educational patterns – staying on rates at school, progression into and out of universities. The changing skills and aspirations of those entering the labour market.

b. The availability of skills within the catchment area of the company.

c. Local unemployment rates.

d. Current and future competition for staff from other local employers.

e. Changes in employee protection.

f. The influence of government training schemes, such as Youth Training (YT) and adult training and re-training.

g. Changes in demands for key categories of workers – such as graduates, technicians, accountants.

h. The general attractiveness of both the company as a place to work and the area as a place to live. This would include the relative price and availability of housing, transport links, shopping and recreational facilities.

Barclays Bank have been accused of planning to use schoolchildren as casual, cheap labour, after the bank announced that it was considering taking on sixth-formers to do routine and administrative work. It is envisaged that the students would work for a couple of hours at a time, up to three times a week and be paid £4 per hour. The bank has said that it sees the plan as an opportunity to develop stronger links with local schools and give paid work-experience to local students. Banking unions claim that the move comes in response to widespread staff shortages, branch closure and redundancy. It is estimated that since 1991 Barclays has closed 500 branches and reduced its workforce from 83,000 to 65,000. (Reported in the *Guardian*, 8 Aug. 1995.)

5. The Internal Labour Market

Consideration of the labour market would be incomplete without giving due attention to the internal labour market that exists in all organizations. The internal labour market concerns the supply and management of, and the demand for, the existing workforce of the organization. It must take account of the ambitions and aspirations of the workforce, their turnover and wastage rates, their current levels of skill and the levels of skill required both now and in the future. Consideration of the internal labour market is often undertaken using a regular manpower audit, which will attempt to profile the workforce on the following dimensions:

Skills Do the skills of the workforce reflect both the current and future needs of the organization? Deficiencies should be identified and quantified. This would be undertaken via training needs analysis, analysis of personnel records, performance appraisal returns, data returns from line managers and trend analysis from activity levels.

Performance Consideration of the level of performance of the various groups of workers should be made. This will typically be via performance appraisal.

Flexibility The degree of flexibility that exists in the workforce should be examined. Increasingly organizations are expecting their employees to be more skilled, more flexible and more proactive in their working lives. Quite clearly flexibility is often associated with the culture that exists in an organization. This cannot be ignored, and indeed will be an important factor in the equation.

Age What is the age profile of the workforce? Have any departments, occupations or grades any age bottlenecks? For instance, if the average age of staff employed in the accounts department was 58 years this might well require some rapid remedial action. It might be considered that an ideal age distribution would be one that has an even spread of ages throughout the organization. This generality, however, would be dependent upon the organization under consideration. For instance, the age profile of supermarket staff might simply reflect the fact that it employs a large number of young part-time workers.

Promotability How ready are junior members of the workforce to step into the shoes of their seniors? Succession planning is a difficult 'game', but normal wastage will require that senior positions will need to be filled, and often from within the organization. Consideration of developmental training needs must be undertaken.

Labour turnover Turnover rates for all groups of staff should be monitored. Monitoring should take place by age, length of service, department, occupation and any other relevant factors. Turnover rates tend to be highest among those groups who have skills that are in short supply, and among the young and also comparatively new staff. High turnover rates will not be a problem if staff can be cheaply and efficiently replaced. However even low turnover rates will be of concern if it is difficult or expensive to replace staff, or if training new staff takes some time. Careful monitoring of turnover should be the norm. The standard method for calculation of turnover is set out below:

$$\frac{\text{No. of leavers (during year)}}{\text{Average number of people employed during the year}} \times 100$$

= labour turnover

This is a crude measure because it tells you little either about the leavers (e.g. a 50 per cent turnover rate could have been achieved by either half the workforce being replaced during the course of the year or by 10 per cent of the workforce being replaced 5 times each), or about those who have stayed. To help overcome this problem many organizations will also consider the 'labour stability index'. This is calculated as set out below:

$$\frac{\text{No. of employees with one or more years' service}}{\text{No. of people employed at the beginning of the year}} \times 100$$

= % stability

This measure is used to calculate how many staff have been in the employ of the organization for at least one year. Many organizations will see value in calculating a stability index for various lengths of service to reflect the needs of their industry. In some organizations employees become most valued after several years of service. Stability amongst this group would be most essential and should therefore be very carefully monitored.

Sickness rates If employees take time off sick this will have a consequent effect on, and cost for, employers. The higher the level of sickness, the greater the cost, particularly if temporary staff or overtime must be used to complete work. Table 2.2 is an extract from a report in *Personnel Today* which details absence in Government departments in 1994.

5.1 The 'induction crisis'
Many organizations can identify what is commonly called the 'induction crisis'. This is the tendency for turnover to be highest among that

Department	Days lost in past year	Days lost as % of days worked
Defence	959,828	3.2
Education	13,926	3.5
Employment	636,709	4.8
Health	69,363	6.2
National Heritage	2,190	2.7
Social Security	1,117,263	5.4

Table 2.2
Sickness absence across
major UK government
departments

Source: amended from *Personnel Today*, 7 Sept. 1994.

group of workers who have been employed the shortest time. It is often particularly acute with young workers. This will be of concern where, for instance, recruitment costs are high, if considerable training is necessary, or if training opportunities occur only at fixed points in the year. A number of explanations have been put forward for this so-called crisis. These include:

a. poor recruitment practice – being less than honest in describing a job to a potential recruit;

b. the culture shock associated with being employed in a new/different organization;

c. the difficulties of being socialized into a new work group.

The problems can be partially overcome by the design and implementation of a sound induction programme. For further discussion see chapter 7, entitled 'The New Employee'.

5.2 Survival rates
Another method by which manpower planners analyse manpower is by examining what is called the 'survival rate'. So, for instance the 'half-life survival rate' would consider the length of time taken for half of a cohort of recruits to leave. Alternatively, consideration of the number of a cohort remaining at a number of points in time (e.g. 3 months, 6 months, 1 year etc.) is also of value. This technique would be suitable for those organizations who have large numbers of staff starting their employment on the same day. This might include the armed forces or the police force.

5.3 Equal opportunities monitoring
The manpower audit is an ideal opportunity to assess the degree of success of the organization's plans towards achieving equality of opportunity. Equality of opportunity in recruitment should be matched by equality of opportunity in progression through the organization. For a fuller discussion see chapter 6.

The answers deduced from the examination of the above questions should allow manpower planners to draw up a profile of the current state of the organization's manpower stock and the trends (e.g. leavers, retirers, etc.) that exist within it. It should be matched against the demand forecast for labour. This should allow the identification and

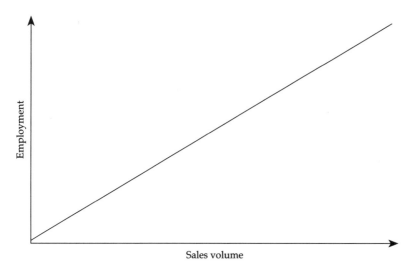

Figure 2.5
Possible relationship between economic activity and employment

quantification of labour shortages and surpluses. In practice it is more likely that it will reveal that the organization has both surpluses and shortages in different areas. If this is the case it will be necessary to reconcile the two and decide how the appropriate adjustments are to be made. This might be through training, redundancy, recruitment or redeployment, or more likely, a combination of all four.

6. The Demand for Manpower

Many of the models for planning the demand for manpower assume that there is a direct correlation between the level of economic activity in an organization and the employment level in that organization (see figure 2.5). While the two are intimately linked many traditional models fail to take account of the other factors that can influence the efficiency with which labour is utilized. This is fully discussed in the next section.

A number of the critics of manpower planning also point to the uncertainty of the economic future as a reason why manpower planning is bound to fail. This criticism contains more than a grain of truth. The future direction and success of the economy is uncertain, and for large organizations operating in global markets the number of variables to consider is immense. Many variables, for instance the policies of foreign governments, are beyond their control or influence. A seemingly minor change of policy taken by a government in a far-flung land can have unforeseen consequences for employment within any particular company. Given even these constraints it is still inconceivable that an organization of any size would fail to plan its manpower in at least a rudimentary manner, for the consequences of not so doing can be considerable.

Some of the more complex statistical models, often called Markov models, try to predict manpower flows (see figure 2.6) based on the age of employees, wastage rates, length of service and career progression. The model cannot take account of 'shocks and unplanned-for

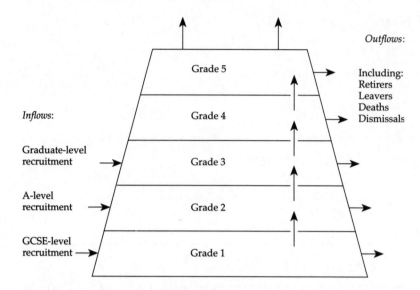

Figure 2.6
Model of manpower flow through an organization

disturbances', but given stable conditions – such as those which, theoretically at least, used to exist in the armed forces, the civil service, local government and the health service – planned recruitment could be projected for a number of years to come.

More sophisticated models, for instance those produced by the Institute of Manpower Studies (e.g. Microprospect, IMS Wasp, IMS Monitor), allow greater scope for questioning, and for asking 'what if?' along spreadsheet lines. A good manpower planning model should:

a. aid understanding of the situation and the variables involved, and increase knowledge of the likely outcome of any decision that is made;

b. allow 'what if' questions to be asked, to aid the generation of new ideas;

c. allow alternative courses of action to be evaluated.

Figure 2.7 usefully illustrates how manpower planning can be undertaken in organizations.

7. The Weaknesses of Manpower Planning

Two of the major weaknesses of manpower planning have been outlined in the preceding section. The first is the assumption made in many manpower models that employment levels will rise and fall in line with changes in business activity. This argument is badly flawed in a number of respects. Employment does not fall in line with decline in economic activity. Many employers will try to hang on to staff in spite of (what they hope to be) short-term falls in demand. The replacement costs of labour can be high, as well as the training costs for new staff. Additionally many employers feel a social responsibility to hold on to staff despite economic logic telling them to do otherwise. Conversely, as

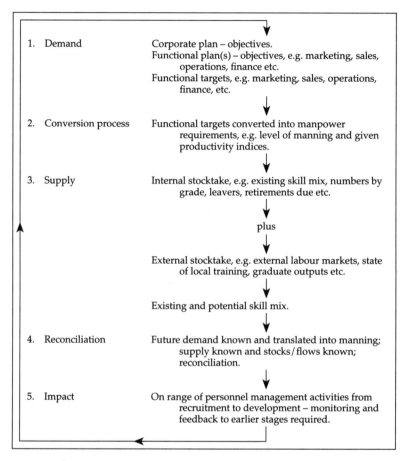

1.	Demand	Corporate plan – objectives. Functional plan(s) – objectives, e.g. marketing, sales, operations, finance etc. Functional targets, e.g. marketing, sales, operations, finance, etc.
2.	Conversion process	Functional targets converted into manpower requirements, e.g. level of manning and given productivity indices.
3.	Supply	Internal stocktake, e.g. existing skill mix, numbers by grade, leavers, retirements due etc. plus External stocktake, e.g. external labour markets, state of local training, graduate outputs etc. Existing and potential skill mix.
4.	Reconciliation	Future demand known and translated into manning; supply known and stocks/flows known; reconciliation.
5.	Impact	On range of personnel management activities from recruitment to development – monitoring and feedback to earlier stages required.

Source: Anderson 1994.

Figure 2.7
The manpower planning process

economic activity picks up jobs do not automatically follow. Initially employers may use overtime to meet the new demands, or sub-contractors or eventually part-time staff and temporary contract staff. Only latterly will the body of full time permanent staff be added to. Employment is what governments would call a 'lagging indicator' of economic growth.

Many employers will take the opportunity of economic downturn to look more carefully at *how* work is done. Factor substitution may occur – labour may be replaced with machinery, or new work methods may be introduced which expect the same work, or more likely more work, to be produced by the same size or a smaller workforce. An example of this may be seen in the case study near the end of this chapter.

New ideas for managing staff, delayering of organizational structures, fresh approaches for reward systems, new systems for monitoring performance, better internal communications systems will all influence not only how work is performed but also how much work is completed and, as important, to what quality. Once these ideas are taken on board many of the statistical models of manpower planning rapidly become obsolete.

The second of the problems outlined earlier concerns the uncertainty of the environment in which most organizations operate. How can coherent manpower planning be developed when the future is so uncertain? This is an argument that is difficult to refute and one that has several dimensions. The level of future demand for products and services is unknown, but also the rapid obsolescence of technology means that future methods of production are also uncertain. Once again traditional manpower planning methods will struggle to cope adequately. The 'solutions', if solutions they be, have been identified by among others Rosabeth Moss Kanter (1986) and Tom Peters (1993), who place emphasis on organizational flexibility, on adaptability, on speed of response and empowerment. They would deride the stability and order necessary for traditional manpower planning models.

The research into the manpower planning practices of British industry have produced mixed results. For instance, MacKay and Torrington (1986) found that although manpower planning is widely practised by businesses, the results of the plan were generally not given much significance in strategic planning. Storey (1992) found that in many organizations even raw data about those employed did not exist in any form that was useable.

8. Manpower Planning – Human Resource Planning?

To many, the root cause of the failure of manpower planning is deep within both the concept and the practice itself. Today many now look to 'human resource planning' (HRP) as the route by which manpower planning can regain its credibility. Torrington et al. (1991: 75) tell us that human resource planning:

> covers a wide spectrum of activities. At one end there are the traditional manpower planning activities concerned with providing the organization with the right number of people with the right skills at the right time. . . . At the other end of the spectrum are plans and activities which are designed to affect the way that people behave in the organization and so ultimately affect the organization's culture.

They claim that examples of this approach would include:

> the planning and implementation of a total quality approach, a performance management culture, a 'customer first orientation', the flexible organization and so on.

Human resource planning emphasizes the importance of linking in with corporate planning in such a way that the strategic planning process takes fully into account human resource implications, and by association human resource practitioners. The casual observer would be forgiven for asking why this has not happened in the past? Burack's

1985 research (quoted in Torrington et al. 1991) indicated that most human resource specialists considered that HRP was included in the corporate planning process. However, a far smaller number of corporate planners considered it to be so!

Human resource planning sees the task as being more than mechanistically fitting the correct number of people into jobs, and sets itself the task of asking fundamental questions about how the job is done, how resources are allocated, how motivation and reward aspects of worker performance can be considered. It tries to question how the culture of the organization can be developed to meet the longer-term objectives of the organization.

Many organizations have focused their human resource planning effort on developing task or functional flexibility in their workforce. Often this has been associated with the abolition of demarcation lines and developing new skills within the workforce. This idea of a multi-skilled workforce is an attractive one, with workers being able to slot into almost any position in the workplace as demand, or sickness, dictates. In practice few organizations have managed to go far along this line, and the main areas where functional flexibility has been achieved have been in the abolition of lines of demarcation and the introduction of attractive bonus schemes.

Other employers have examined carefully the notion of the working day and have tried to get a better output from working hours. In many occupations (see the case at the end of the chapter, for instance) not all parts of the working day, week or year are equally productive, and yet the employer pays an equal amount for each hour of each employee's time. Some employers have introduced 'flexible shifts' whereby shifts might be of unequal length and start and end according to the exigencies of the market, but within an overall constraint of a fixed number of hours per week, possibly aggregated over a number of weeks. Such a situation is illustrated in the case at the end of the chapter. Alternatively, some employers have explored 'annual-hours contracts'. These attempt to get a better and more consistent return from employees' working hours by directing them to work a certain number of hours per year rather than per week or month. An example might be an ice-cream manufacturer who experiences seasonal peaks and demands for his product. If staff were employed working 40 hours a week all year, for part of the year they would be under-employed (idle) and part of the year over-employed, probably necessitating the payment of overtime. To overcome this problem the employer could either lay some staff off during the slacker months and employ them again later in the year (this would involve recruitment and training costs), or employ the staff on annual-hours contracts. Under this arrangement the workers would, for instance, work 30 hours per week for the 6 months when demand is low and work 50 hours per week for the six months when demand is high. Annual hours would be unchanged. This would offer the workforce more secure employment, while allowing the employer to avoid paying overtime at some times of the year, and laying off or under-employing staff at others. Figures 2.8 and 2.9 illustrate both the problem and the solution.

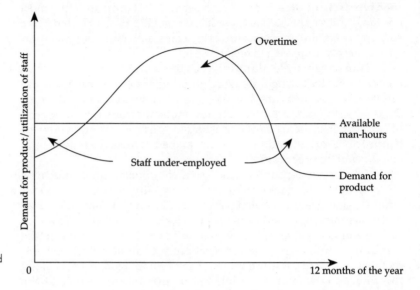

Figure 2.8
Relationship between
demand for product and
utilization of staff

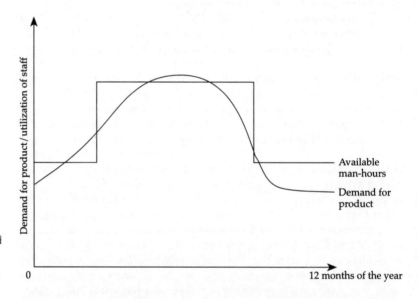

Figure 2.9
Relationship between
demand for product and
utilization of staff
employed under
annual-hours contracts

The Board of Northallerton NHS Trust have approved a plan to employ
nurses on annualized-hours contracts. The features of the new scheme
are:

Nurses will be expected to work 1,670 hours per year.

The old shift system will be phased out.

Nurses on annualized contracts will be paid basic salary plus 12.5 per
cent, but no extra allowances.

> Some nurses not on duty will be placed 'on-call'. If they are not called in to work they will be credited with one hour, if they are called in they will be credited with the hours worked.
>
> Some nurses on duty may be sent home early if not needed. When this occurs they too will be credited with one hour.
>
> At the end of the year positive or negative balances will be rolled into the next year.
>
> It is envisaged that the new scheme will increase staffing flexibility, as well as reduce the use of overtime and agency staff. (Reported in *Personnel Today*, 25 Oct. 1995.)

Other organizations have explored the possibility of numerical flexibility within the workforce. Most discussion here has centred around the idea of retaining a 'core' workforce who would be employed in permanent, salaried, pensionable jobs. These would be those workers who were considered central to the success of the organization. Other work – the periphery – would be done by people employed on part-time, temporary or fixed-term contracts. Other work would be contracted out and extensive use made of out-sourcing. The aim would be to maintain numerical and financial flexibility over labour costs. Such practices, while attractive, are fraught with problems – not least that of needing to recruit and retain sufficient numbers of people with the right skills to make up the 'periphery' part of the workforce. It has also been suggested that many organizations who advocate the 'flexible firm' do so not because it forms part of their long-term strategic plan, but as a reaction to temporary difficulties in economic circumstances.

The three techniques described above form examples of the methods employers are investigating and using to plan for better and more successful utilization of manpower. In practice, many organizations will use the three techniques together with a range of others in their attempts to ensure that they do have sufficient skilled and unskilled staff to meet current and future requirements while maintaining sufficient flexibility to allow adjustments to be made to the plan if and as required.

That HRP is more comprehensive than its predecessor there can be little doubt; whether it will ultimately be more successful is another question, and fundamentally depends on the degree to which human resource managers are able to influence the strategic planning process. As stated earlier, they have a poor track record to date!

Those who doubt the likely success of the incorporation of HRP into corporate planning point to the widely perceived low status of personnel; the failure of personnel specialists to understand business issues; the lack of suitable performance criteria for personnel related issues and the association of personnel with maintenance activities of the organization rather than the strategic issues.

In many organizations it seems human resource planning is something that happens as a result of strategic planning rather than a contributor to it.

THE MEDUSA BUS COMPANY

The Medusa Bus Company operates across the eastern counties of England. It has eight main depots as well as a number of smaller ones scattered across the region. It employs 320 drivers who work a shift pattern. Up until recently the shifts have revolved around the following hours:

06.00–14.00 Early shift

14.00–22.00 Late shift

22.00–06.00 Night shift

The shift system did not necessitate full rotation. For instance, drivers had only to work a night shift 1 week in 7, with the other 6 weeks requiring alternate weeks of early and late shifts.

Basically the drivers worked a 40-hour week, Monday to Saturday, with one day always designated as a 'rest' day. This day moved through the week so that every 6 weeks the drivers had a long weekend off. This was when the Saturday rest day of one week coincided with the Monday rest day of the next week. Sunday working was quite common and always paid as overtime. Overtime was paid at time and a quarter for normal days, time and a half for rest days and double time on Sundays.

Pay for the drivers was considered poor both by the union (who were able to compare it with other bus companies and similar occupations), and also by the management, who felt under pressure to keep basic pay low because of the considerable amount of overtime that had to be worked by most of the drivers.

Because of the regional nature of the bus company's work and the fact that many of the routes were long and cross-country, the first buses left the depots before 6 a.m. This meant that the early shift drivers were regularly being paid overtime before their official shift had started. Additionally they often returned to their home depot with a significant part of their shift remaining (commonly anything up to one and a half hours), and rarely was there any more work for them to do. So, overtime was being paid to drivers who had, in effect (and through no fault of their own), worked considerably less than a full shift. Another problem was that a number of drivers who arrived for work at the start of a shift did not have a bus to take out until some way into the shift. The number and frequency of buses built up with the arrival of the morning rush hour.

The same sorts of problems occurred with the late shift, particularly because few buses ran after 8 p.m. and yet the full shift were still officially on duty until 10 p.m.

The night shift was smaller and generally worked on the longer routes operated by the company.

The management of the company had calculated that during an 8-hour shift, and disregarding statutory breaks, a driver on average worked for only 65 per cent of the shift. Most of the rest was lost in the ways described above. Further, a driver on an average shift worked three-quarters of an hour overtime. Overtime was also routinely worked on rest days (average 4 hours per driver, per week) and on Sundays all driving was paid as overtime. Approximately 40 per cent of the total wage bill consisted of overtime payments.

For a number of years the management had attempted to reduce the amount of overtime worked and to increase the flexibility of the shift system operated. The union was both strong and well represented and had argued consistently against any changes. Indeed it saw the maintenance of these practices, and the widespread use of overtime, as being the only way for the drivers to bolster up their otherwise poor rates of pay.

The pressure on costs which resulted from the effects of competition, recession and falling passenger numbers caused the spotlight to fall more closely on the costs of the drivers. The Operations Manager, together with the Human Resources Manager, had been given the task of improving the situation as outlined.

The company was also aware that the number of hours worked by staff could become a problem, not least if European legislation on a maximum 48-hour working week is enforced in the UK. (See chapter 15 on the influence of Europe.)

The attitude of the union, initially hostile, was later supportive as a package of reforms was put together. The reforms were designed to meet the objectives of both the management and the union and consisted of the following:

1. Flexible shift lengths – between 7 and 9 hours depending on the needs of the service. This would take into account statutory breaks and allow for the average of 40 hours a week still to be worked; but the average would be calculated over a 13-week period (to allow greater rostering flexibility).

2. Rest days and Sundays would be incorporated into the normal working week – drivers would work any 5 of 7 days each week.

3. Most routine overtime would be eliminated.

4. Basic rates of pay were raised by 17.5 per cent.

5. Planned driver utilization rates should rise from the then 65 per cent to a planned 85–90 per cent.

The deal was quite easily sold to the drivers, who benefited from the higher basic rate of pay with far less need to work overtime. The higher rate gave them a more secure income, the prospect of better pensions, and holiday bonuses. The increased driver utilization rate meant that 35 drivers were no longer needed and a programme of enhanced early retirement was introduced to allow this reduction to occur with the minimum of pain. Volunteers were easily found.

The financial effect of the increased utilization rate, the reduced overtime and the increased basic pay was minimal – however, the reduced driver numbers led to a 12 per cent fall in the overall driver wage bill during the first year of implementation. It was generally considered to have been a success.

TASK

Consider the alternatives of using a 'low basic pay high overtime pay system', as against a 'higher pay lower overtime pay system', as a method of getting the best output from the human resources of organizations. What are the strengths and weaknesses of each approach?

QUESTIONS FOR FURTHER CONSIDERATION

1. Consider your own organization (or one with which you are familiar). What arguments would you use to convince your Board that a manpower planning exercise should be undertaken?

2. As the newly appointed HR Manager of the Blackwood Ballbearing Company, how would you go about inaugurating formal manpower planning?

3. Outline the problems that confront the manpower planner in assessing the future demand for and supply of manpower. How can these be overcome or minimized?

4. Consider the ways in which careful manpower planning can contribute to the success of an organization.

5. You are HR Manager for a chain of restaurants. You have identified high labour turnover as a particular problem and brought it to the attention of the HR Director. She is of the opinion that it is not a particular problem yet, but has asked you to monitor the situation. How would you go about this task?

6. Distinguish between manpower planning and human resource planning. Discuss the strengths and weaknesses of each. Why does HRP need to be incorporated into the strategic planning process rather than react to the strategic plan?

•REFERENCES•

Anderson A (1994)
EFFECTIVE PERSONNEL MANAGEMENT: A SKILLS AND ACTIVITY BASED APPROACH
Oxford, Blackwell.

Armstrong M (1992)
A HANDBOOK OF PERSONNEL MANAGEMENT PRACTICE
London, Kogan Page.

Atkinson G B J (1989)
ECONOMICS: THEMES AND PERSPECTIVES
Ormskirk, Causeway Press.

Beardshaw J (1989)
ECONOMICS: A STUDENT GUIDE
2nd edn, London, Pitman

Bennison M & Casson R (1984)
THE MANPOWER PLANNING HANDBOOK
London, McGraw-Hill.

Bowey A (1974)
A GUIDE TO MANPOWER PLANNING
London, Macmillan.

Bramham J (1989)
HUMAN RESOURCE PLANNING
London, Institute of Personnel Management.

Brewster C & Connock S (1990)
Corporate Planning: A No-go Area for Personnel
Personnel Management, July.

Forbes A & McGill D (1985)
UNDERSTANDING WASTAGE
Falmer, Sussex, Institute of Manpower Studies, Report CN 426.

Hayek F (1984)
1980s UNEMPLOYMENT AND THE UNIONS
London, Institute of Economic Affairs.

Institute of Personnel Management (1975)
PRACTICAL MANPOWER PLANNING
London, IPM.

Kanter, R M (1984)
THE CHANGE MASTERS
London, Allen and Unwin.

Livy B (1988)
CORPORATE PERSONNEL MANAGEMENT
London, Pitman.

MacKay L & Torrington D (1986)
THE CHANGING NATURE OF PERSONNEL MANAGEMENT
London, Institute of Personnel Management.

Kanter, R Moss (1986)
WHEN GIANTS LEARN TO DANCE
London, Allen and Unwin.

Osterman P (ed.) (1984)
INTERNAL LABOUR MARKETS
Cambridge, Mass., MIT Press.

Pearson R & Pike, G (1990)
THE GRADUATE LABOUR MARKET IN THE 1990s
Falmer, Sussex, Institute of Manpower Studies.

Peters T (1993)
NECESSARY DISORGANIZATION IN THE NANO-SECOND NINETIES
London, Macmillan.

Rothwell S (1991)
STRATEGIC PLANNING FOR HUMAN RESOURCES
Oxford, Pergamon.

Stainer G (1971)
MANPOWER PLANNING
London, Heinemann.

Storey J (1992)
DEVELOPMENTS IN THE MANAGEMENT OF HUMAN RESOURCES
Oxford, Blackwell.

Torrington D, Hall L, Haylor I & Myers J (1991)
EMPLOYEE RESOURCING
London, Institute of Personnel Management.

Wallum P (1993)
A Broader View of Succession Planning
Personnel Management, Sept.

White J (1983)
LONG TERM UNEMPLOYMENT AND THE LABOUR MARKET
London, Policy Studies Institute.

•CHAPTER•

3

RECRUITMENT:
THE INITIAL STAGES

AS A RESULT OF STUDYING THIS CHAPTER YOU SHOULD BE ABLE TO:

- Distinguish between recruitment and selection.

- Appreciate the importance of good planning in recruitment and the various preparatory stages that should be considered.

- Consider the significance of job analysis and its link with the job specification.

- Appreciate the need for clear, accurate and unambiguous job descriptions and personnel specifications.

- Be aware of the main criticisms of this area of recruitment and the steps that the practitioner should take to ensure reliability and validity in recruitment.

Please note: this chapter should be read together with those that follow, covering 'Recruitment Media', 'Selection' and 'Equal Opportunities'.

1. Introduction

The processes of recruitment and selection are often confused: indeed it is not uncommon for the two words to be used almost interchangeably by some. For the personnel practitioner, however, the two words have very different meanings. As Livy (1988: 94) tells us:

> The purpose of recruitment is to locate appropriate sources of supply of labour; to communicate job opportunities and information through various media; and to generate an interest in vacancies. The recruiter needs to be equipped with two broad sets of information: (i) job specifications as determined by job analysis, and (ii) a knowledge of the labour market.

Dowling and Schuler (1990: 64) add to this by claiming that recruitment is:

> Searching for and obtaining potential job candidates in sufficient numbers and quality so that the organization can select the most appropriate people to fill its job needs.

Recruitment is often distinguished from selection by the claim that recruitment is a *positive* act, that is, it is attempting to attract a pool of suitable candidates for a position, whilst selection is a *negative* process, that is, reducing the likely candidates down to the number that are to be successful. For this reason the two tasks are often undertaken by different people – in fact, recruitment is sometimes managed by recruitment agencies while selection is always decided in-house and generally by the line manager, or senior manager, of the employee to be. It is appropriate to consider the UK Armed Forces, who until recently maintained in many large towns a Recruitment Office. It was the task of the staff employed there to attract suitably qualified candidates to apply for positions in the forces. It is unlikely, however, that these staff would be involved in the 'selection' of new recruits. This task, like recruitment, is left to specialist staff.

Selection is an emerging science. Torrington et al. (1991: 107) tell us that:

> the search for a perfect method of selection continues[;] in its absence personnel managers continue to use a variety of imperfect methods to aid the task of predicting which applicant will be most successful in meeting the demands of the job. Selection is increasingly important as more attention is paid to the cost of poor selection . . .

This chapter and the following two are closely linked and should be considered together. This chapter focuses on the documentation used for recruitment (*job analysis, job description, job specification* and *person specification*), how those documents are prepared, the methodologies available, and the forms which they might take. Chapter 4 considers how recruitment interacts with and uses external media – in other words, alternative recruitment methods and the documentation that supports the process. Chapter 5 considers selection methods and techniques.

The stages of recruitment and selection are flow-charted in figure 3.1. This and the following two chapters will use the flow chart as a guide for the text.

The recruitment process should be systematized and closely managed. This is to ensure not only consistency throughout the organization, but also to maintain procedures that are fair, legal (for instance, see chapter 6 on equal opportunities) and valid. It will also be necessary that recruitment policies are in line with other company policies. These would include:

a. Equal opportunities. This policy will state how the company will treat candidates of differing sex, nationality, ethnic background, age and disability.

b. Manpower planning, and training and development policies.

c. Marketing policies. Recruitment advertising is an act of positive communication with the outside world. There is therefore a marketing aspect to recruitment. Poorly worded advertisements or candidates who feel that they were unfairly treated will not enhance the reputation of the employer.

The rest of this chapter will be devoted to a detailed discussion of these systems and procedures.

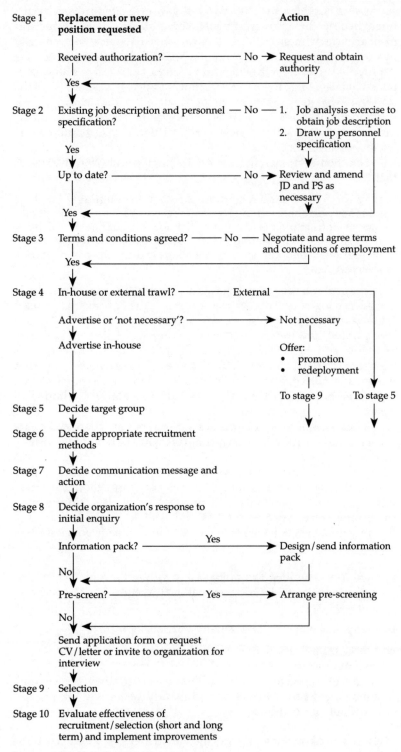

Figure 3.1
Recruitment and selection
flow chart

Source: after Beardwell and Holden 1994.

Falling outside of this flow chart and (arguably) not strictly part of the recruitment and selection process is the 'exit interview'. This is used by many organizations to elicit from the leaver why it is that they have resigned their position. Sometimes exit interviews will be conducted by the line manager or supervisor, or as is more often the case, it will be conducted by a member of the Human Resources Department. Giving responsibility for the interview to someone not directly connected with the employee's work has several advantages, but principally if the behaviour or conduct of the line manager or supervisor is the reason for the employee leaving, then it is less likely that the employee would give such a reason if it is that individual conducting the interview.

Some employees will be reluctant (or possibly unable to articulate) the reasons why they have chosen to leave, but from others will come useful intelligence that can be put to advantage. For instance, if an employee (and particularly if a number give the same or similar reasons) cites such reasons as poor pay, lack of career prospects, or being offered more pay and better prospects by a competitor employer, then that information can be fed back and used appropriately. Some employees may cite sexual or racial harassment as their reason for leaving, in which case prompt action *must* be taken. (See chapter 6.)

2. Authorization

Before recruitment procedures are put under way it is necessary first to confirm that the 'alleged' vacancy does exist. (This might seem rather trite, but in large organizations it is not unknown for advertisements to be placed for jobs that do not, or do not yet, exist.) Once this has been done, and probably it is best to confirm with the payroll department that somebody has left (or indeed is about to), the appropriate authorization can be sought to fill the vacancy. In considering whether to fill the vacancy or not several factors will need to be considered. These will include:

a. the human resource plan and the projected demand for labour (see chapter 2);

b. the financial strength of the organization – when times are tough a 'freeze on recruitment' is not uncommon;

c. consideration of whether the work can be covered by reorganizing the duties of others in the department;

d. questioning whether the job should be replaced 'like for like', or should the opportunity be taken to consider alternative options, such as employing somebody with slightly different skills;

e. considering if the position can be covered by using part-time staff or offering it as suitable for job share;

f. can and/or should the work be contracted out?

g. should the organization take the opportunity to forgo recruitment and instead install capital equipment?

Decisions such as these need to be taken with an overview of the organization in mind and not by simply referring to the relevant line manager, although he or she should be consulted before any decision is taken. It is generally the case that authorization to employ will be made by somebody quite senior in the organization – for example, somebody who is involved with the interpretation of the corporate human resource plan and who is able to take a strategic view of the organization's human resources. The decision will not be left to either the personnel officer responsible for recruitment, or the line manager who has lost the member of staff.

3. Job Analysis and Job Specification

In large organizations, when positions are to be filled, either newly created ones or those that arise as a result of staff turnover, the opportunity is taken to consider fully (or reconsider) the duties of the job. The task is known as 'job analysis'.

The British Standards Institute (1979) have defined job analysis as:

> the determination of the essential characteristics of a job. The process of examining a job to identify its component parts and the circumstances in which it is performed.

If the job under consideration for recruitment is to replace an existing or former member of staff, then it is likely that a considerable amount of information is already in existence about that job. The job analyst (who in large organizations may specialize in this task, or who may be a consultant) will probably be looking to update records. However, if the job is new the analyst will need to prepare his or her information from scratch. Under both sets of circumstances the analyst will have the following objectives at the forefront of their mind when carrying out the analysis:

a. To clarify the details of the post for which new recruits are to be sought.

b. To produce sufficient detail from which to draw up the job description and person specification (see later in the chapter for explanation).

c. To prepare a base of information from which performance appraisal can be considered.

d. To identify where the (new) job fits in with the current organization structure, and identify its relationship with other jobs.

The opportunity to analyse jobs (naturally) will occur when staff leave or reorganization occurs. On such occasions the HR department should take the opportunity to review and update job specifications. The fact that job analysis is taking place may cause some concern among existing staff, who may be fearful for their jobs. The analyst will need to do all he can to gain the trust of staff by use of clear communications (explaining the purpose and method of the analysis), not interrupting the normal flow of work, and giving rapid feedback on the results of the analysis.

The task of carrying out job analysis is far from simple, and a detailed discussion of techniques and methodologies is beyond the scope of this book. However the task is usually carried out by reference to a *pro forma* question sheet which will consider both the 'task-oriented' and 'worker-oriented' aspects of the job.

The *task-oriented* aspects of the job will include:

a. The job title.

b. To whom is the holder responsible?

   For what does the holder have authority?

c. With regard to the work itself:

   what are the component tasks?
   how frequently are these tasks performed?
   how is the work carried out?
   when are the tasks and duties performed?
   how do the tasks fit together?
   where is the work performed?
   what is the relative value of each task in terms of
      frequency?
      difficulty?
      importance?
   to what standards must the worker perform (accuracy, etc.)?

d. With what degree of independence is the worker expected to perform?

e. The working environment. Consideration should be given to the physical and social environment – for example, dirt, noise, hazards, shift working, working alone or with others, etc.

f. Financial considerations.

The *worker-oriented* aspects include:

a. Education and training required.

b. Occupational experience required.

c. The physical and mental demands of the job.

d. Personality and attitudinal considerations.

The (aforementioned) standard form used will need to encompass all the task- and worker-oriented aspects, both in terms of the range of each factor and the degree to which each factor is present. It is common to use a rating scale for this purpose. Job analysis can be carried out using a number of methods. These include:

a. Structured interviews with job holders and line managers. This involves using a *pro forma* questionnaire and asking the worker to explain, describe, quantify and qualify his job and its responsibilities; and carrying out a similar exercise with manager. This method gains two perspectives on the same job.

b. Observation of working practice. This literally involves following an employee for a period of time and recording both what they do, how they do it, and indeed how long they take to do it. This is suitable if the job is repetitive over a short period of time. It is not suitable if the job is significantly varied or repetitive over a lengthy cycle.

c. The use of time diaries. This method requires the employee to keep a diary recording her or his activities over a period of time. Employees are required either to record all activities, what they are doing at regular intervals throughout the day (e.g. every quarter of an hour), or record only critical incidents.

The methodology of job analysis has come under much criticism for being empirically unsound. Principally the methodologies have been questioned both on grounds of validity (do they assess what they purport to assess?) and reliability (if the job analysis was repeated would the same results occur?) Additionally the use of standardized form is not as straightforward as we might believe. Lewis (1985: 109) warns:

> Filling in the form accurately becomes the over-riding objective rather than conveying a real understanding of the job. Also the problem can arise if those writing the specifications are different people from those who will be using them to make selection decisions . . .

However, the needs for speed of information as well as the generally frugal resources devoted to job analysis mean that very often compromises have to be made. To increase both the validity and reliability of job analysis it would be better to use a wider range of techniques over a longer period of time.

The product of a job analysis will be a *job specification*, which should be a detailed account of the duties (physical and mental) involved in a job. It is usually expressed in behavioural terms – worker knowledge, actions, skills, judgements, etc.

The job analysis and the resultant job specification may be used for a number of purposes:

a. In recruitment and selection – to draw up a detailed description of the vacant job.
b. In devising training programmes – to quantify both the skills and knowledge necessary to perform a job.
c. To establish the appropriate rate of pay for the job.
d. To adjust the organization's structure and the roles of other members of staff as necessary.

4. Job Description

A job description is a written 'portrait' of a job at a point in time. It is a statement of the significant facts regarding the job's duties and responsibilities and their organizational and operational interrelationships. The description should focus solely on the job and not the job holder. For an example of a model job description see the case study at the end of this chapter.

It should be emphasized that a job description does not 'set the employee's job in cement': that is, it will not stand for all time. Many commentators see the whole business of job descriptions as too bureaucratic, too inflexible and incompatible with modern business practice, which is characterized by delayering, devolved responsibility and individual initiative. Despite these concerns, most organizations of any size still use systems of job description, and see advantage in formally defining the responsibilities of post holders while also attempting to reconcile the increasing dynamic nature of work.

A job description will be derived from the job analysis and the job specification, and should contain the following:

a. The job title.

b. The department and/or section in which the job is located.

c. A job code number.

d. The title of the person to whom the job holder is responsible.

e. The date at which the job description was prepared (or updated) and by whom.

f. The grade of the job.

g. A brief description of the job purpose.

h. A statement of the key responsibilities of the job.

i. A fuller list of the main duties of the job arranged so as to be consistent with the key responsibilities.

j. The date the job description should be reviewed.

Additionally, though less commonly, some job descriptions will also contain a small organization chart showing where the job sits in relation to others around it.

Although job descriptions are usually prepared by human resource specialists the exact wording and content will be carefully agreed with the relevant line manager.

In describing what is expected of the job holder (responsibilities and duties), active verbs should be used. Cole (1988) provides a useful checklist of the kinds of active verbs appropriate to jobs at different levels in an organization (see figure 3.2).

The job description has uses for both recruitment purposes and for more general matters. Specifically in recruitment, it will be used:

a. To decide what skills should be required of the job holder. These will be articulated in the 'personnel specification' (see section 5, below).

b. To help in deciding the contents of any job advertisements.

c. To help determine a rate of pay (if this is not to be determined elsewhere).

5. Personnel Specification

The information contained within the job description (i.e. the definition of the job in terms of its role and responsibilities) and the job specification (i.e. the definition of the job in terms of the skills, knowledge, aptitudes required) will enable the organization to decide what kind of person is required to fill the position.

The 'personnel specification' is the title of the document used to make explicit the attributes required and expected of the successful candidate, or to describe the ideal job holder. It is a summary of the most

Line Management Jobs	Senior Specialist Jobs	Clerical Jobs
Plan	Analyse	Check
Direct	Propose	Make available
Establish	Interpret	Operate
Implement	Advise	Provide
Achieve	Appraise	Maintain
Ensure	Recommend	Submit
Maintain	Develop	Present
Set		
Review		

Figure 3.2
Relevant verbs by job
category

important knowledge, skills and personal characteristics required for successful performance of the job. For an example of a personnel specification please see the case study at the end of this chapter.

It is common for personnel specifications to list attributes under 'Essential Requirements' and 'Desirable Requirements', indicating the degree of weighting and importance that each feature is accorded.

One of the most common formats for personnel specification is Rodger's (1952), which is commonly known as the 'Seven Point Plan'. The seven points are:

1. *Physical Make-up*: health, strength, personal appearance, energy.

2. *Attainments*: educational qualifications, vocational training and experience.

3. *General Intelligence*: thinking and mental skills, specific intellectual skills.

4. *Special Aptitudes*: the particular skills needed for this job.

5. *Interests*: the personal interests that could be relevant to the performance of the job.

6. *Disposition*: the personality type that is most suitable for the position.

7. *Circumstances*: the special circumstances that might be required of candidates.

Another commonly used form is the 'Five-fold Grading System' developed by Munro-Fraser. This covers:

1. *Impact on Others*: physical make-up, appearance, speech and manner.

2. *Acquired Qualifications*: education, vocational training, work experience.

3. *Innate Abilities*: natural quickness of comprehension and aptitude for learning.

4. *Motivation*: the kinds of goals set by the individual, his or her consistency or determination in following them up, and success in achieving them.

5. *Adjustment*: emotional stability, ability to stand up to stress and ability to get on with people.

The personnel specification in the case study at the back of this chapter is very 'loosely' derived from Rodger's model. It is a framework that should be used as a basis for selection. If used properly, it should enable selectors to make reasonably consistent comparisons between candidates for a job. Many organizations have used Rodger's model to help in the definition of their personnel specifications or adapted it to suit their own needs, as is the case with the example shown.

The processes described within this chapter are not without their critics (e.g. Herriot 1984) who question the assumption that inanimate jobs can be described (via job descriptions) and matched against animate workers (via personnel specifications). The whole process, it is claimed, fails to take account of the dynamic nature of work and the degree of adaptability of workers. Livy (1988) claims that we should take far more account of job candidates' capacities (what they *can* do) and candidates' inclinations (what they *will* do). Livy claims that this will allow recruiters to take account of behavioural versatility and be less hung up on the somewhat crude method for matching job and person.

6. Agree Terms and Conditions

The terms and conditions of employment to be offered with a particular job can be decided at any one of several stages. Where rigid pay scales are in place it is likely that the new employee will be placed on the same scale as his or her predecessor. The point on the scale may be determined by age, experience, qualifications or previous salary. The officer who authorizes the position to be filled may influence the make-up of the job by putting constraints on the level of salary to be offered. This will also influence the recruitment method to be used. If pay is severely constrained, the recruiter may wish to place emphasis on the future potential that the job offers the successful candidate. A maximum age restriction may also be used to deter the 'expensive' applicant.

The job analyst should determine how the job compares with others that are similar and should be able to make a recommendation on pay. However, many employers (while having an idea of the appropriate salary level in mind) prefer to wait and see who applies for the job and then make a judgement on pay according to the experience, qualifications and previous salary of the successful candidate.

THE PUBLICATIONS OFFICER

TASK

Consider the Job Description and the Person Specification for the position of Publications Officer with Casebrook Ltd. Compare it with others that you may have seen or have available.

How useful do you consider they would be as aids to recruitment?

Does the Person Specification 'match' the Job Description?

How would you recommend that the 'essential and desirable' qualities listed in the Person Specification should be assessed by the selectors?

CASEBROOK LTD
JOB DESCRIPTION

JOB TITLE: Publications Officer
LOCATION: Headquarters
CODE: 94/060. MKTG
RESPONSIBLE TO: Publications Manager
PREPARED: TJB 15/5/1995
JOB GRADE: Principal Officer 2

JOB PURPOSE:
To edit, research and write information leaflets, publicity material, reports, articles, or other documents; to work closely with other staff in the Publications Unit to ensure materials are effectively designed and produced; to help with the general workload of the unit.

MAIN DUTIES:

1) To edit documents produced by colleagues or external authors to ensure they communicate effectively with the target audience.

2) To research and write original material, mainly under the direction of the Information Services Manager.

3) To prepare material for publication. This will include marking up copy, and briefing and liaising effectively with design and production colleagues in the Publications Unit.

4) To check proofs and artwork, including colour proofs, to ensure publications are produced to high standards of accuracy and quality.

5) To liaise effectively with clients to ensure their work meets the stated objectives and to keep them informed of the progress of their work.

6) To commission external editors and photographers as necessary.

7) To promote the Company house style, especially on editorial matters.

8) To keep up-to-date records of work in progress.

9) To contribute to the general work of the Department.

10) To undertake other activities as may be necessary.

Date for review: 5/96.

PERSON SPECIFICATION
PUBLICATIONS OFFICER: PUBLICATIONS UNIT

The successful candidate will possess many (if not all) of the qualities listed below.

	Essential	Desirable
The ability to command the respect of colleagues and clients.	X	
Stamina, physical energy; the ability to work to tight deadlines and prioritize work.	X	
Educated to degree standard or equivalent.	X	
Qualification in Journalism.		X
Ability to write and edit copy to high standards, appropriate to different audiences, including the general public and specialist professional groups.	X	
Ability to research new publications, including the ability to use written sources and to interview colleagues and other agencies.	X	
Ability to brief colleagues responsible for design and production of publications.	X	
Ability to proofread accurately and to check artwork.	X	
Knowledge of the complete publishing process.	X	
Ability to commission external editors, photographers and other suppliers as necessary.	X	
Record-keeping skills, including the ability to use computerized records.		X
Typing/editing skills using a word-processor.	X	
Print buying and print production skills.		X
DTP skills.		X
Knowledge of marketing.		X
Experience of working in a multi-disciplinary team.		X
Experience of working on complex multi-media publications.	X	
Genuine team player.	X	
Willingness to travel within the UK, including the occasional overnight stay.	X	
Non-smoker.	X	
Willingness to share an office.	X	

1. Consider your own organization (or one with which you are familiar) and examine the recruitment process. How closely does it follow that described in the text? Examine both the differences and similarities and consider whether they make for better or worse recruitment and why.

2. Your manager (the company HR Manager) has asked you to take responsibility for carrying out job analysis in the company and has suggested that you consider the training that you might require before you start the job. Write a memo to your manager outlining your thoughts.

3. You are the newly appointed HR Manager of P&B Ltd. The Director has expressed concern about the costs of recruitment and the poor quality of staff currently being employed, and has asked you to investigate. How would you convince her of the need to be thorough in the preparation of job descriptions and personnel specifications?

4. Consider job analysis – to what extent is it an 'exact science' and to what extent is it flawed? What could be done to improve its validity and reliability.

5. Consider examples of job descriptions (your own if you have one). Compare it with others that you are able to obtain (or use the example supplied in the case study). To what extent is it a useful document? Is the detail sufficient and precise – or vague and woolly? To what uses could it be put? Make recommendations for improvement.

6. Consider your own organization (or one with which you are familiar). What would be the most appropriate method of carrying out a job analysis in the organization? Consider the advantages and disadvantages of each of the methods described for your organization.

• REFERENCES •

Beardwell I & Holden L (1994)
HUMAN RESOURCE MANAGEMENT
London, Pitman.

British Standards Institute (1979)
GLOSSARY OF TERMS USED IN WORK STUDY AND ORGANISATION METHODS
London, BS 3138.

Cole G (1988)
PERSONNEL MANAGEMENT: THEORY AND PRACTICE
London, DPP.

Dowling P & Schuler R (1990)
INTERNATIONAL DIMENSIONS OF HRM
Boston, PWS-Kent.

Echiejile I (1993)
Job Analysis and the Equal Opportunities Challenge
Training and Development, Feb.

Herriot P (1984)
DOWN FROM THE IVORY TOWER: GRADUATES AND THEIR JOBS
Chichester, Wiley.

Lewis C (1985)
EMPLOYEE SELECTION
London, Hutchinson.

Livy B (1988)
CORPORATE PERSONNEL MANAGEMENT
London, Pitman.

Munro-Fraser J (1978)
EMPLOYMENT INTERVIEWING
5th edn. London, McDonald and Evans.

Rodger A (1952)
THE SEVEN POINT PLAN
3rd edn. London, National Institute of Industrial Psychology.

Torrington D, Hall L, Haylor I & Myers J (1991)
EMPLOYEE RESOURCING
London, Institute of Personnel Management.

• CHAPTER •

4

THE RECRUITMENT
MEDIA

AS A RESULT OF STUDYING THIS CHAPTER YOU SHOULD BE ABLE TO:

- Identify the major principles of good recruitment practice.

- Distinguish the various external agencies that offer recruitment services and be able to identify their suitability for different forms of recruitment.

- Compare a number of different methods of recruitment, highlighting their strengths and weaknesses.

- Appreciate how recruitment policies should be adapted to suit differing labour market situations.

- Be aware of the requirements of recruitment advertising.

- Be able to evaluate the success of recruitment practice in both the short and long terms.

Please note: this chapter should be read together with the one immediately preceding and the two following it.

1. Introduction

This chapter follows on from the last and examines the next stage of the process of recruitment. You will recall from the previous chapter (and to sum up the definitions of recruitment discussed there) that successful recruitment requires us to (a) use job analysis to draw up the various specifications of the job that might be required, and (b) generate interest within the labour market for the job under consideration.

The reader is also referred to chapter 6 ('Equal Opportunities'), which identifies some of the legal requirements governing (b) above. This concerns the need to avoid discrimination in recruitment and selection.

The Institute of Personnel and Development's Recruitment Code (1988) gives guidelines on good recruitment practice and contains the following obligations on recruiters:

1. Job advertisements should state clearly the form of reply desired; in particular, whether this should be by formal application form or *curriculum vitae*. Preferences should also be stated if handwritten replies are required.

2. An acknowledgement or reply should be made promptly to each applicant by the employing organization or its agent. If it is likely to take some time before acknowledgements are made, this should be made clear in the advertisement.

3. Applicants should be informed of the progress of the selection procedures, what these will be (e.g. group selection, aptitude tests, etc.), the steps and time involved and the policy regarding expenses.

4. Detailed personal information (e.g. religion, medical history, place of family background, etc.) should not be called for unless it is relevant to the application process.

5. Before applying for references, potential employers must secure the permission of the applicant.

6. Applications must be treated as confidential.

2. Recruitment Sources

In the discussions that follow it is assumed that the organization has decided to recruit externally – that the vacant position needs to be brought to the attention of the wider labour market. There are numerous organizations willing (and to a lesser or greater degree 'able') to assist you in your search for new employees. Some offer their services for no charge, others will take a considerable fee (generally based on a percentage of the position's salary) and also expenses. Some illustrative examples are considered below:

a.   *Careers Office*   No fee charged. Deals mainly with school leavers. Today they are more proactive in the field of offering constructive advice to young people than was once considered the case. Important to bear in mind that their brief is to assist young people in finding employment rather than acting on behalf of the employer. Perceived by some to be concerned more with unskilled and manual than with technical and skilled employment (it is thought that the majority of more able young people stay on at school or college and proceed to university).

b.   *Job Centres*   Free service. Have made strenuous efforts in recent years to overcome their old 'Labour Exchange' image, with varying degrees of success. They do offer counselling services to applicants and will do a limited amount of pre-screening before recommending people to apply for jobs. Still largely associated with trying to get unemployed people into jobs rather than helping those who wish to change their job, although their services are available to all regardless of employment status. Most of the positions they advertise are for clerical, manual and junior positions.

c.   *Commercial recruitment agencies*   Vary enormously in the range, quality and price of the service offered. Many will specialize by occupation, for instance clerical and secretarial, and some by industry, for instance insurance and banking. Others will specialize in the recruitment of senior staff ('executive' recruitment), while still others will act as an intermediary and approach potential employees to gauge their interest in changing their current job. This service is generally known as 'head-hunting'. Fees charged range between 10 and 50 per cent of the salary of the position, plus expenses. The level of fee is largely dependent upon the degree of perceived exclusivity of the service. Hence general employment-agency fees will be lower (the market is a competitive one), specialist recruitment fees higher, and the recruitment of staff with scarce talents higher still. Many organizations are able to negotiate considerable discounts with agencies, based on the volume of work undertaken.

d. Universities Many employers of graduates will take part in what has become known as the 'milk round'. Large national employers attend recruitment fairs held around the country at universities. This can be both a time-consuming and expensive exercise. It can also generate a number of general enquiries rather than specific ones. Many employers who recruit graduates with specialist skills will use the milk round as one way only in which they maintain a close liaison with those universities that supply the graduates with those skills they most desire. It is often used as an opportunity to develop the interface between employers and universities for courses which have a placement year as part of their requirements.

e. Existing employee contacts Many employees, particularly those with skills or professions, will be in regular formal or informal contact with others who possess those skills. This could be through attendance at professional body meeting or conference, or through less formal contacts. Whatever the method, a lot of knowledge about the availability of certain skills within a given location will be possessed by those with the same skills currently employed in the organization. This resource should not be ignored. However, the equal opportunities implications should be carefully considered. (These are outlined in chapter 6.) It is likely that following up the contacts that existing employees have would be used alongside more formal recruitment methods.

The above catalogue illustrates just a few of the *many* potential methods of recruitment available. It should be remembered that in times of high unemployment many people will wish to assist you actively in your search for good applicants: for example, the Armed Forces Resettlement Services, whose brief it is to help servicemen and women integrate into civilian employment; 'outplacement consultants' (retained by an organization that is slimming down its workforce to help those losing their jobs to find new work), who will be keen to contact employers who use similar skills to those being released and offer information on those workers available.

The retailer Sainsbury recently used the Hippodrome nightclub in London to launch a recruitment campaign to attract up to 200 graduate and A-level management trainees. The two-day event, at which staff dressed casually and music played, was dubbed 'Sainsbury's unplugged'. Those attending were given the chance of first interviews, and offered the opportunity to take a range of aptitude tests. The use of a night club to launch a recruitment campaign has been seen as an attempt to shake off the company's stuffy image, and demonstrate that Sainsbury's can be a fun and exciting place to work. (Reported in *Personnel Today*, 29 Aug. 1995.)

3. Unsolicited Applications

Most employers will also be familiar with unsolicited applications. Indeed, prestigious employers are known to receive many hundreds of these each year. These should be handled with care and courtesy. Those who are likely to apply 'on spec' are also likely to apply for advertised vacancies, and so a similar degree of respect should be shown to both. Many employers will keep on file for a period of time (say, six months) suitable unsolicited applications. Dependence upon unsolicited applications as a source of recruitment can have equal opportunities implications similar to those outlined under sub-section 'e' above.

4. Previous Employees

Previous employees are also a useful source of recruitment and can be utilized in a variety of ways. Early retirers might be used as an easy way of tapping into an immediate source of expert knowledge for (for instance) assignments and projects, or coverage in times of staff shortage or work overload. Women returners are also a source of labour that is likely to possess many of the attitudes and attributes required by the organization. In addition to these two groups, those who have left the organization once to take up an alternative job should not be ignored. It is possible that in the time since they left they have gained new skills, experience and abilities – for some a period with another employer could be viewed as a secondment or a period spent in off-the-job training. Other ex-employees will be viewed with suspicion – they have left the organization once for greener pastures, and it might not be suitable for them to return. Such decisions will have to be taken on an individual basis. It is difficult to propose general rules for re-employment.

5. Recruitment Policies

All policies for recruitment should aim to meet the following basic criteria:

a. To be cost effective.
b. To be consistent with the wider public relations aims of the organization. It is important to remember that potential employees are also actual or potential customers.

c. Not to discriminate against people on the basis of sex, race, age, physical disability or religion.

> The US fighter pilot Captain Scott O'Grady, hailed as an all-American hero after surviving for six days after being shot down behind Serbian lines in the former Yugoslavia, disappointed his military leaders. Following his triumphant return to the United States and lunch with the President, he had been used prominently on posters for a new air-force recruitment campaign. But he decided (much to the disappointment of his superiors, who saw him as an excellent role-model for potential recruits) that he wished to leave the armed forces, though he continued to serve as a reservist. (Reported in the *Guardian*, 8 Aug. 1995.)

6. Recruitment in Practice – Examples

Given that in most organizations of any size a wide range of positions have to be filled, the recruitment policies have to be applied to a range of circumstances. These might include, for example, the recruitment of a senior manager, the replacement of a part-time clerical assistant or the recruitment of a cohort of 25 new graduates to join a management training programme. In each of these circumstances a different approach will be adopted. Some of the alternatives are discussed below.

6.1 The senior manager

In the case of the recruitment of a senior manager, an 'executive recruitment consultancy' might be retained. The consultancy will discuss with the organization the job description and person specification, and will recommend how the search to find the person best suited to fit the brief should be undertaken. This might involve placing advertisements in professional journals, national newspapers and magazines. The agency will send out to those expressing an interest in the position details of the job and application forms (if this is the agreed method of operation). They will act as the receiving point for the completed applications and may act as a filter, sifting the forms to present the employer with either a long or a short list of potentially suitable candidates. In order to produce this list they may interview the applicants, carry out aptitude (or other) tests on the applicants, and carry out some degree of check into their background. It will be for the employer to carry out further interviews (and/or tests) on the short- (or long-) listed candidates and make final decisions about appointments. Most commentators would identify as the crucial stage in this process the drawing up of the initial brief for the consultant. A job description and person specification that is woolly, imprecise or ambiguous will not allow the consultant to target exactly the most suitable candidates for the position. The budget, scope and discretion of the consultant must also be agreed at the earliest stage.

Many consider that the use of consultants is a luxury that can be ill afforded. However, executive recruitment consultants do offer a number of advantages that should not be ignored and which can make them excellent value for money:

a. They should have an expert knowledge of the market within which they advise on recruitment. This will include an appreciation of the best places to advertise various professional and executive positions. This should both reduce the likelihood of wasteful advertising being purchased and increase the chances of attracting a good field of candidates. It is worth bearing in mind that the recruitment of senior managers often takes place within a national or indeed international market-place.

b. Much of the initial filtering of applicants can be undertaken by the consultant. This may be time consuming and labour intensive, particularly if many people apply.

c. The organization may not, for a variety of reasons, wish to reveal (until an advanced stage in the proceedings) that it is trying to recruit a senior manager. The use of a consultant can help the potential employer to remain in an anonymous role until all the preliminary stages have been completed.

d. The consultant, from his position external to the organization, can help the employer determine precisely the qualities that will be required of the new employee. The consultant may help the employer draw up the job description and person specification and consider new ideas and options that had not previously been taken into account.

6.2   Part-time clerical assistant

The recruitment of a part-time clerical assistant might also be undertaken using a recruitment consultancy (or agency) – probably one that specializes in clerical and secretarial staff. One might also refer to the local Job Centre, or place an advertisement in the local newspaper. Each method has its own attractions. The agency will agree with the employer both the job description and person specification for the position under consideration. The agent will then be able to check the specific requirements against the profiles of people currently on their books. If a good match is to be found the agency might recommend an individual (or several individuals) to the employer. Again the employer will conduct final interviews and decide between the candidates. If no good match is to be found with people already on the books of the agency, then either window or display advertising might be placed. If specific skills are required of the job holder (for example, word-processing or computerized bookkeeping skills) the agent will probably require those who put themselves forward to demonstrate their level of proficiency by means of a practical test.

The agency should recommend to the employer only candidates that are generally suitable for the position. Again, the agency will conduct much of the initial sifting and testing of applicants.

If the Job Centre is to be used, no fee will be payable, but the level of service is commensurately poorer. The Job Centre staff will stock your job details and application forms and may also offer general advice on the suitability of various positions to interested people, but will not check skills, offer advice on further advertising, or filter applicants. Hence it is the task of the employer to sift applicants, draw up long- and/or short-lists, test the applicants' skills and conduct all the stages of selection. This can be time consuming and resource intensive.

Placing a newspaper advertisement is a common method of recruitment used by many employers. The design and content of advertisements is more difficult than many would believe. A full discussion is given later in the chapter. Essential points for consideration are:

a. How 'honest' should the advertisement be? If it makes the job sound too attractive you may be overwhelmed with applicants; if you tell the 'truth' you may get none!

b. Where to advertise, and how much to spend – get this wrong and you may attract no interest at all. This will push the process back and the job will need to be re-advertised.

c. In what form and by what date do you wish to receive applications? For instance, by *curriculum vitae* and supporting letter, or by application form? If the latter, then those interested have to contact the employer twice, once to get an application form and once to return it. This will both lengthen and increase the cost of the process.

Clearly recruitment of even part-time staff can be fraught with difficulties.

6.3 Recruitment of graduates

The third example, the recruitment of a number of graduates into a management training programme, indicates a considerable commitment by the organization concerned. It is an investment that will be expected to have long-term benefits in that the recruits will be expected to fill management and senior positions in years to come rather than to have any immediate functional value. Recruitment here must be concerned with attracting those with potential rather than attracting those with immediately usable skills. Most organizations that recruit any number of graduates on a regular basis will have a member of staff with specific responsibility for this task.

The job specification for the graduate recruit will, by necessity, be vague because of its focus on long-term objectives rather than on immediate performance. The person specification, however, may be quite precise in identifying the sort of attributes required of successful candidates. Matching the requirements of the company to what is available in the graduate labour market is a far from easy task. Simple advertisements may attract many hundreds of applicants and the consequent sifting of their details may take much time. It is also likely that the sort of attributes looked for in graduate recruits will not be easily identifiable from completed application forms. Qualities such as leadership, the ability to work in teams, motivation and receptiveness to change can better be assessed by interview, test and assessment centre (see chapter 5 for a full discussion). Such methods are expensive and time consuming. Many graduate recruiters prefer instead (or in addition) to build strong links with those university departments who are likely to supply graduates with the qualities they seek. These links may take a number of forms, but commonly they consist of offering work placements to students whose courses entail a sandwich year, meeting with both students and staff at 'milk round' events, offering vacation employment, offering sponsorships to students, supporting students' projects and research. The objective of all the methods identified is to improve the quality of the interface between the graduate and university and the employer, so recruitment is carried out on the basis of more and better information than is available from a mere application form.

Through the methods described the graduate recruiter can maintain knowledge of the labour market, and of the changes that are occurring within that market, and can hopefully improve the quality (that is, the validity and reliability – see chapter 5 for full discussion of these ideas) of the recruitment process and product for graduates.

The three examples given are illustrative of the range of recruitment methods available and some of the major problems associated with each. While the discussion is not exhaustive, it should give the reader an insight into the techniques and methodologies of recruitment practice.

7. Recruitment Advertising

When placing recruitment advertising a number of factors must be taken into account. These include:

a. The number and location of potential respondents. For instance, it is likely that unskilled staff will be recruited mainly from a local pool of labour, while the recruitment of senior staff may be from a national or even international pool. This will have implications not only for the amount to be spent on advertising, but also where that advertising will be placed.

b. The cost of the advertising must also be considered. It is likely (but not always the case) that the more spent on advertising, the greater the response to that advertising will be. To be efficient, recruitment advertising must aim to attract a satisfactory level and standard of response but at minimum cost.

c. The frequency with which the organization wishes to advertise the position must also be considered. If daily or weekly magazines or papers are used it will be possible to advertise a position several times. If a monthly journal is selected then it is probable that the position will be advertised only once.

d. The readership and circulation of the journal/magazine/newspaper should be investigated. Specialist magazines, such as *Accountancy Age*, *Marketing Weekly* and *Personnel Today* will probably be read mainly by those who are engaged in that area of work, or who are actively seeking work in that area. Advertising more generally (for instance in local newspapers) may well reach a larger audience but probably one that is less attuned to the requirements of the position being advertised.

> The DIY retail giant B&Q report great success in their advertising campaign to recruit older workers to fill managerial jobs in their stores. The company, which targeted people aged around 50 years of age who possessed appropriate retail management experience, used the slogan '*You know your age is not a problem at B&Q – here's another reason why*' and featured older workers. The campaign attracted over 5,000 applicants. By the end of the century B&Q plan to increase the number of their warehouse stores from 19 to 75. Ten are opening during 1996. (Reported in *Personnel Today*, 26 Sept. 1995.)

8. Designing Recruitment Advertising

Whilst it is not the aim of this book to give extensive advice on how to design recruitment advertising, it is possible to give guidelines for the content of such advertisements. In essence good recruitment advertising must meet the following criteria:

a. It should clearly identify the organization, and the industry within which it operates.

b. It should offer a concise summary of the job and its major features.

c. It should outline the essential requirements (skills, knowledge, experience, etc.) expected of the job holder.

d. It should detail the personal characteristics expected of the job holder (for instance, the ability to work to tight deadlines, or the ability to work well as a member of a team).

e. It should detail the main conditions of employment, including an indication of salary.

f. It should state the form in which, and the person to whom, the application should be made.

g. It should conform to all legal requirements.

Moreover, the advertisement should be in a form that is consistent with the wider public relations objectives of the organization. This would include style, tone, layout, colour, use of corporate logos and so forth.

> The advertising agency TCS has established an Internet based electronic recruitment fair known as TAPS (The Appointments Section). It will be aimed at those employers who wish to recruit multi-media professionals and graduates. Employers will be able to advertise on TAPS for a fraction of the cost of national newspaper advertising, while prospective employees will be able to search for attractive vacancies

electronically and then, if interested, complete an on-line standard application form.

The Internet and electronic media are increasingly being used by recruitment consultancies. New vacancies can be rapidly added to the database and updating can be continuous, while prospective employers can access a recruitment consultancy's portfolio of job applicants without leaving their desk, or even making a telephone call. (Reported in *People Management*, 5 Oct. 1995.)

9. Attracting the Scarce Applicant

Whether the economy is in recession or not, it is still common to hear of employers having difficulty in recruiting for some particular positions. This may be due to a number of reasons:

a. A shortage of workers possessing a particular skill or skills.

b. A general shortage of workers in a particular location.

c. The recruiting company is offering poor pay and conditions of service, and line and HR managers do not have the discretion to remedy the situation.

d. In recessionary times those already in work may be reluctant to change their employment if they feel their present position offers relative security.

In such situations the problems of recruitment can be acute. What is required is an adaption of policy to suit the specific circumstances of the labour market. Traditional recruitment procedures have been designed to include a degree of self-selection; in other words, the requirement to complete an application form or to construct a *curriculum vitae* has often been enough to deter many potential applicants from applying. Among the remedies to consider would be to reduce the degree to which candidates self-select and encourage a greater proportion of those who express initial interest to proceed with their application. This could be encouraged by:

a. Reducing the 'barriers' between the potential applicant and the company. For example, simplifying application forms, or using telephone 'hot lines' to allow potential applicants instant access to information about the vacancy.

b. Walk-in interviews. That is, widely advertising the fact that representatives of the company will be available on a number of occasions (during the day and evening) to discuss the opportunities that the company is able to offer. Commonly the sessions will be informal in nature, with refreshments available, and will probably take place in a hotel function room. This will give those currently in employment the opportunity to discuss job opportunities without formally applying for a position.

c. Re-evaluating entry requirements for the positions. If it is decided to lower the acceptable standard of qualification or experience without which people would not be considered, it may be appropriate to give the successful applicants more post-appointment training, to raise their skills to the previously expected standard.

> The Prison Service has put in place policies to increase the number of ethnic minority candidates entering its accelerated promotion scheme. The scheme, which has run since the mid-1980s, has attracted only a very few applicants from non-white backgrounds. The Service has placed a number of advertisements in newspapers read mainly by ethnic minority groups. They include *The Voice, Eastern Eye* and *Asian Times*, in addition to those placed in national daily and Sunday newspapers. (Reported in *Personnel Today*, 22 Nov. 1994.)

10. Evaluating Recruitment

Recruitment can be evaluated using a number of methods that consider both short- and long-term objectives. In the short term, evaluation will be by consideration of:

a. The number of enquiries received.

b. The number of applications received.

c. The suitability of the applicants for the position.

d. Equal opportunities – is the position attracting applications from all groups within the labour market?

e. The relative success of each of the places / times in which the position was advertised.

f. The average cost of recruitment:

$$\frac{\text{Recruitment costs}}{\text{Number starting work}} = \text{Average cost of recruitment}$$

A number of conclusions can be reached from information gleaned from the evaluation. For instance, if many enquiries about a job are received but very few applications, then it is possible that the quality of the information sent to interested parties should be reconsidered. If many applications are received but few are suitable, then it is possible that advertisements have been either incorrectly worded or inappropriately placed. If the profiles of the applicants (in terms of race, sex, etc.) do not match the profile of the labour market in which the job was advertised, then the organization should check its recruitment methods in relation to equality of opportunity.

The results of the evaluation should be fed back to improve the recruitment process for the future.

In the long term, evaluation will be concerned with considering the performance of those appointed and trying to correlate method and source of recruitment with eventual on-the-job performance. Clearly such evaluation will only be possible if the numbers recruited are sufficiently large to make analysis meaningful.

YOUR COUNTRY NEEDS YOU!

In October 1994 the British Army announced that it had awarded the advertising agency Saatchi and Saatchi a £1 million contract with the aim of attracting new recruits to the service. Despite high and continuing levels of unemployment the Army had, for several years, fallen below its recruitment target and manpower levels were perceived to be dangerously low. The army needed to recruit 12,000 young people each year to maintain its strength. It was reported that recruitment for soldiers was 18 per cent behind target, while for officers it was 20 per cent.

It was felt that the widespread publicity given to cuts and redundancies in the armed services had led many to feel that a career in the army was a contradiction in terms – a dead-end job. There was also a suspicion that old methods of advertising (which had laid much emphasis on teamwork, and on the active lifestyle, e.g. soldiers skiing and windsurfing while their bored civilian mates hung out in a pub) would no longer attract sufficient numbers of young people.

The new campaign attempted to show soldiers as skilled professionals, while officers were depicted as managers. The advertising agency talked of 'image repositioning', and trying to demonstrate that the army is about broader values, not just running around with guns. The campaign attempted to show that joining the army is about caring. In one television advertisement a child lay severely wounded in a badly damaged hospital. Three young soldiers were looking on anxiously. They had only fifteen minutes until power supplies were cut. They looked towards the camera at an unseen officer and ask what to do. The advertisement was asking the question of the viewer and inviting those who think they know to call a freephone number. The advertisement was deliberately filmed as a very powerful mini-drama in which a young officer had to make a life-and-death humanitarian decision. The first advertisement was followed by others playing variations on the same theme.

TASK

1. Why do you feel that despite high levels of unemployment the army still had difficulty recruiting?

2. Consider the recruitment campaign described above. How suitable do you feel it to be? What potential problems do you feel it might encounter?

3. Do you feel that the same recruitment campaign could be used to attract both officers and soldiers?

4. How would you evaluate the success of the campaign in the short, medium and long terms?

QUESTIONS FOR FURTHER CONSIDERATION

1. Consider the following:

    THE MANAGER'S CLUB NOBODY WANTS TO JOIN

    I have become a member of the club for 'professional managers' who have experienced redundancy more than once. Membership is growing at an alarming rate, with many companies creating new members.

    I am 39 years old, healthy, with excellent academic and professional qualifications, and am a member of several professional institutes. I have 22 years' work experience, with the last 6 of these being in general management and consultancy positions. Neither of my redundancies were expected or produced any severance payments or outplacement counselling.

    Fourteen months after my second redundancy, I feel I may never work again in the UK because of discriminating trends in the 'executive' recruitment processes. After applying for 30 advertised executive positions and securing only 4 interviews, I telephoned recruitment consultants (most personnel departments would not talk to me) to enquire what was wrong with my applications.

    I was told that my CV was far too long and was not 'professionally presented'. Some recruitment consultants said that because of the number of applications they received for every advertised position, they couldn't read them all. So if they received CVs that were too long, too short, or not laser printed, they would not consider the applicant.

    If this is the case CV presentation becomes more important than the qualifications, experience or skills of an applicant. I paid to have my CV professionally written and started the application process again.

    Another 57 applications resulted in 3 interviews. I also targeted a further 600 firms to receive my CV in a prospecting exercise, but no interviews emerged from this exercise.

    After talking again with recruitment consultants, I was told I didn't fulfil all of the major requirements of the position that employers wanted. Therefore, I wouldn't be short-listed for interview. More importantly, most felt that at 39 and without an MBA I was probably too old for the type of managerial position I was applying for.

    Can it really be that at 39 I am now too old to work as a 'professional manager'? Searching through many newspapers advertisements for 'executive' positions or journals for 'consultancy' positions, I was appalled at the number that have fixed age limits on them – usually between mid-20s and early 30s.

    My question is: How can I hope to find full-time employment when I am so blatantly discriminated against on the basis of my age by recruitment consultants and organizations who cannot even decide what style of CV they would like to receive?

    T.N., London

    (Letter published in *Personnel Management Plus*, June 1994.)

    You are the Secretary of the local branch of the IPD and have been asked to speak to the local Executive Job Club on the topic of 'Modern Recruitment Practices – Attracting the Good Applicant'. You know that TN will be a member of the audience – prepare notes for your talk, outlining possible responses to the queries raised in the letter.

2. Consider the methods of recruitment that you would consider for the following groups of workers:

Trainee Animal Technicians (to be employed in a role supporting scientists who carry out medical research using animals).

Labouring Staff for Oil-rigs (roughnecks and roustabouts).

Postal Delivery Workers.

Trainee Accountants.

Drummer for a local semi-professional band.

3. Under what circumstances would you consider using an employment consultancy/agency for recruitment?

4. You have been given the brief to recruit a new HR Manager for your organization. The role of the job encompasses manpower planning, reward management and developing a performance management system. Describe the recruitment methods to be followed in order to generate an acceptable number of applicants.

5. Consider some examples of recruitment advertising – to what extent are they 'good' or 'bad'? Relate your answers to the criteria outlined in the chapter.

• REFERENCES •

Courtis J (1989)
RECRUITING FOR PROFIT
London, Institute of Personnel Management.

Curnow B (1989)
Recruit, Retrain, Retain – Personnel Management and the Three Rs
Personnel Management, Nov.

Equal Opportunities Commission (1990)
THE SEX DISCRIMINATION ACT AND ADVERTISING
Manchester, Equal Opportunities Commission.

Fowler A (1990)
How to Write a Job Advertisement
Personnel Management Plus, Oct.

Herriot P (1989)
RECRUITMENT IN THE 90s
London, Institute of Personnel Management.

Hogg C (1988)
Graduate Recruitment: Factsheet No. 1.
Published in *Personnel Management*, Jan.

Institute of Personnel Management (1988)
CODE OF PRACTICE ON RECRUITMENT
London, IPM.

Lewis C (1985)
EMPLOYEE SELECTION
London, Hutchinson.

Paddison L (1990)
The Targeted Approach to Recruitment
Personnel Management, Nov.

Personnel Management Plus – Letters, June 1994.

Plumbley K (1985)
RECRUITMENT AND SELECTION
London, Institute of Personnel Management.

West A (1983)
Recruitment and Selection, in **A TEXTBOOK OF TECHNIQUES AND STRATEGIES IN PERSONNEL MANAGEMENT**
Guest D & Kenny T (eds). London, Institute of Personnel Management.

Wheeler D (1988)
How to Recruit A Recruitment Agency
Personnel Management, April.

• CHAPTER •

5

SELECTION

AS A RESULT OF STUDYING THIS CHAPTER YOU SHOULD BE ABLE TO:

- Describe the main features of the selection process and distinguish it from recruitment.
- Identify the criteria upon which selection should be based.
- Be aware of the various stages of selection and how they all should fit together.

- Comment critically on a range of selection methods and appraise their suitability for different selection situations.
- Be aware of the major techniques for candidate testing and the difficulties and problems associated with each.

Please note: this chapter should be read together with chapters 3, 4 and 6.

1. Introduction

The reader will recall the lengths to which the author went in earlier chapters to distinguish clearly between recruitment and selection. To summarize, recruitment is concerned with the production of the 'definitions' of a job (job descriptions and personnel specifications), and also with attracting the interest of suitably qualified candidates in the vacant position. Selection takes the process to the next stage and, as Lewis (1985: 30) suggests, can be defined as:

> The activity in which the organisation uses one or more methods to assess individuals with a view to making a decision concerning their suitability to join that organisation.

However, Lewis also raises a concern over the use of the term 'selection' itself, suggesting that what is involved is not a one-way process but a two-way exchange of information, and the employer not only has to 'select' the best candidate for the job, but the candidate also has to choose the employer!

Cole (1988: 141) builds on Lewis's concerns in stating that:

> Even in times of high unemployment, selection is very much a two way process, with the candidate assessing the organisation as well as the other way round. From the organisation's point of view, selection is just as much a 'selling' operation as the initial recruitment.

As we will see later in the chapter, selection can be undertaken using a variety of methods. However, whichever method is chosen, two over-riding criteria must be borne in mind: the need for validity and reliability in the selection methods used. These fundamental requirements are discussed below.

2. Validity

In this context, validity refers to the degree to which the selection methods chosen are a predictor of future job performance. For instance, those registering with a recruitment agency with the aim of seeking work as a secretary may well be expected to give a demonstration of their word-processing and short-hand skills before they are put forward for positions. However, this test would have no validity if the position under consideration was for a receptionist/switchboard operator. This remarkably obvious piece of information can only be put in context when it is further pointed out that many of the selection methods used by employers are also of dubious validity – not least of all, the interview. Any selection 'tool' used must in some way be able to test likely future job performance. That is, the test should be a valid method of assessing the suitability of the short-listed applicants for the position for which they have applied.

Many employers will give potential employees some sort of 'test' to assess likely job performance. These might include personality tests, psychometric tests, in-tray exercises and presentations, to name but a few. However, all employers should be aware of the potential equal opportunities problems of employment testing. Inappropriate or badly designed tests have been shown to discriminate unfairly against some candidates.

All selectors should seek to use methods that are *valid* in deciding who to appoint to a position.

3. Reliability

Tests are reliable if, when repeated on a number of occasions, they produce the same result. Clearly all tests for employment need to have a high degree of reliability. If unreliable methods were to be used then it is *probable* that a candidate appointed one day might be rejected the next. An application of the concept of reliability would be the driving test. If, for instance, a candidate was deemed to have passed by one examiner, but would have failed if tested by another examiner, then the test is unreliable. Reliability implies clear standards and trained assessors all working to those clear standards.

4. Choosing the Tools for Selection: The Main Criteria

4.1 Cost

The more complex the selection process, the greater the cost will be. If a number of techniques are used in series it is probable that not only will the time taken increase but also it is likely that a larger number of staff will need to be involved. The amount to be spent on selection will depend on a number of factors, among which will be:

- the relative importance of the position

- how crucial the appointment of the 'right' person is

- if the job requires the performance of a 'critical' skill (e.g. airline pilot), then more time and effort may need to be devoted to selection.

The overriding concern may well be cost-effectiveness rather than cost *per se*.

4.2   Time
The process of recruitment and selection can be quite long and drawn out. The period of time that may elapse between permission being granted for a position to be filled and final selection (and the successful candidate taking up the job) might quite easily run to several weeks and in some cases several months. The priority should be to select the right person for the job rather than merely to fill the vacancy. Mistakes in selection can be expensive, and rued over a number of years!

4.3   The need for particular skills and attributes
Many jobs will require the holder to have particular attributes, skills or qualities. These might include physical fitness, the possession of a Heavy Goods Vehicle (HGV) licence, programming skills in various computer languages, to name but a few. If such qualities are essential then it is best to test them yourself rather than rely on either the word of the candidate or on some ancient certificate.

4.4   The expectations of the candidates
As suggested earlier, selection is a two-way process: the candidate will have expectations of the employer just as much as the employer about the candidate. Most job candidates would find it unusual if a job interview did not form at least some part of the selection process, despite (as we shall see later) its lack of reliability and validity.

5. The Basis for Selection

The basis for selection should be the job description and person specification (as discussed in chapters 3 and 4). If constant reference is not made to these documents throughout the selection process it is easy to forget that what is required is not to select the 'best' person but *the best person for the job*; in other words, the one who most exactly fits the characteristics outlined in the job description and the person specification.

The Director General of the Imperial Cancer Research Fund, Sir Walter Bodmer, has told a Recruitment Society meeting that the science of genetic engineering is developing at such a pace and in a way that could be useful to recruiters. Simple tests may soon be available to assess whether job candidates are prone to mental instability, susceptible to fatal diseases, or have a propensity towards a particular skill which could be developed. The tests, if and when available, could be simple, cheap and quick to administer, not unlike the standard test for colour blindness – which is, after all, the result of a simple genetic defect. (Reported in *Personnel Today*, 10 Oct. 1995.)

6. The Stages of Selection

6.1 The application form/*curriculum vitae*

Those who have expressed an interest in a position will make known that interest by applying for the job. Most jobs require that candidates apply by either completing a *pro forma* application form and supporting it with a letter of application, or by forwarding a *curriculum vitae* (CV), which should also be accompanied by formal letter of application. The application form is an employer standard CV. It will contain much of the detail of a self-devised CV, but in the order, form and style that most suits the prospective employer. The self-constructed CV may well tell you a little more about the abilities of the applicant to present a comparatively large amount of information in a clear, simple and readily understandable form, but also allows the applicant to obscure in amongst the more florid details their less flattering achievements and times.

The application form requires all questions to be answered and does not allow the applicant to 'conveniently forget to mention' the little hiccups in his career. Additionally if it is expected that a large number of people might apply for a particular position, then a well-designed application form should allow rapid short-listing decisions to be made if (for instance) it locates in one place the key pieces of data that are to be used for short-listing.

Most large organizations will have several standard application forms. One for manual staff, one for clerical and supervisory staff and one for technical and managerial staff. The style of the forms should be consistent with what is expected (in performance terms) of the job holders. So, for instance, the manual staff application form may only require factual details to be supplied. This should reflect the fact that proficiency in the written form of the English language is probably not a requirement of the job. On the other hand, the management form will probably require applicants to be more expansive and provide answers to such questions as:

Give examples of difficult situations that you have faced and how you have coped?

What do you consider to be the major achievements of your career to date?

In what ways do you feel that you will be able to contribute to the
Company?

This additional information should aid the processes of short-listing,
and will provide such information about the candidates as:

Their ability to express themselves clearly in the written form.

Their motivations and aspirations.

Their ability to relate their past achievements to the requirements of the
post under consideration.

Additionally, some employers place a great deal of store by the
ability to write neatly and to fill in forms correctly. Indeed, both of these
attributes may be requirements of the position (for example, clerical and
administrative staff), and so quite correctly are considered at the earliest
stage.

Examination of the completed and returned application forms
(or CVs) should allow applicants to be sorted into three piles. The 'possibles', the 'definitely nots' and the 'look at agains'. If there are plenty of
'possibles' then they will have to be whittled down further into a short-
list, and the 'look at agains' will join the 'definitely nots'. If there are
insufficient 'possibles', then the 'look at agains' will indeed have to be
looked at again until a sufficient number of possibles (if there are a
sufficient number) are found.

6.2   The interview

The interview is a two-way process and therefore as much of an opportunity for the applicant to find out about the employer as for the employer
to find out about the applicant. It has long been argued that interviews
have a very low predictive validity, and that used alone they are a poor
method for selecting from among candidates. Good interview skills do
not necessarily indicate good job skills. They also have a number of
other inherent problems. These include:

a.   The 'halo' effect   This is the tendency to give greatest credit or
value to the candidate who is most like ourselves. After all, is it not a
truism to claim that if we are 'good' employees (and we perceive
ourselves to be so), then those most like us also will probably be good
employees. This assumption has clear equal opportunities problems,
and would potentially mean that interviewers would only ever offer
appointments to those who are very similar to them.

*b.   The tendency to stereotype candidates on the basis of insufficient
evidence*   This might include dress, hair, accent. This would also include
the incorrect assumptions that all women are physically weak, or all
Scotsmen mean (and thereby probably very good accountants). This
tendency to make assumptions about individuals based on our (probably very minor) experiences of, or prejudices about, other members of
that group lies at the heart of the concern about unequal access to
workplace opportunity.

c.   Cultural bias   The rituals and customs of employment interviewing are essentially features of Western workplace practice and may not be familiar to members of other ethnic groups. For instance, one of the unwritten rules of interviewing is that strong eye contact between interviewee and interviewer indicates honesty and integrity, while weak eye contact is said to indicate shiftiness and dishonesty. This 'unwritten rule' does not take account of the accepted practice among many members of the Asian community, who would regard a young person holding strong eye contact with an older person (e.g. an interviewer) as rude and insolent. The interviewer must be aware of the degree to which our culture impinges upon our perception of others.

d.   The strength of first impressions   It is claimed, and indeed there is considerable research to back this up, that the interviewer generally makes up his or her mind about an interviewee within the first few minutes of the start of an interview. Some would claim that it takes less time than that – and that interviewers decide as soon as the person walks through the door. Whatever the truth of the matter, common sense tells us that we have all had experiences whereby we have changed our opinion of those we have met as we have got to know them better. The interviewer must guard against making instant (or too rapid) decisions about candidates.

e.   The lack of training of many interviewers   It is probable that in most organizations the only people that will have regular experience of interviewing are the HR specialists. Most other managers will be called upon to interview infrequently, and probably only when a vacancy exists in their own department. It is also widely accepted that interviewing is a skill, and like most skills will deteriorate if not practised regularly. So no matter what training is given to line managers, their interviewing skills may well be rusty.

Despite all of these difficulties with interviewing, Torrington et al. (1991) still claim that:

> They [interviews] cannot be surpassed as a method of allowing the candidate and the employer to 'tune in' to each other and to establish whether they could develop an effective working relationship.

HR can help to overcome the weaknesses identified above in a number of ways:

By ensuring that high-quality job descriptions and person specifications are available for the interviewers.

By providing a simple, jargon-free, set of criteria from which interviewers can construct their interview strategy.

By providing training and retraining for staff involved in interviewing.

7. Procedure and Practice for Interviewing

7.1 Procedure

Many of the 'housekeeping' arrangements for good interviewing will be the responsibility of HR. These will include:

a. Agreeing the time, date and the place in which the interviews are to be held.

b. Notifying the candidates in good time, providing directions, maps, etc. if needed, and making it clear to candidates the policy of the organization with respect to reimbursing travel and other expenses.

c. Ensuring that a suitable reception/waiting area exists in which candidates can wait before they are interviewed and in which tea or coffee can be taken. If refreshments are to be offered it is probably best that they be taken before the interview to spare the candidates the difficulty of trying to eat a biscuit and answer a question at the same time!

d. Ensuring that the furniture and configuration of the interview room gives the degree of formality that the interviewers would wish. The room to be used should be tidy and free of clutter, and provide the candidates with space to leave a coat or bag. The interviewee's chair should be positioned in such a place that there is no confusion as to where he should sit.

e. Ensuring that there will be no disturbances during the interview. This would include no telephone calls or other interruptions.

7.2 Practice

Questions asked during the course of the interview should meet the following broad set of criteria:

a. All questions should be related to the job requirements as laid out in the person specification and job description.

b. Questions should not be asked to test ethnic minority candidates' knowledge or understanding of British customs or to check their skills in English, unless these are particular requirements of the job under consideration.

c. The style of questioning should be 'open' as opposed to 'closed'. So for instance, the question 'did you enjoy your time at University'? should be rephrased as 'what particular aspects of your time at University did you enjoy'?

d. If a job requires the working of irregular or unsocial hours all candidates should be presented with the full facts and then asked if such requirements would present any difficulties. There should not be an assumption that female candidates would have greater difficulty in working irregular hours.

e. Questions should not be asked about marriage plans, plans to start a family or family commitments. All are likely to discriminate against women.

It is an unwritten rule of interviewing that the interviewer should speak for no longer than one third of the time, with the other two-thirds left for the applicant to respond to questions and ask questions of his or her own.

Candidates should be interviewed with the aim of finding the best match between the applicants and the person specification. It is probable that no candidate will exactly fit the list of 'essential' and 'desirable' attributes that are to be detailed in the person specification. So the best match with 'essential' attributes must first be found and then the less important 'desirable' attributes considered. The successful candidate should be the one that 'best fits' the person specification, while having no significant demerits.

An alternative scenario to that painted in the previous paragraph may also emerge. This could be when all, or a number, of the short-listed candidates meet the 'essential' and 'desirable' attributes required. If this is the situation then the selectors must choose additional criteria upon which to make their selection. The problem with this is that the additional criteria selected may well not be relevant to the job, for all of those that are relevant should have been identified in the person specification. If this happens the selectors are then using what are known as 'spurious criteria'. Alternatively the selectors can make a random selection from the candidates.

The University of East London has used video conferencing in order to interview an applicant for an academic post. The applicant had only recently returned to the United States following a visit to the United Kingdom, when she found that she had been short-listed and invited to return to the UK to attend an interview. In discussions with the University it was agreed to conduct the interview using the video conference facilities of the University and of the University of Pennsylvania.
(Reported in the *Times Higher Education Supplement*, 10 Nov. 1995.)

8. Types of Interview

8.1 Individual, or one-to-one, interviews

These are by far the most common, and offer the best opportunity for a rapport to be developed between the interviewer and the candidate. They do, however, have a number of problems. For instance, if the interviewer lacks objectivity, then since he is the sole judge this weakness will go unchecked. Additionally the interviewer may find that he lacks knowledge of some of the areas in which he has to question the candidates. The judgement may then be made more on *how* the person answers rather than on *what* is actually said. A further problem may be that the very fact that the interviewer and the candidate did establish a rapport may act to cloud the judgement of the interviewer, to the extent that the person appointed is the one with whom the interviewer got on best, rather than the most suitable candidate in terms of experience and quali-fications. Once again this would go unchecked.

8.2   Panel interviews

To a degree at least, panel interviews should overcome the problems identified above. Generally speaking, a 'panel' will consist of two or more people who will together interview the candidates. It is common practice for the panel to be made up of the line manager of the vacant position, an HR specialist, plus others who may have a significant inter-est in the appointment. This might, for instance, be a senior member of staff from the department who might be able to question the candidates about their specialist knowledge or experience. The panel interview has a number of advantages, but principally the fact that any decision made will be a group decision and based upon the feelings of all panel mem-bers and not one individual. Each panellist can ask questions relevant to their own specialist knowledge and interest and a more fully rounded picture of each candidate can be developed.

Variations on panel interviews include the selection board, in which a comparatively large number of people (all of whom have a vested interest in the selection) convene to interview the candidates. The board may number up to a dozen people in all and form quite a formidable battery for the candidates to face. Rarely are all members of the board expected to participate fully in the interviewing, most will perhaps ask only a nominal question or two, but all will get the chance to see and hear the candidates and pass an opinion as to their suitability. Although cumbersome, the use of a board can make for subsequent ease of communication and liaison, and allow the solicitation of wide range of expertise and opinion.

An alternative method of using the panel method is to conduct 'interviews in series', where each candidate is interviewed by a number of people in turn. That is, each interviewer will spend (say) 20 minutes with each candidate before the candidate moves to another room to see another interviewer. The first interviewer will then be joined by another candidate, and so on. This should take no longer than all the panel together seeing all the candidates, and (theoretically at least) combines the best features of both the panel and individual interviews. However, no one member of the panel hears all that is said (or not said) by any of the candidates, and so each interviewer will independently form his opinions. When using this method it is not uncommon for the members of the panel to form very different opinions of the candidates, and reconciling these differences can be difficult.

The panel interview (and its variations) do produce problems of their own. These include:

a. The likelihood that the views of the chairman will dominate decision-making. Not all panel members will feel equally able to contribute their views and opinions and may tend to defer to the wishes of the chairman or a dominant member of the panel. This will particularly be the case if the chairman is prepared to 'bully' other members of the panel by, for instance, challenging them to disagree with his assertion that 'we couldn't possibly appoint the second candidate could we'?

b. The panel acting collectively may be prepared to appoint a far higher-risk candidate than would any of its members interviewing alone. This tendency towards risk when decisions are made collectively is well researched and probably occurs because no one individual can be held responsible for the consequence of the error.

c. The tendency to go for a compromise candidate satisfying nobody but appointing the candidate who is least offensive to all the panel members. This sub-optimal decision-making is again a well-documented feature of group behaviour.

8.3 Interviews: conclusion

Undoubtedly interviewing is a vital and necessary part of the process of selection. It also meets the expectations of candidates by offering them the opportunity to meet their future supervisor, and possibly other future work colleagues. However, to depend upon an interview alone as a selection tool is often a mistake. As stated before, interviews have a low predictive validity for assessing future job performance. For many positions employers will wish to use other measures to aid selection. Amongst the most common of these is the taking up of references. Generally references are taken up after the person has been offered the job. The reference then performs a confirmatory role.

8.4 Taking up references

All applicants should be asked to supply the names, addresses and positions of at least one, and preferably two, employer referees. In the case of school, college or university leavers, a teacher or lecturer would suffice for this purpose. Employers also often ask for a personal referee. However, this is widely discredited – most people are able to find someone to say a few kind words about them!

The value of employer references also is often questioned. Today many companies simply send the referee a *pro forma* document to complete which requires boxes to be ticked and brief comments to be made. The aim of the form will be:

a. To gain confirmation that the person was employed by the organization as claimed.

b. To confirm the title of the job and a brief description of duties and responsibilities.

c. To confirm that the referee considers the candidate to be honest and trustworthy.

d. To confirm that the candidate's time-keeping, attendance and attitude to work were all satisfactory.

e. To give a brief space for the referee to add additional comments.

Research shows that very rarely are references bad, and that references are not a predictor of future job performance. At best they can perform the confirmatory role outlined above. Every HR manager can tell tales of a florid reference that contained phrases such as 'any company that gets Mr Brown to work for them will be fortunate indeed', or 'Mr Brown leaves this company as he joined it; fired with enthusiasm'!

The application form, the interview and the reference are not the only selection tools available to recruiters. Many employers will choose from a range of other techniques in an attempt to try and increase the validity and reliability of their selection. These techniques are discussed below.

9. Selection Testing

9.1 Introduction

For many jobs it is appropriate to supplement an interview with some form of selection test or tests. To be of value tests need to meet a number of criteria, but principally they must be:

a. Valid (as explained earlier in this chapter).

b. Reliable (as explained earlier in this chapter).

c. If possible the test should also have face validity; that is, it should also be closely linked in content to actual job performance. For instance, the driving test closely replicates the 'real world' and therefore probably has high face validity.

d. The tests should be discriminating – they should be designed in such a way as to allow the differences between the candidates to be made clear.

e. Tests should also be relevant to their purpose.

f. All tests should also be standardized in order that they measure the same thing in different people.

g. Tests should not either intentionally nor unintentionally discriminate against any group or groups. Many tests have run into problems in this area. This is particularly so if the tests assume a degree of cultural orientation or linguistic skill that is not a requirement of the job itself.

Given these requirements it is unlikely that the average human resource manager will have the skills to devise suitable tests for any but the simplest jobs. This is really the specialist area of the 'industrial and organizational psychologist', who can offer advice on testing procedures, techniques and methodologies. It is recommended that the advice of an industrial psychologist be sought before tests are embarked upon.

9.2 Assessment centres

Very often tests are grouped together and a range of tests used to aid selection for a position. When this occurs it is often known as an 'assessment centre'.

By exposing candidates to a range of tests, each closely related to one or more aspects of the job, an assessment centre aims to develop a high degree of predictive validity about the ability of candidates to perform the job under consideration. Typically an assessment centre may run over a couple of days and therefore require considerable resources devoted to it. These might include food and refreshment, accommodation, and the availability of several skilled assessors. Assessment centres can only justify such expenditure if (a) the position is comparatively senior, or (b) costs can be absorbed easily and (c) the degree of predictive validity that they are able to offer is sufficiently high.

It is not uncommon for assessment centre type testing to be used for reasons other than just selection. Indeed some organizations use them for promotion and diagnostic purposes.

Selection tests and assessment centres will call on a range of types of tests, however they can be categorized into four broad types:

a.   *Personality tests*   These aim to measure a variety of characteristics, such as the candidate's degree of introversion, or extroversion, and their emotional stability. Generally they take the form of questionnaires. Such tests should only be administered by a trained psychologist, who should be able to analyse the results to give feedback about the candidate's motivations and characteristics. This might include (for example) ambition, skills at dealing with others, or determination.

Personality tests can prove difficult to analyse if candidates fail to answer questions honestly, or try to give the answer that they think is expected. Additionally, the wording of tests must be clear and unambiguous if they are not to be interpreted differently by each candidate.

The tests used by psychologists must be validated and standardized if they are to be of any value in selection.

b.   *Intelligence tests*   These are aimed at measuring the general intelligence of the candidate. Testing 'intelligence' is a very controversial area and the tests used are, generally speaking, far from infallible. For instance, test scores can be improved with practice, and examples of intelligence tests are available in many bookshops. Intelligence tests are probably best used for diagnostic purposes and for this reason 'intelligence' is grouped into a number of areas. These include mathematical skills, reasoning skills, skills of logic, problem solving skills, etc. The relative performance of the candidate in each of the areas can then be assessed and a diagnosis of strengths and weaknesses made.

c.   *Proficiency tests*   These are designed to assess and measure the candidate's ability to do the work involved with the position. They may be attainment tests, which assess the degree to which a candidate can perform the skills which they possess in some degree already (e.g. word-processing speeds). Alternatively, they may be more predictive in nature, trying to assess how past experiences relate to the new position. Among the tests used here might be in-tray exercises, chairmanship exercises and oral and written presentation exercises.

d.   *Aptitude tests*   These are designed to test the potential of an individual to perform a task. For instance, flying an aeroplane requires the coordination of hand and foot movement. The aptitude of an individual to perform this skill can be assessed well away from an aircraft using quite simple manual or computer technologies.

10. Following Up

Once the selection has been made the successful applicant should be quickly told. The unsuccessful applicants (with the possible exception of the second choice) should also be politely informed that on this occasion they were not selected, and thanked for their interest in the position. The successful applicant should be promptly contacted and told that she is to be offered the job *subject to satisfactory references and medical examination*. Hopefully, this should be a mere formality and the organization should soon be in a position to confirm the offer. At this stage the second-choice candidate can also be told that she too is unsuccessful on this occasion.

In many organizations it is the practice to offer debriefing to the unsuccessful candidates. Here, one of the selectors (often the HR manager), will offer feedback to the candidates as to why, on this occasion, they were unsuccessful. The debriefing should relate the candidate's application and interview performance to the requirements as specified in the job description and person specification. Debriefing should identify weaknesses in the application and selection performance, and if done correctly and sympathetically will not only inform unsuccessful candidates why they did not get the position, but will also give them useful pointers as to how they might improve for the future. The opportunity for useful feedback is often appreciated by job applicants, and will help them to feel confident that the successful candidate was selected for the correct reasons, namely because they presented the best match with the person specification.

Table 5.1 lists a selection of reasons given to unsuccessful candidates that would *not* give applicants confidence that due process had been followed.

11. Conclusion

Recruitment and selection is an area fraught with difficulties for the unwary or ill-prepared. This and the preceding chapters have attempted to outline some of the techniques that managers should use if common pitfalls are to be avoided. It is easy to be wise about selection errors after they have been made, less easy to put them right. It is always better not to employ someone in the first place rather than to have to dismiss them once they have commenced work and been found to be unsatisfactory. Why is dismissal 'difficult'? Well, apart from the legal niceties that must be observed, an employee is someone that you know, and despite their shortcomings as an employee, they may have personal qualities that make them popular with their colleagues. You may have come to know the employee's partner and family and also to be aware of the financial and other difficulties that loss of employment would cause to that family. Given these circumstances, it is not surprising that many employers and managers are very reluctant to dismiss unsatisfactory employees, and where they do, they find the experience to be both stressful and distasteful. It is far better not to have employed the person in the first place.

'You didn't get the job because . . .	Problem
your CV was too long/short.'	This might be a reason for not long- or short-listing an applicant, but usually a good CV is merely an *entrée* to the next stage of selection.
you're too young.'	Is this a valid basis for rejecting a candidate? Surely if you are suitably qualified and experienced, then age is not of significance?
the Chairman wanted Kate, but if it were up to me alone you would have got the job.'	So, the selection panel seemed to be split. More careful consideration of the person specification might have helped them reach a common decision.
the panel thought that a young woman such as yourself would soon be getting married and therefore wouldn't have the commitment to the job.'	Clear sexual discrimination, and the applicant would be well advised to seek legal redress. There should be no assumption that married women or working mothers could not offer the degree of commitment required for employment. All candidates should have the demands of the job (e.g. hours of work, unsocial hours, weekend work, etc.) clearly explained to them and all should be asked if this presents any problems.
on the day Mary performed better.'	Better, but making an employment decision can have long-term consequences, and should marginally better interview performance alone determine such an important decision? Far better to relate selection to the criteria in the person specification.

More appropriate reasons might include:

'You didn't get the job because . . .

we really wanted a fully qualified, rather than a part-qualified, accountant for this job.'

although your application had many strengths, your lack of project management experience was crucial.'

you told us that you would not be prepared to do shift work, and as this is a requirement for all our drivers we had to turn you down.'

Table 5.1
'You didn't get the job because . . .'

THE CASEBROOK HOSPITAL TRUST

You are employed in the Human Resources Department of the Casebrook Hospital and have specific responsibility for coordinating recruitment and selection. Although the hospital is situated in an area of relatively high unemployment and one that has been quite badly affected by the recession, the Hospital still has significant problems filling some vacancies, particularly those for junior doctors and theatre nurses. You have managed to overcome the problem to some degree by advertising widely and imaginatively, and considering a wider pool of candidates. This contrasts with the recruitment of clerical and manual staff, where the high rates of local unemployment ensure many applicants for each and every vacancy.

For clerical and manual grades the Trust has an agreement with unions that all vacancies will be advertised in the local press and local Job Centres. The Trust also has a commitment to ensuring equality of opportunity.

In recent months two local factories have closed down, making 940 mostly skilled and semi-skilled people redundant. The local authority has also announced 250 redundancies, mostly among clerical and manual grades. The local unemployment rate currently stands at 15 per cent, with most of the people registered either unskilled, semi-skilled, or with clerical and administrative skills.

Two of the hospital's porters are due to retire at the end of the month and a third has handed in his resignation (he is taking up a place at college). Budget cuts have meant that the porterage service has had to operate below full strength for several months, and the loss of three more porters will stretch the service further. Approval has been granted to fill all three vacancies quickly.

The jobs were advertised and a closing date two weeks from the date of advertisement announced. By the closing date over 3,500 applications had been received. Currently they are standing in a pile by your desk. The pile is several feet high. You have quickly looked at the top fifty and of those about forty applicants seem to fit your requirements. If a similar proportion of the rest are satisfactory, then over 2,500 could fit the specifications of the job.

TASK

You have apprised the General Services Manager (who is responsible for porters) of the number of applications received and are due to meet her this afternoon to consider how best to proceed. The GSM has said that she would wish to reduce the number by considering one of the following methods:

a. Rejecting those who have not got GCSE-standard Maths and English, and those who are educated to A-level standard or above, or

b. Looking only at the first 50 applicants and selecting from those, or

c. Rejecting all of those aged under 25 and over 40, or

d. Only considering applicants who are married and have children ('they need the jobs more than the others . . .'), or

e. Only considering those applicants who live within a two-mile radius of the hospital ('easier to call them in if we have a flap on . . .').

Consider the alternatives outlined by the GSM and consider others that might be more suitably used as a basis for the selection. How would you wish to proceed once the applicants had been whittled down to a manageable number?

1. 'Recruitment is a science, selection is an art.' Discuss.

2. If the interview is widely regarded as a selection tool that has low predictive validity, why is it still the primary method by which the vast majority of employees are selected?

3. You are the Human Resource Manager of the Blueplate Engineering Co. The post of Marketing Manager is vacant and interviews for the short-listed applicants are due to take place in two weeks' time. The MD, who is taking a personal interest in the appointment, has asked you to *investigate some tests that we can give them, to see what they're made of*. No budget is available for this purpose. Outline your reply, with justifications, in a memorandum to the MD.

4. From your own experiences of applying for jobs, what are the rituals that are part of job interviewing? Consider the extent to which they are necessary. Do you consider that they can work against the interests of equal opportunities? Explain your answers.

5. What major functions does the selection interview fulfil?

•REFERENCES•

Cole G (1988)
PERSONNEL MANAGEMENT: THEORY AND PRACTICE
London, DPP.

Collinson D (1987)
Who Controls Selection?
Personnel Management, May.

Fletcher C & Johnson C (1989)
A Test by Any Other Name
Personnel Management, March.

Goodworth C (1979)
EFFECTIVE INTERVIEWING
London, Hutchinson.

Hackett P (1978)
INTERVIEW SKILLS TRAINING
London, Institute of Personnel Management.

Herriot P & Fletcher C (1990)
Candidate Friendly Selection for the 1990s
Personnel Management, Feb.

Langtry R (1994)
Selection, in **HUMAN RESOURCE MANAGEMENT: A CONTEMPORARY PERSPECTIVE**
Beardwell I & Holden L (eds). London, Pitman.

Lewis C (1985)
EMPLOYEE SELECTION
London, Hutchinson.

Ludlow R & Panton F (1991)
SUCCESSFUL STAFF SELECTION
Hemel Hempstead, Prentice-Hall.

Pearson R (1991)
THE HUMAN RESOURCE
Maidenhead, McGraw-Hill.

Plumbley K (1985)
RECRUITMENT AND SELECTION
London, Institute of Personnel Management.

Rodger A (1951)
THE SEVEN POINT PLAN
London, National Institute of Industrial Psychology.

Torrington D & Hall L (1992)
PERSONNEL MANAGEMENT: A NEW APPROACH
Hemel Hempstead, Prentice-Hall.

Torrington D, Hall L, Haylor I & Myers J (1991)
EMPLOYEE RESOURCING
London, Institute of Personnel Management.

West A (1983)
Recruitment and Selection, in **A TEXTBOOK OF TECHNIQUES AND STRATEGIES IN PERSONNEL MANAGEMENT**
Guest D & Kenny T (eds). London, Institute of Personnel Management.

• CHAPTER •

6

EQUAL OPPORTUNITIES

AS A RESULT OF STUDYING THIS CHAPTER YOU SHOULD BE ABLE TO:

- Be aware of the relative disadvantage that many groups in society operate under in the field of employment.

- Appreciate the economic and social benefits that can accrue to organizations that have sound policies and procedures for equality of opportunity.

- Be aware of the major pieces of legislation in this area and the responsibilities that employers have under the law.

- Understand how employers can introduce policies (and how these policies should be monitored) to ensure that equality of opportunity is promoted.

- Consider the relative merits of some of the employment-related initiatives introduced to promote greater equality of opportunity.

- Be aware of the situations in which employers may still legitimately (and indeed should) discriminate in the employment situation.

Please note: this chapter should be read in conjunction with the chapters on recruitment, selection and training and development.

> *The 20 year olds of today probably have little awareness that 20 years ago it was common to see women's rates for the same jobs done by men, discriminatory job advertising, and restrictions on women's ability to obtain credit . . . Today, the picture shows that irrespective of whether women are high or low earners, overall, they are in a considerably worse financial position than men at all stages in their lives.*

UK Central Statistical Office, *Social Focus on Women* (1995)

1. Introduction

EQUAL OPPORTUNITIES – THE COMPANY POLICY

The company is committed to equality of opportunity for all, irrespective of race, colour, creed, ethnic or national origins, gender, marital status, sexuality, disability or age.

We are committed to taking positive action to promote equality of opportunity and our recruitment, training and promotion procedures are based on the requirements of a job.

> In this policy the company includes all staff whether full-time, part-time or temporary, and any person who acts as an agent on behalf of the company on employment matters. All company employees are made aware of the provisions of this policy.

This statement could be taken from any one of many British companies that claim to be 'equal opportunities' employers. This chapter attempts to consider the employment-related disadvantages suffered by many groups in British society, the response of the law and specific pieces of legislation, as well as the policies that can be, and indeed are being, used by employers to enhance and promote equality of opportunity.

Coussey and Jackson (1991: 4) claim that:

> achieving equality of opportunity essentially means changing how we do things, how we behave and how one's organization looks. It means that more women, ethnic minorities and disabled applicants and employees will be given the same chances to take part, progress and succeed as white males.

Further, they state:

> The basic premise is that talent and ability is evenly spread throughout all groups and between men and women; however, women and ethnic minorities are unevenly distributed in employment and concentrated in lower grade jobs because of the effects of past and of present discriminatory practices, and of social and educational disadvantages. People with a disability are also most likely to be found in lower level jobs and this is unlikely to be entirely because of limited capacity. The long term objective of an equal opportunity programme is to remove any barriers which prevent these groups fully taking part in an organization, and thereby achieve a random distribution; that is, a workforce which fully reflects the population at all levels.

Setting aside legal considerations for the moment, there are two major ways in which equal opportunities are of importance to employers in general and to the human resource specialist in particular. The first is to do with maximizing the utilization of available human capital. It is fair to say that employers who promote equality of opportunity should be able to achieve a better return out of the workforce, simply because they are more likely to have the best people filling all available positions. The absence of equality of opportunity is likely to see a sub-optimal use of human resources, and although difficult to quantify is none the less a potentially significant factor. This of course has a real cost in terms of lower output and/or reduced efficiency.

The economic reasons are probably compelling enough for some employers, but they are often intertwined with the second reason for promoting equality of opportunity – the need for social justice. This primarily involves taking an ethical focus that seeks to identify the processes that give rise to inequalities and seeks to address them by putting in place education, training and policies that promote acceptance and understanding.

The two reasons outlined above may be seen by many as ample evidence of the need to promote a greater awareness of equal opportunities within employing organizations. However, the fact that great inequality of both opportunity and achievement exists in the workplace seems to indicate that many (if not most) employers still have a considerable way to go in developing appropriate attitudes and policies.

The UK Central Statistical Office's 1995 report *Social Focus on Women* showed that although women form 53 per cent of the workforce, they are most highly concentrated in lowly paid occupations such as clerical and secretarial work, childcare, personal services and sales. On average, women are paid less than men (up to 27 per cent), and reach their peak of earnings in their early thirties, ten years before the average man. Taking breaks to raise families will disrupt a woman's career and most never make up the lost time. Many women working in traditional female areas such as education or clerical work, although surrounded by female colleagues, will still answer to a male boss.

2. Equal Opportunities and the Law

It is also of course the case that the law has quite a lot to say about equal opportunities, but principally via the following pieces of legislation:

Disabled Persons Acts 1944 and 1958, and the Disability Discrimination Act 1995

Race Relations Act 1976

Equal Pay Act 1970 (amended 1983)

Sex Discrimination Act 1975

These are considered below.

2.1 The Disabled Persons Acts 1944 and 1958
The Disabled Persons Acts require that employers with 20 or more staff employ at least 3 per cent from among the ranks of the disabled. However, this percentage may be varied where the work is particularly suitable or unsuitable. Although it is not an offence to be below quota, it is an offence to employ somebody who is not registered disabled while below quota unless a permit has been obtained from the Secretary of State for Employment. None the less, prosecutions under these Acts are extremely rare, and it seems fair to assume that most employers are either ignorant of their responsibilities under the Act or are prepared to ignore them.

2.2 The Disability Discrimination Act 1995
The employment-related implications of the new Act which came into force in 1996 will affect every employer in the country. The Act makes it illegal for employers to discriminate against disabled people in employment, and will put a duty on all employers with more than 20 staff to make any *reasonable* adjustment to working conditions or the workplace

to overcome the practical effects of a disability. Additionally, those organizations that supply goods and services to customers will have to make such adjustments as are reasonably possible to allow access for disabled customers.

At the time of writing some of the key terms in the Act were still seen to be imprecise and ill-defined. For instance, what constitutes 'disability' or 'reasonable access' is the subject of considerable debate. What is more certain is that the Act has implications for all aspects of employment, including recruitment advertising, selection, training and re-training.

In considering their response to the Act employers are recommended to be proactive. They should review their employment practices and the facilities they provide, give consideration to the costs of making them more accessible to disabled people, and act quickly where it is reasonable or necessary to do so. If costs are prohibitively high the employer is recommended to record all calculations made and estimates taken. Such data may well be of use in future legal cases.

The UK government has not made provision for a body to monitor the new Act, along the lines of the Equal Opportunities Commission or the Commission for Racial Equality. This is unfortunate because the EOC and CRE are excellent sources of advice for employers seeking to apply other areas of the law.

Employment-related disputes arising out of the new Act will be handled by industrial tribunals. Under the provisions of the Act employers will be liable if it can be shown that they have unreasonably discriminated against disabled people. They will also be liable for the discriminatory acts of their employees unless they are able to show that they had provided adequate training for their staff.

At present, the cost of making adjustments to equipment and the workplace will be met by the government's Access to Work Scheme. This can cover such diverse areas as taxi fares or computer equipment, but the future of the scheme is uncertain and it is likely that a greater burden of the costs of the new Act will fall on employers.

2.3 The Race Relations Act 1976

The Race Relations Act has as its aim the prevention of unfair discrimination on the grounds of race, colour, nationality and ethnic or national origin. It is concerned with both direct discrimination – for example, where an employer refuses to employ or promote Asian workers – and indirect discrimination – for example, using an employment test for applicants for a job that required the display of skills not directly related to the job and which were not likely to be possessed in equal measure by all candidates. This could include tests of proficiency in written or spoken English, when proficiency in these areas is not a direct requirement of the job.

Employers must take great care with their methods of recruitment to ensure that neither by accident nor intent do they discriminate against any particular group. For instance, the Commission for Racial Equality's Report of its Formal Investigation into Massey Ferguson Perkins Ltd concluded that:

The main reason for the under-representation of blacks, we found, was not direct discrimination, but the company's method of recruitment for hourly paid jobs. They did not advertise or use Job Centres . . . they simply relied upon letters of application. (Commission for Racial Equality 1982)

This practice tended to favour friends and relatives of the existing (and largely white) workforce, who were made aware of the procedure for application by the current workforce.

The Commission served a 'non-discrimination notice' on the company requiring the company to cease its discriminatory practices.

> In 1994 an industrial tribunal awarded £1,900 damages to a black barmaid who was dismissed when she took offence at a video featuring the comedian Jim Davidson. She had been the only black person present in the pub when the landlady played the video. The barmaid became distressed and telephoned her mother. As she made the call the landlady approached her, and there followed an argument in which the landlady told the barmaid to 'go and not come back'. At the industrial tribunal the landlady claimed that she never thought of the barmaid as black and would not have given her the job if she had been a racist. The decision to dismiss, she said, was taken in the heat of the moment.
>
> The tribunal unanimously decided that the landlady was in breach of section 2 of the Race Relations Act, and awarded £1,900 damages.

The Immigration and Asylum Bill unveiled in the Queen's Speech in November 1995 will, if passed into law, make employers criminally liable if they employ illegal immigrants. Employers will face very large fines if it is shown that they fail to check the immigration status of new staff. It is feared that the bill will not only force employers to become untrained (and unpaid) immigration officers, but will also encourage racist recruitment practices. In order to comply with the proposed law employers will need to understand passport stamps, and the various residence rights accorded to different groups. In order not to be accused of racial discrimination employers will need to check the immigration status of all job applicants, not only (for instance) blacks, Asians or members of other ethnic minority groups.

2.4 The Sex Discrimination Act 1975

The Sex Discrimination Act is similar in its intention to the Race Relations Act, but of course applied to discrimination on the grounds of sex and marital status. It identifies both direct and indirect discrimination as being illegal. An example of indirect discrimination in this case would be height: expecting applicants for a particular position to be of at least a certain height. This would clearly discriminate against women and would not be allowed unless it can be shown that it is a 'genuine occupational qualification'.

Employers must take great care not to discriminate against women in the way they decide issues such as promotion or redundancy. For example, see *Price* v. *Civil Service Commission and Another* (1977 ICR 27), in which Mrs Price applied for a post in the Civil Service. She was not considered because she was over the age limit of 28. She contended that this was unfair since many women in their twenties took career breaks. The Employment Appeal Tribunal agreed and held that the practice constituted indirect discrimination. The Civil Service was therefore required to raise its age limit.

In *Dick* v. *University of Dundee* (1977 ICR 14), the fact that the university wished to make a number of staff redundant, and decided that it should be part-time staff who should go, was also held to be discriminatory, since by far the vast majority of part-time staff were women.

Another leading case is that of *Martin* v. *National Car Parks* (1976 ICR 26), in which a woman and her husband were both employed by the same company. The women was not considered for a more senior position because her husband was a subordinate of the person for whom she would be working. It was held that under these circumstances discrimination was not unlawful.

For the Sex Discrimination Act to be workable it was recognized that (as with the Martin case) there would have to be legitimate exceptions. These can be summarized as follows:

a. Privacy or decency – for example, public baths or lavatory attendants.

b. Accommodation – where there exists sanitary and sleeping facilities for only one sex and it is *unreasonable* to expect the employer to make additional provision.

c. Physiological reasons – this would include the recruitment of a woman to model women's clothing, but would not include strength or stamina.

d. Education and welfare – an example of this would be a housemaster in a single-sex boarding school; and other such cases where personal services promoting education or welfare can be best provided by members of only one sex.

e. The character of the establishment – one sex is appropriate because of the basic character of the establishment. This would include, for example, prison warders.

f. Married couples – the Act permits discrimination against one partner in a marriage because of the particular employment circumstances of the other partner. For an example, see *Martin* v. *National Car Parks*, mentioned above.

g. Overseas working – it would not be unlawful to discriminate against a woman where a job involves working overseas and the laws and customs are such that the work could not be performed by a woman.

h. Statutory bar – there exist a number of legal restrictions on the employment of women in certain categories. These come from various Acts and have been brought together in the Employment Act (1989), detailed below.

In 1991, following a challenge in the European Court, the UK government admitted that it had failed to properly implement the 1975 Sex Discrimination Act in line with European Law requirements. This was because the Act was drafted in such as way that it did not apply to women serving in the armed forces. As a result, thousands of servicewomen who became pregnant were dismissed from their employment. The government, in admitting its error, allowed all those who were affected to claim unfair dismissal and sue for damages.

Between 1991 and 1995 the Ministry of Defence paid £36 million to 3,527 women who claimed damages, with over 1000 cases still outstanding.

In February 1995 the government announced changes to the Sex Discrimination Act, bringing it in line with European Law requirements, and giving the women affected a further three months to lodge their claims. Had the law been changed in 1991, the women's lawyers would have had only three months to bring their claims, instead of three and a half years. This failure to act sooner was welcomed by the women's lawyers, but criticized by public expenditure watchdogs.

The Court of Appeal dealt a further blow to the UK government's employment law policy when it ruled in August 1995 that legislation introduced in 1985 barring employees who have worked less than two years from bringing unfair dismissal claims, discriminated against women. The law, which increased the qualifying period from one to two years, was introduced with the aim of creating new jobs and was challenged by two workers, Nicole Seymour-Smith and Laura Perez, who had both been dismissed by different employers after 15 months in their jobs. Neither was given a reason for the dismissal and both felt that they had been dismissed unfairly. They took their claim to an industrial tribunal, who ruled against them on the grounds that they had not been in continuous employment with their employer for two years. Their appeal to the High Court was rejected for the same reasons. The Court of Appeal, however, held that the law as it stood went against a European Union Directive of 1972 which enshrines the principle of equal treatment. The court accepted the women's argument that because women tended to change their jobs more regularly (due to family commitments) than men, they were less easily able to gain protection of employment with the two-year rule.

The implications of the judgement are that the UK government may be called upon to compensate other workers who lost their jobs after 1985 and had worked between one and two years for the same employer. (Reported in *The Times*, 11 Aug. 1995.)

2.5 The Employment Act 1989

There are still some restrictions on the employment of women that fall outside the genuine occupational qualification test. These are to be found incorporated into the Employment Act (1989), and operate in those areas in which it is considered that women need protection. In these circumstances it would be lawful to discriminate against women in order to comply with the Act. These restrictions are:

a. The prohibition of the employment of women in a whole range of processes involving lead or lead compounds.

b. The prohibition on the employment of women in a number of processes in the pottery industry.

c. Protection from exposure to ionizing radiation.

d. The prohibition of the employment of women in factories within four weeks of childbirth.

e. Restrictions on working on ships and aircraft while pregnant.

All of the reasons listed are intended to protect women from exposure to working situations or substances that might do damage to their health and their actual or potential capacity to bear children.

The Equal Opportunities Commission and the Commission for Racial Equality have both issued codes of practice for the elimination of discrimination and the promotion of equality of opportunity in employment. They advise employers to extend the range of employment sources used, to consider carefully the hurdles that they put in the way of applicants (age, height, qualifications, experience, etc.), and carefully consider what is genuinely required for successful performance in any particular occupation. The codes also suggest that employers have a policy on equal opportunities, monitor the proportion of people from different backgrounds who apply for positions, and consider the success rate of different groups as compared with the local labour market.

One of the more controversial aspects of the codes is that they recommend that the ethnic origin of the workforce be monitored. (An example of a monitoring form can be found in figure 6.1, and illustration of how monitoring should be undertaken is to be found in the section entitled 'Equal Opportunities' later in this chapter.) As far as recruitment and selection are concerned, this can have serious implications. A full discussion is to be found in the relevant chapters.

The codes do not have the force of law, but their provisions can be (and often are) taken into account by industrial tribunals in deciding whether or not an employer has discriminated. Both codes are essential reading for all involved in the recruitment, selection, development and promotion of staff.

2.6 Positive discrimination

Both the Sex Discrimination Act and the Race Relations Act make it lawful to encourage and provide training for members of one sex or racial group who have been under-represented in particular work in the previous twelve months. However, positive discrimination at the point of job selection is illegal.

The TSB, for example, have in recent years developed policies to encourage more members of ethnic minority groups to apply for jobs in banking (see Arkin 1991). Their 'Access to Banking' course, set up and run with South West London College, was a pre-recruitment training course designed to allow members of ethnic minorities who had the right potential but insufficient academic qualifications to try for a career in banking.

```
┌─────────────────────────────────────────────────────────────┐
│            EQUAL OPPORTUNITIES MONITORING FORM                │
│                                                               │
│  As part of its equal opportunities policy the company        │
│  analyses its recruitment practices and procedures. To        │
│  assist us with this process please complete and return       │
│  this document, duly completed, together with your            │
│  application form. The details supplied will be treated as    │
│  confidential and will not be taken into account when         │
│  making the appointment to the post under consideration.      │
│                                                               │
│  Surname..................................  Forenames.......................................  │
│                                                               │
│  Post Applied For...................................................................  │
│                                                               │
│  1.  Where did you see the post advertised?......................  │
│                                                               │
│  2.  Date of Birth.....................................................  │
│                                                               │
│  3.  Are you              ........Male                         │
│                           ........Female                       │
│                                                               │
│  4.  Are you              ........Single                       │
│                           ........Married                      │
│                           ........Widowed                      │
│                           ........Separated/Divorced           │
│                           ........Other                        │
│                                                               │
│  5.  Are you registered disabled? ........Yes                  │
│                                   ........No                   │
│                                                               │
│  6.  To which of the following groups do you consider you     │
│      belong?                                                  │
│              ........White European, including UK             │
│              ........White other (please specify)             │
│              ........Black Afro-Caribbean                     │
│              ........Black African                            │
│              ........Asian                                    │
│              ........Black other (please specify)             │
│              ........Other, including mixed (specify below)   │
│                                                               │
│  (Please tick as necessary)                                   │
│                                                               │
│        Thank you for taking the time to complete this form    │
└─────────────────────────────────────────────────────────────┘
```

Figure 6.1
Equal opportunities
monitoring form

2.7 Equal Pay Act (1970)

The Equal Pay Act, passed in 1970 but not operative until 1975, established for the first time the rights of men and women to receive equal treatment with regard to pay and terms and conditions of employment when they are employed by the same employer to perform the same (or broadly similar) work. Indeed, where work is different, although assigned a similar value under a job evaluation scheme, pay should also be the same.

The Equal Pay (Amendment) Regulations came into effect in 1974, widening the operation of the original Act. Under these regulations if a women feels that her work is of equal value – that it calls for the same level of skill, carries similar responsibility or requires the same amount of effort (or other valid criteria), as that of a job performed by a man – she can claim equal pay. The existence of a good, properly implemented job evaluation scheme (see chapter 12 for examples) will make the substantiation or refutation of such a claim easier. But matters are further complicated by the tendency of many job evaluation schemes to overvalue male characteristics (such as physical strength) while under-valuing female characteristics (such as manipulative dexterity). Particular problems may occur when different groups of workers are covered by different schemes: for example, if a company's clerical (and predominately female) staff were covered by one scheme and its manual (and predominately male) staff were covered by another scheme. It is recommended that as a general rule, and whenever possible, one system of job evaluation be used to cover all employees.

In some of the leading legal cases in this area, supermarket chains have been forced to raise the pay of their check-out operators to bring it in line with that paid to warehousemen. For instance, in 1987, J Sainsbury faced just such a claim from a check-out operator and they settled out of court, raising the pay of their check-out staff by 4 per cent above the annual wage settlement. Similarly, the check-out staff employed by the Co-operative Retail Societies were also the recipients of significant pay increases and job restructuring. Marks and Spencer also reviewed their pay structures, and as well as giving pay rises to check-out staff, froze the pay of warehouse staff for a period of time, in order that differentials might be eased.

3. Discrimination Against the Older Worker

An area that is attracting considerable attention in both the press and the human resource literature is the issue of discrimination on the grounds of age (see, for instance, *PM Plus*, June 1991). Of course it is not illegal, and many job advertisements contain a clause that states the likely age range of the successful candidate. This often indicates that applicants over a certain age (typically the top end of the range is 40) will not be considered. However, Megginson (1972: 64) tells us that employers should give much more consideration to employees over the age of 40, because they possess:

> Greater experience and better judgement in decision making; more objectivity about personal goals and abilities, as the older men have already satisfied many of their needs for salary and status and are able to concentrate more on job responsibilities, increased social intelligence and the ability to understand and influence others.

In the United Kingdom many employers are reluctant to employ the older worker and the law does little to challenge their prejudice. The situation is very different in the United States (see Dessler 1986), where the Age Discrimination of Employment Act (1967) makes it illegal to discriminate against job applicants or employees who are aged between 40 and 65 years. The Act was amended by Congress in 1978, extending protection to the age of 70 for most workers.

Many would like to see protection of a similar form introduced into the UK. The government has chastised companies for not giving due consideration to the older employee. However, given the stated intention of the government to reduce its interference in the relationship between employer and employee, it is unlikely that legislation will be brought forward in the foreseeable future.

A number of employers are reconsidering their attitudes towards the older worker. The charity Age Concern England have joined with a number of major employers, including British Airways, NatWest and Midland Banks, the Nationwide Building Society and Unigate, to highlight the benefits of recruiting and retaining the older worker. The Carnegie Third Age Programme has also recruited many well-known employers to combat ageism. These employers include Mercury Communications, Costain, Higgs and Hill and the NatWest Bank. Among the advantages of employing older workers often cited are lower turnover (and reduced recruitment costs), lower absenteeism, and in some organizations, a customer preference for dealing with an older employee.

Currently the armed forces, the senior echelons of the Civil Service and the European Commission all set recruitment age limits for certain categories of staff. (Reported in *People Management*, 7 Sept. 1995.)

4. Rehabilitation of Offenders Act (1974)

Another group who feel that they are discriminated against in employment are ex-offenders. However, the provisions the 1974 Act allow for most convictions to become 'spent' after a stated period of time. This allows the ex-convict to answer quite honestly (once the conviction is spent) *No* to the question, *have you ever been convicted of a criminal offence?*, on a job application form.

The law is more generous to young offenders (aged under 17 years) than it is to adult offenders. See table 6.1 for details.

So, for instance, if somebody had been convicted of a criminal offence and sentenced to six months in prison, the conviction would be considered 'spent' after a period of 7 years if the person is aged 17 or over, and after 3.5 years, if aged under 17.

Some convictions can never be considered 'spent'. These are offences for which the sentence was longer than those outlined in table 6.1. Further, for entry into some occupations all previous offences should be disclosed. The areas of employment covered here are lawyers, accountants, teachers and those in the medical profession. The Amendment Regulations of 1978 brought into the above group those whose occupations brought them into contact with young people under 18 years of age.

The implication of the Act and the Amendment Regulations is that, with the exceptions stated above, an applicant for a job can honestly state that he has never been convicted of a criminal offence if he has undergone the period of rehabilitation without further offence. Indeed, if an employer subsequently discovers that an employee has a 'spent' criminal record this would not be reasonable grounds for dismissal.

5. Equal Opportunities Policies

The equal opportunities policy that appears at the start of this chapter is not untypical of that which might be adopted by many organizations. It

Sentence	Aged under 17 on conviction	Aged 17 or over on conviction
Prison or young offender institution for more than 6 months but less than 2.5 years	5 years	10 years
Prison or young offender institution 6 months or less.	3.5 years	7 years
Dismissal from HM Services	3.5 years	7 years
Fine or community service order	2.5 years	5 years
Probation, supervision, care order, conditional discharge or bind over		1 year, or until order expires
Attendance care order		1 year after order expires
Absolute discharge	6 months	6 months

Table 6.1
Rehabilitation periods

states the coverage of the policy and the intention to promote equality of opportunity in a range of personnel-related areas. The final paragraph tells us who will be involved in the policy and that the policy will be communicated to all staff. What the statement does not tell us is how the policy will be implemented, how it will be monitored, whether it will be reviewed (and if so by whom). As it stands the policy is of little value other than as a statement of intent – it needs to be put into operational effect.

For many of us, ensuring equality of opportunity does not come naturally. This is not to imply that most of us are overtly racist or sexist, merely to recognize that for a number of reasons many people find it difficult to (for instance) consider all applicants for a job equally. One of these reasons is the so-called 'halo-effect' which (when interviewing for new employees) tends to make us favour those candidates who are most like us at the expense of those who are least like us. This tendency can be reduced with training and by monitoring.

It is the practice for many employers to include with their job application forms a document which is commonly called an 'Equal Opportunity Monitoring Form' (see figure 6.1). This document should be completed by all applicants and returned together with the form. At this stage they should be parted, the application forms going to the person responsible for short-listing, while the monitoring forms should be examined separately. Analysis of the monitoring forms by sex, age, ethnic/cultural background and disability should take place, and the results should be compared against both the number of application forms returned, the numbers in each category interviewed and the number eventually appointed. The results should also be used cumulatively for comparison against labour-force surveys, census data and industrial sector information. A great deal of useful data is to be found in the *Employment Gazette* (published by HMSO).

It should be remembered that it is likely that different groups of staff are recruited from different labour markets. For instance, unskilled staff may be recruited from the local pool, while highly skilled staff may be recruited nationally or even internationally. This will have a bearing on the results of the monitoring. Larger employers might be able to compare practice between occupations, departments, branches or regions, allowing differences to be identified, examined and where necessary addressed. Monitoring should identify where practice does not meet the aims stated in the policy. The action that should follow might well include changes in recruitment advertising, training (or retraining) of recruiters and selectors, and, if staff show themselves unwilling, or unable, to work within codes of equal opportunities, further training or disciplinary action.

It is unlikely that any organization will find it easy to become an equal opportunities employer. The process of recording and monitoring practice will go some way to identifying the problems that might exist in different departments or sections of the company; or indeed more general problems with, for instance, attracting workers from one particular ethnic group. Those organizations who boast in their recruitment literature that they are 'Equal Opportunities Employers' are probably being ambitious. More accurate is the employer who claims to be 'working towards equality of opportunity for all'.

OPPORTUNITY 2000

Over the years a number of initiatives have been launched in the UK to improve the opportunities for disadvantaged groups in employment. A comparatively recent initiative, launched with the support of the government, is Opportunity 2000. The initiative was business led and has as its aim to increase the quality and quantity of women's participation in the workforce. Sixty-two organizations participated in the launch, and each has set goals and targets to increase employment opportunities for women by the year 2000. Although a number of the largest companies in Britain have not signed up, over 275 major employers have now agreed to participate. There is no equivalent scheme for members of ethnic minorities.

The National Health Service is the largest employer in the UK (in fact, it is the largest employer in Europe). It has over one million staff, three-quarters of whom are women. Thus it is the largest employer of women in Europe. As part of its commitment to Opportunity 2000 the NHS has adopted the following goal:

> *To take advantage of the potential of women in the NHS so we can provide the best health care for all members of the population.*

To achieve the goal the NHS has set a number of interim goals which it hopes to achieve by the end of 1994. This it sees as the first milestone towards the year 2000.

According to <u>Women in the NHS</u> (Department of Health, 1992), the interim goals are:

Goal 1: Increase the number of women in general management posts from 18 per cent in 1991 to 30 per cent by 1994.

Goal 2: Increase the number of qualified women accountants in the NHS.

Goal 3: Increase the percentage of women consultants, necessitating an annual increase of 10 per cent, from 15.5 per cent in 1991 to 20 per cent in 1994. Accelerate the rate of increase in the number of women consultants in surgical specialities from the current 9.7 per cent per annum to 15 per cent per annum.

Goal 4: Increase the representation of women as members of Authorities and Trusts from 29 per cent in 1991 to 35 per cent by 1994.

Goal 5: Introduce a programme allowing women aspiring to management positions to go through a development centre with a view to establishing and addressing their own personal development needs.

Goal 6: Introduce initiatives on recruitment and retention to ensure that the numbers of qualified nurses and midwives leaving the profession do not rise.

Goal 7: Ensure that following maternity leave or a career break all women, including those returning to nursing part-time or as a job share, are able to return at a grade commensurate with their leaving grade and to work of similar status.

Goal 8: Monitor the time taken for nurses to reach management positions to ensure that men and women have equal access to these positions.

The NHS has also established plans for implementation; identified responsibilities for both the local area and the centre; set guidelines for monitoring progress; and established a complaints procedure for any women who consider that they have not been treated fairly.

TASK

You are the HR Director of an NHS Trust. How would you go about the task of implementing Opportunity 2000 within the Trust? The Trust employs 1,800 staff of whom 1,450 are women. What problems do you anticipate that you might encounter? How might they be overcome?

1. The Superior Supermarket Company has an equal opportunities policy but receives very few applications for employment from either men or members of ethnic minority groups. How would you go about investigating the reasons why?

2. Your employer is reluctant to consider introducing a policy on equality of opportunity. Draw up a paper that you would put to your employer outlining why an equal opportunities policy should be introduced.

3. Outline the steps that an organization should take in order to ensure the absence of discrimination in its policies related to such areas as recruitment, selection, promotion and redundancy. How would such policies be validated?

4. You are the personnel manager of a chain of dairies operating across the east of England. Your board are keen to devolve more responsibility to individual dairy managers. To date recruitment has always been managed centrally with due care paid to equality of opportunity. What potential equal opportunities problems would you envisage with the new policy (with locally managed recruitment, selection, training) and how would you recommend that they be overcome?

5. Consider the interim goals, listed above, that the NHS has set as part of its commitment to Opportunity 2000. Look at your own organization (or one with which you are familiar) and consider what might be appropriate objectives for that organization. Consider how you might go about getting the proposals accepted, implemented and monitored. What problems do you consider would have to be overcome?

6. 'Equal Opportunities policies are too bureaucratic, too time consuming and too paper based. The best companies don't need an EO policy – they just do it.' This statement is the opinion a fellow personnel manager. Consider the merits of his argument.

•REFERENCES•

Arkin A (1991)
The TSB Banks on Equal Opportunities
Personnel Plus, Jan.

Beardwell I & Holden L (1994)
HUMAN RESOURCE MANAGEMENT: A CONTEMPORARY PERSPECTIVE
London, Pitman.

Bowers J (1990)
A PRACTICAL APPROACH TO EMPLOYMENT LAW
London, FT Publishing.

Commission for Racial Equality (1978)
EQUAL OPPORTUNITIES IN EMPLOYMENT AND MONITORING ON EQUAL OPPORTUNITIES POLICY
London, CRE.

Commission for Racial Equality (1982)
MASSEY FERGUSON PERKINS LTD: REPORT OF A FORMAL INVESTIGATION
London, CRE.

Coussey M & Jackson H (1991)
MAKING EQUAL OPPORTUNITIES WORK
London, Pitman.

Dickins L & Colling T (1990)
Why Bargaining Won't Appear on the Bargaining Agenda
Personnel Management, April.

Dessler G (1986)
PERSONNEL MANAGEMENT
Reston, Va., Prentice-Hall.

Employment Institute (1991)
OLDER WORKERS AND THE RECESSION
London, Employment Institute.

Equal Opportunities Commission (1985)
A MODEL EQUAL OPPORTUNITIES POLICY
London, EOC.

Equal Opportunities Commission (1985)
EQUAL OPPORTUNITIES: A GUIDE FOR EMPLOYERS TO

THE SEX DISCRIMINATION ACT
London, EOC.

Income Data Services (1987)
EQUAL RIGHTS OR EQUAL RITES
IDS Study 392, Aug.

Institute of Personnel Management (1990)
RECRUITMENT CODE OF PRACTICE
London, IPM.

Kidner R (1990)
STATUTES ON EMPLOYMENT LAW
London, Blackstone.

Manpower Services Commission (1984)
CODE OF GOOD PRACTICE ON THE EMPLOYMENT OF DISABLED PEOPLE
Sheffield, MSC.

Megginson L (1972)
PERSONNEL: A BEHAVIOURAL APPROACH TO ADMINISTRATION
Homewood, Ill.., Irwin.

North S-J (1992)
Ex-offenders Silent
Personnel Today, Oct.

PM Plus (1991)
Age Discrimination Makes the Over 40's Almost Unemployable
London, June.

Straw J (1989)
EQUAL OPPORTUNITIES: THE WAY AHEAD
London, Institute of Personnel Management.

Torrington D & Hall L (1991)
PERSONNEL MANAGEMENT: A NEW APPROACH
2nd edn. London, Prentice-Hall.

UK Central Statistical Office (1995)
SOCIAL FOCUS ON WOMEN
London, HMSO.

UK Department of Health (1992)
WOMEN IN THE NHS
London, HMSO.

• CHAPTER •

7

THE NEW EMPLOYEE

AS A RESULT OF STUDYING THIS CHAPTER YOU SHOULD BE ABLE TO:

- Appreciate the value for both employer and employee of sound induction procedures.

- Consider the alternative methods that may be employed to facilitate induction.

- Be aware of the so-called 'induction crisis' and how to identify it, consider its causes and

methods that may be employed to counter its effects.

- Appreciate the legal nature of the employment contract and the rights and obligations that spring from the contract.

> *With no traffic to fight the office was ten minutes away. He had decided his day would start at five-thirty, unless someone could top that, then he would be there at five, or four-thirty, or whatever it took to be first. Sleep was a nuisance. He would be the first lawyer to arrive at the Bendini Building this and every day until he became a partner.*
>
> John Grisham, *The Firm*

1. Introduction

The new employee is a precious commodity and should be treated as such. It is likely that considerable resources will have been committed to securing the new employees' services for the organization, and it is vital that everything be done to ensure that he or she settles in smoothly and quickly begins to make a contribution to corporate objectives. For the new employee, starting a new job is also a time of excitement and trepidation: the excitement of the new challenge and new colleagues; trepidation because starting any new job will bring some measure of anxiety and insecurity.

2. The Need for Induction

Most large organizations will have a formalized procedure for inducting new employees to the organization. However, smaller employers should also give some thought as to how they intend to welcome their new colleague and ensure that they settle in as quickly as possible.

Armstrong (1992: 376) identifies three main aims for the induction process:

a. To smooth the preliminary stages when everything is likely to be strange and unfamiliar to the starter.

b. To establish quickly a favourable attitude to the company in the mind of the new employee so that he or she is more likely to stay.

c. To obtain effective output from the employee in the shortest possible time.

So, induction serves both a 'social' and a 'performance-related' function, to initiate the new employee into the culture of the organization as well as enabling her to become proficient at her job in the shortest possible time.

Some activities must be performed before the new employee even commences work. These will include ensuring that physical facilities are ready (e.g. desk, telephone), allocating a locker or locker-room key, making the appropriate security arrangements (e.g. issuing a site pass) arranging for standard clothing to be issued (e.g. overalls, safety equipment, etc.). It will also be necessary to make certain that the appropriate person is available to meet the new staff member and introduce her to new colleagues and other key contacts.

3. Induction Training

Inducting the new employee into both the social and performance-related aspects of the job can be undertaken in two main ways. First, the new employee can be put alongside experienced members of staff. This so-called 'learning from Nellie' method has the advantages of being cheap and easy to arrange, but has the disadvantage of allowing the new employee to pick up bad as well as good methods of working, and of finding out only what the experienced worker will, or can, tell her. Many organizations prefer to conduct at least a proportion of their induction training away from the workplace. This, although more difficult and time consuming to arrange, allows the employer to determine the input, to take steps to ensure understanding and adherence to accepted working methods.

Many employers recognize the value of spreading induction over a period of time. It is unlikely that the new employee, bombarded with information on her first day, will be able to remember much of it by the second day. It is common then for new employees to come together on their first few days for initial induction, this to be followed up with regular sessions over the next six months or so, until the employee can be considered to be satisfactorily integrated into the workforce.

However undertaken, it is important that the new employee receives in some form, and has explained to her, the following information as a minimum:

a. A brief outline of the organization, its background, history, development, products or services and management.

b. Basic conditions of employment – hours of work, holiday entitlements, pensions, etc.

c. Pay – when and how it is paid, queries, deductions, pay-scales.

d. Disciplinary procedure.

e. Grievance procedure.

f. Work rules.

g. Sickness, notification of absence, certificates, etc.

h. Health and safety arrangements.

i. Opportunities for training and development.

j. Medical and first-aid facilities.

k. Social and welfare arrangements.

l. Restaurant and canteen facilities.

Much of this information can (and should) be contained in a staff handbook. If the organization is too small to justify a handbook, then a collection of loosely bound typed sheets should be prepared. This should summarize the information as best as is possible.

The performance-related aspects of induction will probably need to take place far closer to the place of work, and are likely to be delivered (formally or informally) by superiors and peers. It is here that the standards of work and levels of output expected will be outlined, the methods of working explained, key contacts introduced and procedures demonstrated. It is vital that good methods are demonstrated and high standards expected. The role of the inductor is crucial, for bad habits learned at this point may contaminate the new employee for the rest of her time with the organization. Once again, it is best if the induction process is proceduralized, written down and then made the specific responsibility of an experienced member of staff.

Figure 7.1 is a checklist used for the induction of new employees in a small manufacturing company.

4. Mentoring

Very often new employees will be allocated a mentor, an experienced and respected member of staff who can act as a 'friend and guide' to the new employee as she picks her way through the workplace. The mentor can adopt a semi-formal role arranging regular meetings with her new colleague to discuss progress to date, or more of a 'hands-off' role, simply keeping an eye on the new employee, offering the occasional piece of advice as and when it is needed.

Collin (in Beardwell and Holden 1994: 317) claims that for those organizations who have introduced mentoring programmes:

TJB HYDROPARTS LTD

NEW EMPLOYEE INDUCTION PROGRAMME CHECKLIST

NAME.. DEPARTMENT...

	FACTORY	OFFICE
CONDITIONS OF EMPLOYMENT		
Company rules and disciplinary procedures	(..........)	(..........)
Sickness pay rules	(..........)	(..........)
Hours of work	(..........)	(..........)
Pay rate and arrangements	(..........)	(..........)
Overtime	(..........)	(N/A)
Holiday rules	(..........)	(..........)
Holiday pay entitlement and rate	(..........)	(..........)
Pension scheme	(..........)	(..........)
PERSONNEL INTRODUCTIONS		
Production/works manager	(..........)	(N/A)
Department manager	(..........)	(..........)
Chargehand/supervisor	(..........)	(N/A)
Directors(s)	(N/A)	(..........)
WORKFLOW		
Machinery locations	(..........)	(N/A)
Origin/destination of materials	(..........)	(N/A)
HEALTH AND SAFETY		
Company safety policy	(..........)	(..........)
Safety video	(..........)	(N/A)
Fire procedure and alarm operation	(..........)	(..........)
Fire extinguishers, location and operation	(..........)	(..........)
Fire exits: location	(..........)	(..........)
Reporting of fire and accident hazards	(..........)	(..........)
'Learn, Don't Burn' video	(..........)	(N/A)
Tidy work area	(..........)	(..........)
Waste bags	(..........)	(N/A)
Smoking policy	(..........)	(..........)
Lifting equipment	(..........)	(N/A)
Accident procedure	(..........)	(..........)
First aid room location/first aiders	(..........)	(..........)
Forklift regulations	(..........)	(N/A)
Safety guards/emergency stops	(..........)	(N/A)
Protective clothing/safety wear	(..........)	(..........)
TRAINING		
Quality standards	(..........)	(..........)
Production records	(..........)	(N/A)
Materials and stores requisitions	(..........)	(..........)
QUALITY ASSURANCE		
BS5750 Pt. 2 (copy of quality policy given)	(..........)	(..........)
Q.A. procedures	(..........)	(N/A)
Introduce quality assurance personnel	(..........)	(N/A)
GENERAL		
Canteen arrangements	(..........)	(..........)
Location of toilets	(..........)	(..........)
Location of noticeboards	(..........)	(..........)
Social club	(..........)	(..........)
OFFICE		
Issue clock card	(..........)	(N/A)
Request P45	(..........)	(..........)
Request bank details	(..........)	(..........)
Termination of employment	(..........)	(..........)

A copy of the company rules and regulations should be given to the new employee.

Induction Carried Out By:

Signed:... Position held:..

Print name:.. Date:...

DECLARATION

I have been instructed in the company's rules, regulations and safety information and fully accept their obligations and responsibilities:

Signed:... Name:...

Date:...

Figure 7.1
Induction checklist

experience suggests that mentoring facilitates the learning to learn of their employees, contributes to the process of meaning-making in the organization and hence to its responsiveness to its environment, while meeting the developmental needs of employees.

5. The 'Experienced' Worker

In planning a programme of induction the inductor should have in the front of her mind the standards, behaviours and qualities expected of the experienced worker. The induction programme then should aim to bring the new worker up to the level of the experienced worker as quickly as reasonably possible. Many would argue that the new worker left to learn from her new colleagues would, over a period of time, acquire many of the skills of the experienced worker without the need for intervention in the form of an induction programme. This *may* be correct and, if it is, then one test of an induction programme is that it should raise the new worker to the standard of the experienced worker more quickly than if it had been left merely to chance. This is illustrated in figure 7.2.

One way of justifying the cost of induction training would be to consider the reduced time in which properly inducted new employees can make a significant contribution to achieving the objectives of the organization. The absence of induction training should result in a longer lead time before full operational efficiency is achieved.

6. The Induction Crisis

The so-called 'induction crisis' is well documented. Kenney and Reid (1988: 241) tell us that the term is used to describe:

> the critical period when new starters are most likely to leave. A well planned induction course can help to decrease labour turnover by ensuring that new starters settle quickly in their jobs and reach an efficient standard of performance as soon as possible.

Induction training, then, can be seen as positive action to help the new employee to adjust to her new surroundings and quickly to gain

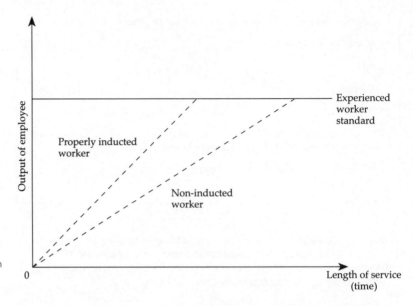

Figure 7.2
The relationship between
induction training and
output

confidence and commitment. Tyson and York (1982: 146) claim that
to minimize the induction crisis employers need to be aware of the
following:

a. The induction phase is much more critical and stressful than it is
    often recognized to be.

b. The length of the critical phase will naturally vary and depend on the
    adaptability of each individual, but it may well last for many months.

c. The causes contributing to the general problem may be found in the
    psychological and sociological factors affecting organizational and
    group behaviour.

d. The induction phase needs to be planned carefully and supervised,
    as the first stage in staff development.

It is in the first few weeks and months of taking up a new position
that an employee is most likely to leave. The longer an employee
remains with an organization, the less likely he is to leave. This can be
illustrated as an inverse relationship (as shown in figure 7.3) between
length of service and likelihood of leaving.

High rates of labour turnover can be very costly and very
disappointing. If considerable time, effort and expense have been put
into recruiting staff it is very wasteful if they choose to leave after an
uneconomically short period of time. High labour turnover (and hence
the induction crisis) will be particular problem when:

Recruitment costs are high.

Labour is in short supply.

Training is expensive and / or time consuming.

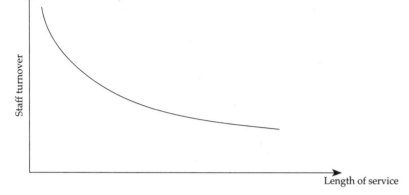

Figure 7.3
The relationship between
length of service and staff
turnover

Of course, the effect of the induction crisis is often made worse by poor recruitment and selection. That is to say, that if poor methods of recruitment and selection are used (and the 'wrong' people are selected for employment) then no induction programme can hope to stop staff from leaving, and leaving feeling dissatisfied and cheated. Notwithstanding this problem, it is vital for recruiters and selectors to communicate with inductors so that induction can be appropriate to the needs of staff. For instance, in times when the labour market is tight, many organizations may be forced to recruit less skilled and experienced workers than they would consider ideal. In cases such as this the role of induction (and post-employment training) would be to develop in employees the skills that are vital for them to function effectively in the organization. The style and content of induction training would be very different from that to be delivered under other circumstances. Induction training, then, must be tailored to meet the requirements of the different groups of staff employed. When staff do leave it is important to carry out an exit interview to elicit the reasons why the person has chosen to resign. Information gained can then be fed back to change practice and improve retention.

7. New Employees and the Law

The employer and employee have entered into a 'work–wage bargain'. That is, so long as the agreement is not for unlawful purposes (for example, a 'contract' to kill someone), and both parties are competent to enter into the agreement, then a legally binding contract of employment has been formed.

An employment contract is much like any other form of contract in that there must be:

a. An offer: generally the offer of the job with certain terms and conditions.

b. Acceptance: that is, an agreement to accept the position on the terms offered.

c. Consideration: the employee's promise to work in return for the employer's promise to pay.

It is important to note that the 'contract of employment' only exists between an employer and an employee. That is, no such contract will exist between the company and someone who supplies services to the company but none the less remains self-employed.

There is no legal requirement for the contract to be in writing (except in the special cases of seamen and apprentices). However, the UK Employment Protection (Consolidation) Act 1978 EP(C)A, and as amended by Schedule 4 of the Trades Union Reform and Employment Rights Act 1993 (TURERA), requires that the new employee must be issued, within two months of the commencement of her employment, with a written statement of the terms and conditions under which she is to be employed. This provision now applies to all employees. It was extended to part-time workers in the Employment Protection (Part-time Employees) Regulations 1995. In almost all respects part-time workers should now be treated in the same manner as their full-time counterparts.

The written statement (which is often called the contract of employment) must contain the following details:

a. The names of the employer and employee and the date from which the contract is effective.

b. The method to be used for calculating remuneration and the intervals at which it will be paid.

c. Details of terms and conditions relating to hours of work.

d. Holiday entitlements, including public holidays and holiday pay.

e. The title of (or a brief description of) the job that the person is employed to perform.

f. The place of work and the employer's address.

g. When the job is temporary, the date at which employment will cease.

h. Terms and conditions relating to sickness and sick pay. Note: there is no legal requirement to pay sick pay other than 'statutory sick pay'.

i. Terms and conditions relating to pensions and pension schemes.

j. The length of notice required by the parties to terminate the contract.

Employees should also receive, or have (in writing) their attention drawn to:

k. Disciplinary rules relevant to the employment.

l. The method by which redress of a grievance should be sought.

m. How the employee can appeal against the results of a disciplinary decision.

It is common for the details under points (k) to (m) above to be contained in separate documents to which reference is made in the statement of terms and conditions.

In entering into an employment contract both employers and employees undertake certain responsibilities. Principally, the duties of an employer are:

a. To pay wages. The contract places employers under a clear obligation to pay wages even if no work can be provided.

b. To provide work. Employers are not (in the main) obliged to provide work unless a failure to do so would result in a breach of the contract.

c. To take reasonable care of the employee. This means that the employer is obliged to provide and maintain a safe working environment.

The duties of the employee are:

a. To cooperate with the employer – to obey reasonable orders and not to impede the employer's business.

b. Employees have a duty of good faith – they should not (for instance) accept rewards other than from their employer, aid a competitor or disclose information confidential to the employer.

c. Employees are expected to take reasonable care and exercise a reasonable degree of skill in carrying out their duties.

8. Notice Entitlement

Generally speaking, the period of notice to which the employee is entitled is as set out in the contract of employment. However, employees also have a statutory right to the periods of notice listed in table 7.1. This entitlement does not apply to (among others) merchant seamen, Crown employees or House of Commons staff.

Period of continuous employment	Notice entitlement
Up to one month	Nil
One month to two years	1 week
2–3 years	2 weeks
3–4 years	3 weeks
4–5 years	4 weeks
5–6 years	5 weeks
6–7 years	6 weeks
7–8 years	7 weeks
8–9 years	8 weeks
9–10 years	9 weeks
10–11 years	10 weeks
11–12 years	11 weeks
12 years or more	12 weeks

Table 7.1
Employees' entitlement to notice

An employee, employed for at least one month, is required to give at least one week's notice. This does not increase with length of service. However, many contracts of employment make provision for longer periods of notice.

9. Beyond Induction

Induction usually is only concerned with the period immediately following recruitment and commencement of employment. Once the employee is settled in, the employer will wish to consider the longer-term needs of the employee. Training and management development are considered in the next two chapters. The performance of the employee will also need to be regularly assessed, commonly through methods of performance appraisal or, as is becoming increasingly popular, performance management. These are both considered in chapter 11.

CASE STUDY

CORNWALL BROWNE AND ASSOCIATES: EXECUTIVE RECRUITMENT (OVERSEAS) LTD

Cornwall Browne are recruitment consultants specializing in advising governments and employers wishing to consider British scientists, technologists and managers for positions in the Middle East. To date the company has specialized in the petrochemical industry (both installation and extraction), and more recently in hospital staffs. Most staff are employed on a fixed-term contract, generally between two and four years in duration. The company has an enviable client list which it works hard to maintain, and of which it is justly proud.

In recent years, with the gradual maturing of the Middle Eastern economies, clients have fewer vacancies to fill and those that are available tend to be more specialist in nature. Conversely, a recession in the UK has seen a greater number than ever of highly skilled and experienced staff seeking employment overseas.

The company has always prided itself on the care it has taken to achieve the best possible match between the requirements of the client and the skills and attributes of the worker. In recent years, however, a worrying trend has begun to emerge. A greater than normal number of employees are returning to the UK before the end of their contracts. This is despite the fact that the company has been able to recommend better and better qualified and experienced staff to its clients.

Several clients have expressed disquiet about this trend. Two major clients have threatened to move their accounts elsewhere.

TASK

You are a partner in Cornwall Browne and have investigated the problems outlined above. Your conclusions lead you to believe that the staff employed, while possessing all necessary professional and technical skills, are not being adequately prepared to work overseas. You and your partners agree to provide training for your clients' new employees to help prepare them for the problems and challenges that they might encounter while working overseas.

Consider the likely content of such a course, how it should be run, and what objectives you would wish to achieve in running it.

QUESTIONS FOR FURTHER CONSIDERATION

1. What steps might an organization take to reduce the effects of the 'induction crisis'?

2. Consider your own induction into either your present employment or your course of study. (a) What fears or concerns did you have and to what extent did the process of induction allay your concerns? (b) Design an induction programme for either a new employee in your organization or a future student in your course of study. Be prepared to justify its contents.

3. You are employed as a personnel officer in a large engineering company. You have been asked to investigate the problem of high rates of labour turnover among graduate engineers. The losses are particularly worrying among those who have been employed for between 6 and 12 months. Your initial investigations have found that the Training Manager blames poor recruitment, while the Graduate Recruitment Manager blames poor training. Consider how you might take your investigations further.

4. You have been asked to set up a mentoring scheme for new employees. Outline the steps that you would take to (a) find suitable mentors, (b) prepare them for their role, and (c) monitor their effectiveness.

5. Your Manager has suggested that in order to reduce costs all induction training should be scrapped. How might you try to justify expenditure on induction training?

6. Consider the 'new employee induction procedure checklist' in figure 7.1 (amended from one used by a small manufacturing company):

   a. To what extent do you consider it adequate for the task? Does it have major deficiencies?

   b. Factory and office staffs are treated slightly differently by this company. Why do you think this is so, and do you believe it to be either necessary or good practice? Make suitable suggestions for amendment.

•REFERENCES•

Advisory, Conciliation and Arbitration Service (1982)
INDUCTION OF NEW EMPLOYEES, ADVISORY BOOKLET NO. 7
London, ACAS.

Armstrong M (1992)
A HANDBOOK OF PERSONNEL MANAGEMENT PRACTICE
London, Kogan Page.

Beardwell L & Holden L (1994)
HUMAN RESOURCE MANAGEMENT: A CONTEMPORY PERSPECTIVE
London, Pitman.

Fowler A (1983)
GETTING OFF TO A GOOD START: SUCCESSFUL EMPLOYEE INDUCTION
London, Institute of Personnel Management.

Hackett P (1989)
SUCCESS IN PERSONNEL MANAGEMENT
London, John Murray.

Kenney J & Reid M (1988)
TRAINING INTERVENTIONS
2nd edn. London, Institute of Personnel Management.

Pigors P & Myers C (1977)
PERSONNEL ADMINISTRATION
8th edn. New York, McGraw-Hill.

Tyson S & York A (1982)
PERSONNEL MANAGEMENT
London, Heinemann.

UK Department of Employment (1981)
GLOSSARY OF TRAINING TERMS
London, HMSO.

TRAINING AND DEVELOPMENT: THE UNITED KINGDOM EXPERIENCE

•CHAPTER•
8

AS A RESULT OF STUDYING THIS CHAPTER YOU SHOULD BE ABLE TO:

- Appreciate the approach taken to training and development in the United Kingdom by government and employers, and the resources devoted to it.

- Consider the role of those organizations charged with directing the vocational training and development effort: namely the TECs and NCVQ.

- Appreciate the National Training Framework as developed by NCVQ, and how academic, vocational and quasi-vocational qualifications fit into it.

- Offer comment on the range of initiatives introduced by the UK government in recent years to promote a training and development culture.

> *Mao offered a magic cure to the peasants: 'doctors' who could be turned out en masse – barefoot doctors. 'It is not at all necessary to have so much formal training,' he said. 'They should mainly learn and raise their standard in practice.' On 26th June 1965 he made the remark which became a guideline for health and education: 'The more books you read, the more stupid you become.' I went to work with absolutely no training.*
>
> Jung Chang, *Wild Swans*

1. Introduction

The European countries with the best general and vocational education systems will increasingly possess a competitive advantage as West European economic integration progresses. Well-trained labour forces are productive (hence off-setting the higher wages that trained workers normally command), cohesive, motivated and (most importantly) capable of accommodating change and introducing new technologies . . . It follows that the long-term neglect of industrial training in any European nation is sure to put its businesses at a disadvantage when faced with intense competition from rival countries. (Graham and Bennett 1995: 254)

This chapter examines the United Kingdom experience of training and development and attempts to consider why it is so often the case that training is done infrequently and poorly in this country. It will also consider several recent UK government initiatives designed to give training and development a far higher profile. These initiatives include National Training Awards and the 'Investors In People' Training Standard. In recent times the government has set national training targets for UK industry and commerce, most recently through its 1995 *Competitiveness* White Paper. Most of the support to aid industry achieve these targets is channelled through the Training and Enterprise Councils (TECs). These are also given due consideration here. In addition, the government's national training and education framework is discussed. This framework attempts to draw comparison and develop parity between traditional academic qualifications and their (apparently) less prestigious vocational counterparts. It is the aim of the government that their national framework will offer complementary and parallel pathways through which young people (and others) can achieve qualifications which are equal in value but reflect a diversity of needs and ambitions encompassing the vocational, non-vocational and quasi-vocational portfolio of awards, both available and developing.

2. Training and Development in the United Kingdom

> Two-thirds of British workers have no professional or vocational qualifications, compared with only a quarter in Germany . . . [as a result] . . . Britain has a lumpenproletariat unlike any other advanced nation, and this shows not only in British factories but also on football terraces around the world. (Layard 1992: 5)

Many British employers claim that they give great importance to training. For instance, the Manpower Services Commission (MSC 1985) found in a survey of 500 employers that 95 per cent recognized that training was necessary to update the workforce in response to changing business and economic circumstances, 88 per cent agreed that training was necessary to maximize productivity and profits, 49 per cent claimed that training was part of their formal business plan and was a regular item for discussion on the board's agenda. The same survey, however, also found that although training may be talked about at high levels, and indeed considered to be important, comparatively little of it actually took place. The survey found that employers spent only 0.15 per cent of turnover on training. Comparable figures for our major competitors indicate that employers in our competitor nations (such as Japan and Germany) spend up to 3 per cent of turnover on training. Other surveys have indicated that the little training that does take place in the UK is disproportionately concentrated on managers, with less being spent on technical, administrative or manual employees.

Study after study, over a number of years (e.g., Prais 1985 and Layard and Mayhew 1995) have repeated the assertion that at the top end of training and education, the United Kingdom does as well as any other nation with, for instance, the proportion of young people achieving university degrees. It is at the intermediate level of qualification, the technician, the apprenticeship, secretarial and clerical training, that we do so poorly. It is generally recognized that the UK trains about half the number of young people with these skills as do many of our competitors.

Other reports have investigated the quality of management training in Britain. The most influential of these were produced by Handy (1987) and Constable and McCormick (1987). The reports painted a startling picture. Of 3 million managers in Britain the majority received no formal training at all. The average manager received only one day's training per year. Newly appointed managers generally received no training at all.

Handy put these figures into an international context and claimed that not only did our competitors do more management training, they also did better, more systematic and better-planned training. The methods used varied widely – the United States placed great emphasis on the MBA, while the Japanese produced hardly any MBAs, relying instead on in-house training and development of graduates carefully selected from universities. Germany, meanwhile, follows an approach not dissimilar to the Japanese model, with little postgraduate business training in university business schools but instead reliance on in-house training.

Both reports were shocked by the apparent amateurism of British management, the lack of training and development, and the lack of a clear vision as to what skills and abilities were required of managers. A number of recommendations came from the reports; Constable and McCormick called for the expansion of MBA programmes with widened access for full-time employees via part-time and modular courses, and a structured management 'apprenticeship' scheme whereby 'articled' managers would, over a period of time, go through a planned development programme which would lead to recognition as a qualified manager. Handy called for employers to commit themselves to 'benchmarks of good practice', whereby they would (for example) guarantee 5 days per year off-the-job training to all managers.

The British government plans to reform the training of probation officers. At present probation officers are required to undertake a two-year university-based qualification in social work; moreover, many are graduates. The government wishes to open up the service to a far wider range of applicants by making the training on-the-job and competence based. It is hoped that this will attract to the service more older people and people with a military background – many of whom would not be able to devote two years to getting a certificate.

The National Association of Probation Officers (NAPO) has refused to cooperate with the plans, as has the Association of Chief Officers of Probation (AcoP). They argue that it is not appropriate to reduce the qualities, skills and professionalism of the service at a time when its work is becoming increasingly complex.

It is estimated that currently 10 per cent of probation officers have a uniformed background. A further 10 per cent of new recruits are aged over 30, and 30 per cent aged over 40. (Reported in *People Management*, 19 Oct. 1995.)

3. Why Do British Firms Train Their Employees So Little?

The question of why British firms have not trained their staff, or more precisely why they have chosen to train them less fully than our competitor nations, has been the subject of much debate and research over the years. For many the answer lies in the intangible nature of training and the fact that monies spent on training do not always give an immediate or visible benefit. Additionally, the benefit of training may be felt over a number of years, may be ill-defined and unquantifiable. Many employers see that training gives the employee a higher intrinsic market-place value, allowing the employee to take expensively acquired skills elsewhere, or demand a higher salary. Trained employees are then often associated with higher wage bills, and this too may be a disincentive to train. Many smaller employers feel that they may be able to 'poach' skilled workers from other employers. Indeed, this argument will hold good when skilled workers are plentiful, but when they are in short supply prices will indeed be bid up – that is, assuming that there are workers with the requisite skills to be bid for. It is a fact that even in the depths of recession skill shortages are a feature of the UK economy. When the economy begins to pick its way out of recession those skill shortages become ever more acute, particularly in those occupations and industries which represent the newest technologies and therefore the best bet for the long-term viability of the economy.

To many cost-conscious employers the training budget is an easy budget to prune in times of economic hardship. Many still consider training to be an expensive luxury to be supported by the productive parts of the organization, rather than an engine of renewal and development.

Trainers too have been in part to blame for the problem. It has been argued that they have been unable or unwilling to demonstrate clearly the vital contribution that training is able to make to the success of the organization. In part this may be due to the fact that training, and human resource issues in general, are often not adequately represented at the highest levels of industry and commerce in the United Kingdom.

4. Training and Enterprise Councils

Training and Enterprise Councils (TECs) and Local Enterprise Councils (LECs) in Scotland were set up in 1991–2. In all there are 81 TECs and 22 LECs. They are established along geographical lines. Their brief is to identify the employment-related training needs in their area and direct training schemes which are of obvious need and relevance to local employers. Only rarely are they providers of training themselves; more often they fund other training providers who undertake to train in the particular areas identified. The training providers that they fund may be local colleges or private-sector training establishments. Training contracts are awarded for a limited period of time (one to two years), and, for many, payment is dependent upon outputs, on the number of people who achieve the qualification or skill for which they are being trained. This is as opposed to the number who enter the training in the first place. TECs employ staff to carry out their work, but they are managed by a board made up of senior local business people. TECs have the brief of identifying and addressing local skills deficiencies. In carrying out this work they manage multi-million-pound budgets. In 1994 the total government funding to TECs exceeded £2 billion. The major areas of their responsibility are Youth Training (YT) and Training for Work (TFW); adult training and retraining.

TECs have not been without their critics. The South Thames TEC had a deficit of £5 million in 1995 and called in the receiver. It was eventually taken over by three neighbouring TECs. Other have criticized TECs for bureaucracy and waste, and argued that they are simply too many in number. The way TECs are funded has also been criticized. At present they negotiate funds with government based on the number of people in their area that they identify as in need of their services. They then sub-contract to training providers for the provision of the training while attempting to retain a surplus of income over expenditure in order to fund their own initiatives and activities. It is this requirement that has led some to claim that TECs choose to go for the cheapest provider, or indeed choose to fund training only for those who are easy to train. Others have criticized TECs for taking a narrow or parochial view: for funding training for the short term and local need rather than considering longer-term factors or the needs of the economy as a whole.

The continued squeeze on government expenditure has led some to question the need for TECs at all. Some see considerable potential for savings within their £2 billion budgets. The government Budget of November 1994 cut the funds going to TECs by up to 20 per cent. The cuts fell particularly harshly on the 'Training for Work' budget. This is designed to help unemployed people back into the workplace. Funding was cut partly as a result of falling unemployment, but also because of what many saw as the failure of the scheme to help significant numbers back into work. At the moment of writing, government thinking seems to favour the employer or trainee paying an increased proportion of what is now provided free by the TEC. It is generally agreed that the number of TECs will fall in the years to come as they reorganize themselves along more strategically advantageous lines, to work ever more closely with business and commerce on a regional or geographical basis.

Large employers who, for instance, operate across the country, have experienced some difficulties in trying to deal with a large numbers of TECs at the same time. Each TEC has developed its own bureaucracy and methods of operating, leading to considerable delay and operational problems for those companies who wished to establish national training schemes. The government has given its approval for 'lead TECs' to be established, so a large employer will be able to coordinate training programmes through one TEC only. As well as reducing bureaucracy the new scheme should make planning and coordination of training considerably easier. (Reported in *Personnel Today*, 7 Nov. 1995.)

5. The National Council for Vocational Qualifications and the 'National Training Framework'

In 1986 the government established the National Council for Vocational Qualifications (NCVQ) and gave it the task of developing a national system of vocational qualifications and determining standards of occupational competence on a national scale. The government was concerned that literally hundreds of bodies awarded occupational qualifications, with little real regard to overall quality standards, and little or no cooperation between the bodies. The brief of NCVQ was to establish a national framework for qualifications through which awarding bodies could apply for accreditation, if their qualifications met the requirements of the Council. NCVQ thus is not an awarding body but is an accreditation authority.

The National Framework has been developed in liaison with representatives of industry, professional bodies, commerce and public service, who are brought together in what is called 'Industry Lead Bodies'. These Lead Bodies will, in conjunction with NCVQ and the awarding bodies, jointly develop the occupational standards for their particular industry. NCVQ will be concerned to ensure that the proposals fit into the National Framework that they have established. The framework draws comparisons of standard between vocational qualifications and academic qualifications, and the growing band of qualifications that straddle the divide (e.g. GNVQs or General National Vocational Qualifications).

The NCVQ does not award qualifications but instead gives its 'hallmark' to qualifications. Qualifications are awarded by awarding bodies, such as BTEC, City and Guilds, The Royal Society of Arts, and others. These too must be accredited by NCVQ.

A distinctive feature of NVQs is that they accredit competence. That is, they are concerned with the ability of the trainee to utilize her knowledge directly in her place of work. To this end NVQs are written and tested in such a way that they relate directly to workplace activities and give significantly less weight to more general educational considerations. Wherever possible trainees following NVQ programmes should be tested in, or close to, the workplace. This means that for those not in employment, gaining NVQs can be problematic.

In the last few years it has been realized that many young people would value a work-related qualification but are not able to access a workplace in order that the necessary assessment can take place. This has led to the development of the General National Vocational Qualification (GNVQ) in a number of work-related areas. These are also awarded by the awarding bodies who have developed GNVQs in conjunction with Lead Bodies and NCVQ. GNVQs are considered to be more appropriate for those in full-time education.

NCVQ has developed a number of levels within their National Framework. Table 8.1 illustrates how qualifications stand against one another.

NVQ 5 (to be developed)	Higher Professional Qualifications	GNVQ 5 (proposed)*	Middle Manager, Senior Professional
NVQ 4	HND/Degree/ Professional Level	GNVQ 4 (proposed)*	First Line Manager
NVQ 3	2 A-levels	GNVQ Advanced	Supervisor
NVQ 2	GCSEs	GNVQ Intermediate	Junior Employee
NVQ 1	Sub GCSE	GNVQ Foundation	

Table 8.1
The National Training
Framework

* NCVQ 1995.

It is envisaged that in time all qualifications will fall within the boundaries of the National Framework, and to date many awarding and professional bodies have brought their qualifications within the NVQ system. Many others are in the process of developing their qualifications into the appropriate style and will come on board in the next few years.

NVQs go beyond what many of us would recognize as occupations from our own experiences of industry and commerce. For instance, not only can you now qualify for NVQs in such areas as accounting (via the Association of Accounting Technicians) and marketing (via the Chartered Institute of Marketing), but also in radio operations. The Signals Division of the Army School of Mechanical Transport has been accredited as an approved training centre, and NVQs at Level 2 in 'Telecommunications Equipment: Radio' have been developed. It is planned to introduce qualifications at Levels 3 and 4.

> Research by the Basic Skills Agency . . . has shown a need for better 'core skills' within the British workforce. Core skills are defined as literacy, numeracy and communications skills. Core skills are increasingly part of the education and training curriculum via (for instance) NVQs and GNVQs, and as well as those listed above also cover IT, team working, learning skills and problem solving, but are less common for other members of the workforce. The Basic Skills Agency is concerned to promote ways in which older employees will be able to develop their own core skills, by encouraging employers to set up their own training programmes. (Reported in *Personnel Today*, 10 Oct. 1995.)

6. National Vocational Qualifications in Practice

6.1 The assessment of competence

National Vocational Qualifications are based on the notion of 'competence', which has been defined by the Department of Employment (1989) in an early document as:

> the ability to perform activities within an occupation. Competence is a wide concept which embodies the ability to transfer skills and knowledge to new situations within the occupational area. . . . It includes those qualities of personal effectiveness that are required in the workplace to deal with co-workers, managers and customers.

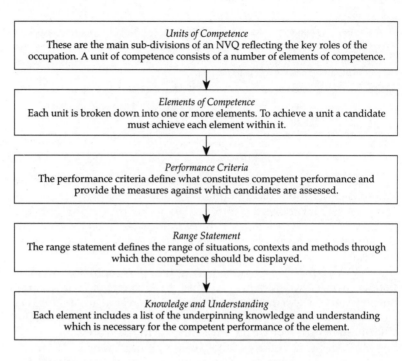

Figure 8.1
The structure of an NVQ

NVQs are essentially measures of workplace competence, and, as stated earlier, assessment of this competence should, whenever possible, take place in the workplace, or very close to it. For this reason NVQs are particularly suitable for those in employment, and less suitable for those out of work or seeking employment, because of the difficulty they would experience in finding work or work-based assessment opportunities.

An NVQ is made up of a number of *units*, and to achieve the qualification all units within the qualification must be achieved. All units are made up of several *elements* each of which must be assessed and passed. Each element will contain the following sub-sections: *performance criteria, range statement*, and *knowledge and understanding*. Each of these is briefly defined in figure 8.1. The definitions are adapted from BTEC's NVQ Accounting Standards (1992).

To illustrate, the NVQ Level 2 in Accounting has 5 Units which are made up of a total of 16 elements. An example of one of the units (taken from BTEC 1992, *Accounting at Level 2: Part 2: Standards*) is given in figure 8.2, with one of the elements of that unit detailed fully.

6.2 Routes to an NVQ

National Vocational Qualifications can be achieved in a number of ways. These include:

a. A planned training programme. This might take place through a college or private training provider. The provider will arrange a series of varied assessment opportunities, which should include wherever possible work, or work-based, assessment.

UNIT 1 *RECORDING AND ACCOUNTING FOR BANK TRANSACTIONS*
ELEMENTS: 1.1 Record and bank monies received
  1.2 Make and record payments
  1.3 Maintain petty cash records
  1.4 Account for cash and bank transactions

ELEMENT 1.1 *RECORD AND BANK MONIES RECEIVED*

PERFORMANCE CRITERIA:

- Monies are banked in accordance with the organization's policies, regulations, procedures and time-scales.
- Incoming monies are checked against relevant supporting documentation.
- Monies received are correctly and legibly recorded.
- Written receipts are correctly issued where required.
- Totals and balances are correctly calculated.
- Paying-in documents are correctly prepared and reconciled to relevant records.
- Documentation is correctly filed.
- Cash handling, security and confidentiality procedures are followed.
- Discrepancies, unusual features or queries are identified and either resolved or referred to the appropriate person.

RANGE STATEMENT:

- Monies received: cash, cheques, inter-bank transfers, payable orders, credit card transactions, but not foreign currency.
- The primary recording of monies received: remittance lists, cash books, cash registers or other methods with a similar purpose.
- Discrepancies, unusual features or queries including wrongly completed cheques, out-of-date validation cards, credit limits exceeded, disagreement with supporting documentation.

ELEMENT 1.1 *KNOWLEDGE AND UNDERSTANDING*

THE BUSINESS ENVIRONMENT:
  Types of business transactions and documents involved
  General principles of VAT
  Trade discounts and cash
  Legal aspects of cheques including crossings and endorsements
  Legal relationship of banker and customer
  General bank services and operation of clearing-bank system
  Characteristics of forms of payments (as in range statement)
  Functions and form of banking documentation

ACCOUNTING TECHNIQUES:
  Calculation facility, including use of equipment provided
  Methods of posting from primary documents to ledger accounts
  Methods of coding data
  Operation of manual and computerized accounting systems
  Methods of handling and storing money, security
  Functioning of cash register equipment
  Credit card procedures

ACCOUNTING PRINCIPLES AND THEORY:
  Functions of a ledger account system
  Main types of ledger account
  Interrelationship of accounts – double entry system
  Nature and function of primary records
  Distinction between capital and revenue (in general terms)
  Principles of internal check

THE ORGANIZATION:
  Background understanding that the accounting systems of an organization are affected by its organizational structure, its administrative systems and procedures and the nature of business transactions.

Figure 8.2
A sample NVQ unit –
Accounting

b. Assessment only. This would be appropriate for those in employment who have the opportunity in the workplace to acquire and be assessed in the competencies required for the award.

c. Through Accreditation of Prior Learning (APL). Many people wishing to achieve an NVQ will find that past study or work-based learning will correlate well against the requirements of the qualification. If the trainee is able to provide appropriate evidence of this prior learning it can be accredited against the award, thus reducing the period of study.

d. A combination of the above. Many trainees will find that they will be able to achieve their NVQ through a combination of each of the three methods described. For instance, they may have some work-based experience that can count, some opportunities for assessment will be present in their job, and some competencies will be acquired via off-the-job training.

6.3 Assessment of NVQs

The preceding section describes the variety of ways through which an NVQ might be achieved. Equally diverse are the methods through which NVQs should be assessed. The awarding bodies approve colleges, private training providers, employers' training centres and others (which meet certain criteria) to be NVQ centres. This means that they have the resources to deliver the qualifications for which they have been approved. As part of this the staff who are to carry out the assessment should receive training, and be accredited as, 'assessors'. Where there are a number of assessors, or a number of awards being delivered, the approved centre should also have an accredited 'internal verifier'. This will be the person who has the responsibility to act, in effect, as the internal auditor of the assessment processes and products. Additionally the awarding body will appoint an 'external verifier' who will visit the centre regularly and through sampling provide an external check on the quality of the assessment that is taking place.

6.4 Criticisms of NVQs

The introduction of NVQs has not been smooth and they have been criticized on a number of grounds. Industrialists have argued that they are too prescriptive, too complicated, and in many cases not related to 'real-life' requirements. Colleges and trainers have argued that the assessment model is too paper based and bureaucratic, allowing insufficient time for training input. Others claimed that the NVQ model itself is flawed with its reliance on the 'achievement of competence' as a measure of success. This line of argument suggests that NVQ trainees often fail to grasp the underlying principles that go with the competence: that is, though they can perform the required tasks, they have not acquired the underlying knowledge necessary to apply the skill to new or varied situations. The systems of APL and work-based assessment have led some to claim that NVQs only accredit what the trainee already knows rather than challenging them to aspire to new knowledge and skills. It has also been claimed that NVQs are a 'quick fix' designed to give a high percentage of the workforce vocational qualifications with the minimum cost and effort, while failing to tackle the underlying problems within industrial training in the UK. Problems have also become apparent as attempts are made to develop the higher-level NVQs. These require the trainee to demonstrate more abstract and conceptual skills. Arguably such skills are not suited to the highly prescriptive, task- and performance-related NVQ model.

6.5   NVQs – conclusion

Despite the criticisms of NVQs, and those outlined above probably do not do full justice to the wide-ranging attacks made on them, it is probable that the competence-based model of training has made an indelible impression on vocational training in the United Kingdom and is here for some time to come. What is less certain is that NVQs will actually lead to a workforce that is better qualified to compete into the twenty-first century, or instead merely produce a workforce that possesses more qualifications.

7. The Management Charter Initiative

Concerns about the standard of education and training of British managers, best expressed in the Constable and McCormick (1987) and Handy (1987) reports, led to the setting up of the Management Charter Initiative (MCI). The aim was to give management a greater training profile, in the hope that one day it would become a chartered profession like accountancy or banking. One of the prerequisites for this to happen would be for a body of knowledge that could be called 'management' to be agreed so that standards of assessment could be arrived at; another would be for professional standards of behaviour (or professional ethics) to be developed. The MCI looked at the management qualifications as they stood in the 1980s – principally the Certificate in Management Studies or CMS (one year of part-time study for the junior manager), the Diploma in Management Studies or DMS (two years of part-time study for the middle manager – often graduate or CMS entry), and the Master of Business Administration or MBA, for senior managers (usually graduate or senior professional qualification entry). These were redefined, and respecified as:

Certificate in Management (replaces CMS), roughly equivalent to NVQ 4.

Diploma in Management (replaces DMS), roughly equivalent to NVQ 5.

The Master in Business Administration (MBA).

The respecification of qualifications was undertaken with reference to NCVQ, and an outcomes-based method was adopted (similar to NVQs). Awarding bodies for the CIM and DIM include BTEC, the Open University, and the Management Verification Consortium (a consortium of a number of universities working together). MBAs are of course still awarded by individual universities.

The new qualifications have been very popular, and many more managers than ever before are working towards achieving one of the new awards. Many companies have set up formal agreements with qualification providers to provide training specific to the needs of that organization. By far the most popular route for achieving one of the new awards has been via the Open University, who are now the biggest provider of management education and training in Europe.

8. Investors in People

The 1988 White Paper (*Employment for the 1990s*) led to the introduction of the 'Investors in People' (IIP) scheme. It is designed as a training standard for investment in employees. Those aspiring to or holding the award must make an ongoing commitment to the training of their staff. This commitment is outlined below. As part of the process of becoming an IIP an organization will first have to audit its current training practice and provision. This is done with the assistance of the survey instruments available through the scheme. Once the survey is complete the organization should take the appropriate action to meet the standards. The organization will be required to produce evidence of its achievements and of its training standards and objectives. These will be considered by an assessor. The job of assessing the standards was given to the TECs (LECs in Scotland), and those who achieve the standards are given public recognition and entitled to display the 'Investors in People' logo on their headed paper and advertising material.

AN INVESTOR IN PEOPLE IS . . .

The 'Investor in People Commitment' reads as follows:

- An Investor in People makes a public commitment from the top to develop all employees to achieve its business goals.

- An Investor in People regularly reviews the training and development needs of all employees.

- An Investor in People takes action to train and develop individuals on recruitment and throughout their careers.

- An Investor in People evaluates the investment in training and development to assess achievement and improve effectiveness.

(Employment Department 1991, *Investors in People: A Guide for Top Managers*.)

---

9. National Training Awards

National Training Awards were introduced by the government in 1987 as a method by which corporate and individual excellence in the field of training could be recognized. They are administered by the Department for Education and Employment on behalf on the Secretary of State. Entries can come from organizations or individuals, who can nominate themselves. The judgements are made by a national panel. Winners are permitted to display the fact that they are winners of National Training Awards on their letter paper and advertising material. The 1993 NTA Handbook tells us that the awards aim to:

a. identify excellence in training development and practice;

b. demonstrate the link between effective investment in training and improved business performance; and,

c. Encourage greater personal commitment by individuals to self-development.

10. The Modern Apprenticeship Scheme

The decline in the apprenticeship system in the UK, compared with (for instance) Germany, has been marked. Today the traditional apprenticeship has all but gone in the UK, while in Germany up to half a million young people choose to commence a three-year apprenticeship each year. A considerable proportion of these young people will have university entrance qualifications but choose to delay their entry until after the completion of their apprenticeship. The system could not be more different in the UK, where apprenticeships and vocational qualifications are often seen to be suitable for those who are less academically gifted.

In its 1993 budget the government announced its intention to introduce what it called a 'modern apprenticeship' scheme. To this end it provided £1.25 billion to launch a number of pilot schemes. In 1994 approximately 2,000 young people entered modern apprenticeships in 17 industrial and commercial sectors, and in September 1995 up to 40,000 young people were able to join. The apprenticeships will be available in a wide range of occupational areas and not just the traditional engineering trades. Among those areas available are childcare, tourism and the travel trade.

The apprenticeship, which should last three years (although it is being touted that those who enter with A-levels may be able to complete in 18 months), will be based around an NVQ Level 3, core skills development (e.g. interpersonal skills, communication skills, numeracy skills, etc.), and extensive hands-on experience with the sponsoring company. The apprentices, although attached to a particular employer, will not be guaranteed work at the end of the training: the contract (which will be between the TEC and the employer) will be for training only.

Currently the Youth Training model is based around an assumption that trainees will achieve an NVQ Level 2 after two years of training. The modern apprenticeship scheme is designed to raise standards and skills and involve industry ever more closely in the development of young people with the skills needed for future industrial success. It is too early to assess the extent to which the scheme will succeed.

11. The 1995 *Competitiveness* White Paper

The 1995 White Paper, launched by the President of the Board of Trade in May of that year, once again emphasized the vital role training must play in the development of the British economy in the latter years of the twentieth century and beyond. The White Paper set new training targets for the workforce, for individuals and for employers. These are summarized below:

TARGETS FOR THE YEAR 2000

The 1995 *Competitiveness* White Paper suggests the following targets:

For the Workforce:

- 30 per cent Qualified to NVQ4 or above
- 60 per cent qualified to NVQ3, Advanced GNVQ or two A-level standard

For Young People:

- 75 per cent to achieve NVQ Level 2 competence in Communication, Numeracy and Information Technology by age 19, and 35 per cent to achieve Level 3 in these core skills by age 21
- 85 per cent to achieve 5 GCSEs at grade C or above, an Intermediate GNVQ or an NVQ Level 2 by age 19
- 60 per cent qualified to NVQ Level 3, Advanced GNVQ or two A-level standard

For Employers:

- 70 per cent of all firms employing 200 or more, and 35 per cent with 50 or more employees, to achieve the Investors in People training standard

---

12. Conclusion

Arguably the government is taking training more seriously now than any time for a generation. The development of TECs, NVQs, national training targets, more rigorous standards for training, the national training framework, all indicate the commitment of the government to develop a workforce fit to face the challenges of the twenty-first century. Many, however, still remain unimpressed. Layard and Mayhew (1995), in their report *Britain's Training Deficit*, argue that still more needs to be done to close the skills gap with our major competitors. They claim that over the past decade the country has been 'groping around in the dark', and recommend a reinvigoration of policy. Specifically they call for all off-the-job training to be funded by the state, and for all under-19s to be employed as trainees. Up until the age of 21 they argue that all workers should have the right to a day off per week to attend training. They are firmly in favour of increasing the wage differential between young and adult workers (between skilled and unskilled workers). A starting salary of 30 per cent of the skilled-worker rate would be an appropriate reward for young people. The wage rate would rise as young people progressed towards skilled status. Additionally they argue for all vocational learning to be funded by the state, and are critical of the 'fallacy' that firms should pay for training because they benefit from it. State funding, they claim, is the only way in which vocational education and training can be given parity with traditional academic routes which, of course, are fully funded by the state. Treating both equally (in terms of funding) is the first step towards their being regarded as equals by young people, parents and employers.

KENNEY-REED LTD.

Kenney-Reed are a manufacturer of various high-precision steel components, which are produced in the main for the defence industry. Most of their contracts come from the major defence industry suppliers. The industry was comparatively stable until the last twenty years or so, when orders became harder to win, margins were cut and the defence industry as a whole began to feel the effects of public expenditure cuts, closer scrutiny of contracts, a drive for higher quality and, latterly, the end of the cold war.

Kenney-Reed has cut its workforce from a peak of 2,500 in 1981 to a core workforce of less than 800 now. It has also abandoned its apprenticeship system (up until the early 1980s it regularly took on up to 80 apprentices each year); none have been taken on since 1987. The wages paid to the core staff have not kept pace with the general rise in earnings. The training budget has been frozen at the bare minimum.

The volatile nature of the market that the company has found itself in in recent years has meant that it has had to be more proactive and responsive, not least in the field of recruitment and training. For the last eight years it has been the policy of the company to employ an increasing proportion of staff on short-term contracts, to make greater use of sub-contractors, and where necessary consultants. As a result it has maintained a core workforce of about 780 while employing anything up to another 300 temporary and contract staff. The contract and temporary staff are particularly useful when the core staff do not possess all of the skills needed to complete a contract won by the company. Temporary staff are employed (at the market rate, which has sometimes been considerably above that paid to core staff) for the duration of the contract and then released. Some, however, have been employed almost continuously for several years.

Locally the company has gained something of a reputation for 'hiring and firing' staff – advertising extensively for skilled workers one month while announcing redundancies a few months later.

The quality of work produced by the company has come under criticism recently and several customers are unhappy. Kenney-Reed directors are very concerned because profit margins are already tight (and falling), and they are not sure how to develop the quality of their products nor how to gain greater economies. One of the directors has recently argued that the company should re-appraise how it recruits and develops its staff. He has argued for a many-fold increase in the training budget. His ideas have been met with resistance, largely on the grounds of cost. As a compromise the board have agreed to employ a consultant to consider the director's proposals and review the whole staffing policy.

TASK

Adopting the role of the consultant, consider how you would go about your task, the investigations that you would make and questions you would ask.

QUESTIONS FOR FURTHER CONSIDERATION

1. Why is training important to organizations, individuals and for the country as a whole?

2. Consider the advantages and disadvantages of leaving the responsibility for training to employers, rather than the state taking an active role in determining a national training policy.

3. Why do you think vocational training is considered to be less prestigious than academic study in the UK?

4. Traditionally, many British employers have chosen to recruit staff already skilled rather than train staff themselves. Consider the merits and demerits of this practice for the individual, the company and the economy.

5. What weaknesses exist in the UK system of training?

•REFERENCES•

BTEC (1992)
ACCOUNTING LEVELS 2–4: PART 1: GUIDANCE TO CENTRES
London, BTEC.

BTEC (1992)
ACCOUNTING AT LEVEL 2: PART 2: STANDARDS
London, BTEC.

Constable J & McCormick R (1987)
THE MAKING OF BRITISH MANAGERS: A REPORT OF THE BIM AND CBI INTO MANAGEMENT TRAINING, EDUCATION AND DEVELOPMENT
London, British Institute of Management.

Graham H & Bennett R (1995)
HUMAN RESOURCES MANAGEMENT
London, Pitman.

Handy C (1987)
THE MAKING OF MANAGERS
London, National Economic Development Office.

Keep E (1989)
A Training Scandal?, in **PERSONNEL MANAGEMENT IN BRITAIN**
Sisson K (ed.). Oxford, Blackwell.

Layard R (1992)
Call for a Training System Reform
Financial Times, 11 Dec.

Layard R & Mayhew Sir G (1995)
BRITAIN'S TRAINING DEFICIT
Aldershot, Avebury Publishing.

Manpower Services Commission (1981)
GLOSSARY OF TRAINING TERMS
London, MSC.

Manpower Services Commission (1985)
ADULT TRAINING IN BRITAIN
Sheffield, HMSO.

National Council for Vocational Qualifications (1995)
GNVQs AT HIGHER LEVELS: A CONSULTATION PAPER
London, NCVQ.

Prais S (1985)
What Can We Learn From the German System of Vocational Education and Training?, in **EDUCATION AND ECONOMIC PERFORMANCE**
Worswick G (ed.). London, Gower.

UK Department of Employment (1989)
CLARIFYING THE COMPONENTS OF MANAGEMENT COMPETENCE
London, HMSO.

UK Department of Employment (1991)
**INVESTORS IN PEOPLE:
A GUIDE FOR TOP MANAGERS**
Sheffield, Employment Department.

UK Department of Employment (1993)
NATIONAL TRAINING AWARDS: HANDBOOK AND ENTRY FORM
Sheffield, Employment Department.

UK Department of Trade and Industry (1995)
COMPETITIVENESS (Government White Paper)
London: HMSO.

•CHAPTER•
9

TRAINING AND DEVELOPMENT METHODS

AS A RESULT OF STUDYING THIS CHAPTER YOU SHOULD BE ABLE TO:

- Appreciate the importance of training and development provision relating to the short-, medium- and long-term strategic needs of the organization.

- Appreciate the benefits that might accrue to an organization from a commitment to developing properly its employees.

- Understand the need for, and the stages of, developing a systematic approach to training based on the need for a clear identification of needs.

- Consider the range of training and development techniques that are available and the advantages and disadvantages of each.

1. Introduction

> As we have mentioned tirelessly . . . , the competitive edge will be maintained by those organizations which use their workforce most efficiently. From this it follows that effective training is paramount in the fight for survival and growth. (Molander and Winterton 1994: 78)

> We continue to put great emphasis on development and training and, during the year, provided more than 800,000 training days – equivalent to over 5 days per person. (British Telecom Annual Report and Accounts 1995)

Despite the historic problems of United Kingdom employers with regard to training (as outlined in the previous chapter), the need for and the importance of training has never been greater, and more and more organizations are giving it their due consideration and attention. Among the benefits that organizations might expect from an increased training effort are:

a. Greater productivity and better quality.

b. Greater versatility from the workforce.

c. Better job satisfaction (as evidenced by lower absenteeism and lower turnover) and greater motivation.

d. A reduced need for supervision.

e. Greater understanding of and adherence to employer values.

f. Reduced accident rates.

g. Less scrap and fewer mistakes.

h. The development of a more confident and competent workforce.

Despite its importance and the alleged benefits that it might actually bring, what is training? A commonly used definition is that produced by the now defunct Manpower Services Commission (MSC 1981):

> A planned process to modify attitude, knowledge or skill behaviour through learning experience to achieve effective performance in an activity or range of activities. Its purpose, in the work situation, is to develop the abilities of the individual and to satisfy the current and future needs of the organization.

This definition is wide, sufficiently wide to cover the range of training methods discussed later in the chapter. Perhaps the key terms in the definition are that it is a: *planned process designed to modify attitude, knowledge or skill behaviour*. Development, on the other hand, takes a longer-term view, and although still based on behavioural change or learning, adopts a far longer timescale. It encompasses such areas as 'life-long learning', the 'learning organization' and 'organizational development' – all of which, except in the most general sense, are beyond the scope of this book. Development focuses on the longer-term needs of the employer and the employee and is seen in its most developed form in Japan (Bratton and Gold 1994: 226):

> the Japanese presumption in larger organizations of lifetime employment for core workers . . . allows organizations to recruit employees for a career rather than for a job which may soon become obsolete. Employees are expected to retrain and indeed many employees undertake courses of self-study in order to continue their learning. Employees are therefore selected carefully as much for their ability to learn as for their current repertoire of skills.

The recent problems in the Japanese economy have called into question the whole idea of lifetime employment, and in the United Kingdom the idea of job security has long been abandoned as redundancies have cut into even the most secure occupations. This puts the responsibility for development securely onto the shoulders of the employee – for lifetime learning, and development, will be one of the key ways that the individual can ensure that they are able to adapt to the changing needs of the world of employment.

The UK Institute of Management (IM) launched in November 1995 their new policy on Continuous Professional Development. This initiative, which is designed to act as a framework to help managers keep up to date and is consistent with those issued by many other professional bodies. Indeed many now see CPD as a requirement for continued membership of the institute. The CPD principle is centred around the individual and predicated on the assumption that each manager must take responsibility for assessing and meeting their own needs, using help available from their professional bodies, educational institutions and employer.

The IM claim that for the manager as well as for other professionals, initial qualification is only a start, and that technological and legislative changes, the growth of knowledge, development of new techniques, changing economic and competitive pressures and social priorities demand continuing updating of knowledge and skills. (Reported in *Professional Manager*, Nov. 1995.)

Training and Development, although different in their focus, are or course closely related. Training activities which are directed at addressing a short-term problem will also help the employee develop the portfolio of skills necessary for longer-term success. Because of its shorter-term focus, training is inevitably able to operate in a more planned and structured manner. Many employers will direct their training in a way similar to that outlined in figure 9.1.

2. Training Policy

In considering its training policy the organization will need to ask the fundamental questions – why do we train, what purpose will training serve, who do we train, when do we train, where will the training take place. In other words, the organization is asking itself to make a commitment to training, and to ensure that it serves the purpose of developing the long-term interests of the organization.

Too often in the past training has been seen to have too little relevance to the real business of the organization. In many ways it has been seen as peripheral to what the organization is really about. In order to be really effective training must be related to the corporate plan of the organization; that is, it must be directed to helping the organization develop its manpower in such a way that short-, medium- and long-term objectives can be achieved in an efficient and effective manner. Training policies, then, need to be developed in line with the human resource planning activities of the organization; in such a way to gain

Figure 9.1
The stages of training

the support of line managers; so that the current and future problems of managers and their staff can be identified and overcome. Consultation with line managers will be vital if any training effort is to succeed. It is also important to keep at the forefront of thinking and planning the fact that training will not be the solution to all problems. Too often in the past, training has been seen as the solution to all ills, from lack of motivation and poor reward policies, to poor management and outdated technology. Quite clearly training will not solve all problems, and part of the objective of undertaking a training needs analysis is to determine not only what can be addressed with training, but also what can (and should) be left to other methods.

3. Identification of Training Needs (Training Needs Analysis)

In order to train effectively it is necessary first to decide in some detail what specific knowledge and skills the jobs involve, what the individuals already possess, and what gaps in such knowledge and skill training can fill. (Gode 1972: 9)

Training needs analysis will need to take account of both long- and short-term issues. In the short term training will need to address the current and immediate problems of the organization. Some of this may be 'fire-fighting', some may be in response to rapid changes in the market-place. Whatever the cause, if the issue is correctly identified it can often be speedily addressed. Longer-term training will relate to the strategic and developmental needs of the organization, will require planners to have a view of what the organization will look like at some predetermined point in the future (e.g. five years), and will also attempt to quantify and qualify the skills, attributes and attitudes that the workforce of the future will need to possess. The 'gap' between how the workforce measures up now and the model for the future should also be quantified, and then a plan put in place to develop a workforce that will meet the organization's requirements for the future. The process requires a degree of abstraction and clearly must be developed in conjunction with the human resource plan. At the strategic or longer-term level many fundamental questions will need to be asked. These might include 'how many staff will be needed in the future?', 'do the current staff possess the basic "raw material" that can be developed to meet future requirements?', 'what culture will best suit the organization in the future?'

Any training needs analysis should be undertaken in close consultation with line managers. They should be able to identify the problems they and their staff have in meeting the requirements of their position. Gaining their support is vital because any training undertaken must impact most quickly where it is seen by individual line managers – it must make a contribution to workplace performance. If it does not, then it may well be viewed with suspicion and given little support by those whose support can make it work best of all – line managers.

Pepper (1984: 17) identifies nine key areas where training will be needed in most organizations on an ongoing basis. These are:

a. new recruits to the company

b. transferees within the company

c. promotions

d. new plant or equipment

e. new procedures

f. new standards, rules and practices

g. new relationships and authorities

h. the maintenance of standards

i. the maintenance of flexibility.

While it is probable that training will be needed on an ongoing basis in all of these nine areas, the actual and specific training required should be determined by application of the following formula:

Current and future organizational needs, *minus*   Skills currently possessed by workforce, *equals* the skills gap.

It is this gap that training needs analysis must identify, qualify and quantify.

4. Determine Training Objectives

In recent years much attention has been given to ensuring that training is clearly focused and directed at the real needs of the organization. In large part this is done by setting clear and unambiguous (and wherever possible, measurable) goals for training. Many organizations will direct training at developing the ability of the individual to carry out specific tasks, usually in relation to their job. The development of the 'competence movement' and NVQs has aided this approach considerably. These developments are discussed in the previous chapter.

With pressure on training budgets ever tighter and a requirement upon training managers to justify the real benefits of their training provision, less and less scope is available for training and development to be done 'for its own sake'. More and more organizations expect training to meet some clearly defined and pre-set goal.

So, all training should be directed to address specific targets, which once addressed will improve the workplace performance of staff. As a bare minimum the trainee should be told what he should be able to do as a result of undertaking the training. This will also, of course, aid the process of evaluation.

5. Plan the Training Provision

Trainers must consider the methods available for delivering the training required. For many areas training can be delivered in a number of ways, and these may be either on or off the job. As a general rule in deciding the best way to deliver, the trainer should bear in mind not only speed, cost and effectiveness but also the axiom that the further away training occurs from the workplace the more acute the problem of transference to the workplace will be. A number of the techniques available to trainers are discussed later in this chapter.

In planning the training provision the priority to be given to any particular area of training should be considered. The training needs analysis should identify the urgency with which the training areas should be addressed. However, because needs are quite likely to exceed the budget to support training, it is likely that some difficult decisions will need to be made either about provision, timing or method of training selected.

6. Undertake the Training

The manager of the training should ensure that the training, when it takes place, relates clearly and specifically to the identified training needs. This is to ensure maximum value from the training effort. In undertaking this the manager will need to liaise carefully with all training providers, including outside agencies. Specific training methods are described later in this chapter.

7. Evaluate the Training

All trainers, managers and writers about training are agreed on the importance of evaluating training. Where there is less agreement, is how this can and should be done. Hamblin (1974: 65) has defined the process of evaluating training as:

> Any attempt to gain information (feedback) on the effects of a training programme, and to assess the value of the training in the light of that information.

This definition has several implications but principally that the *costs* of training should be weighed against the *benefits* and a judgement made about the *value* of the training. This may sound a simple concept, but in reality can prove to be very difficult. In practice the costs of inadequate training can often be clearly seen (and measured). They might include customer complaints, excessive scrap, spoiled work, low output or variable quality. However, the real contributions that training is able to make are far more difficult to capture, and indeed they may appear over a longer period of time than any exercise to evaluate the benefit of training might allow. Additionally the well-trained worker might be better motivated, require less supervision, be absent less often, have less accidents and be more in tune with the wider aims and objectives of the organization. Few of these benefits will come out of formal training evaluation.

Costing training can also be fraught with difficulties. Off-the-job training is most easy to cost and will include the direct cost of the employee attending the training course, plus the work lost as a result of the individual's absence from work. On-the-job training can be more difficult to cost, and although the cost may appear to be very low, this may not always be the case. Additionally, on-the-job training can appear to be both haphazard and unstructured and may result in little real benefit accruing to the trainee and hence the organization.

The preceding paragraphs should leave the reader in little doubt that evaluating training in any meaningful way is fraught with both procedural and practical difficulties. These difficulties do not mean that evaluation should not be undertaken, they simply underline the need to take care in evaluating and the necessity for caution when considering its results.

Hamblin (1974) has proposed that evaluation can be undertaken at five different levels. They are:

a. *Reactions Level*. At this level the trainee is asked about the training experience itself, which parts she found useful, which parts less so. The trainee might be asked to pass judgement on the speakers, the facilities, the organization of the event and what improvements they might like to see made.

b. *The Learning Level*. At this level evaluation requires that the trainees should be tested on what they have learned as a result of the training. This might be an end-of-course test and would aim to assess the degree to which the trainee had acquired the knowledge, skills or abilities that the training aimed to deliver.

c. *Job Behaviour Level*. This level of evaluation considers the degree to which knowledge and skills acquired in training are used back in the workplace. The objective of all training must be to influence workplace behaviour in a desired way. No matter how successful training appears to be as a result of any evaluation undertaken at levels one and two; if it does not result in the desired changes in workplace behaviour then it will probably be deemed to have failed. When evaluating at this level it is important to note that any failure to transfer new skills to the workplace may not be the fault of either the training nor the trainee. It may be that the culture of the workplace, or the attitudes of the boss mitigate against the trainee displaying her new skills to best effect, and the newly trained worker will continue to behave as though no training had taken place. Generally speaking new skills will be best displayed in an environment that is receptive to change.

d. *The Organization Level*. Evaluation at this level considers the effect of training on the functioning of the workplace. The evaluator will be looking for improvements in output, quality, productivity, less waste, or whatever measure is most appropriate for the type of training undertaken. Evaluation at this level will focus on the areas of concern that gave rise to the need for training in the first place, and consider to what extent they have been addressed by the training. Evaluation at this level is less concerned with behavioural changes and more with changes in workplace performance as measured by key workplace indicators.

e. *The Ultimate Level.* Ultimately all training should have some positive effect on the performance of the organization and the highest level of evaluation will attempt to assess this effect. However, while it is easy to accept that all training should make a contribution to corporate success, it is more difficult to measure that contribution, let alone make a judgement as to whether that contribution is satisfactory or not.

Ideally training should be assessed at all five levels. Practically the higher the level the more difficult the evaluation will become, and the more prolonged the timescale. Trainers like to have an immediate feedback for their training, not only for their own satisfaction but also so they can fine-tune their procedures in order that future trainees can receive a better experience. All of this mitigates against taking a long-term view of training and its evaluation. However, with pressure on corporate budgets ever greater the need for trainers to justify the value of their work and demonstrate that it can and does contribute to organizational success has never been greater.

8. Feedback

On the basis of the short-, medium- and long-term evaluation undertaken the training manager will need to decide:

a. To what extent the training programme(s) has met it objectives.

b. Which, if any, training objectives remain to be satisfied.

c. How the training provision should be revised, improved or replaced.

The decisions made should feed back into future training provision.

9. Training Methods

Training is traditionally described as falling into one of two categories – on-the-job or off-the-job. On-the-job training takes place when the trainee is not removed from the workplace. Training undertaken in this way has the advantage of being immediately transferable to the work situation and is generally considered to be cheap and cost effective. However, it can also appear to be random and haphazard in its rigour and application. At the other extreme is off-the-job training, which occurs when the trainee is removed from the workplace to (for instance) attend a training course. While the content of off-the-job training can be more certain, the degree to which it can be applied back to the workplace is not. Examples of the range of locations for training is considered in table 9.1.

Decisions about the location of training will inevitably be made in conjunction with decisions about the form in which training should be undertaken. The are many, many methods by which people can be trained. Some of the most popular are considered below.

Option choice	Advantages	Disadvantages
College or university courses	General principles covered; thinking skills developed; often leads to qualification.	Insufficient practical work; training may take considerable period of time.
Private training agency	Meets special needs in professional way; fills gaps in the organization's resources.	May have to accept an off-the-shelf package; may be costly.
Secondment; special projects	Authentic setting; widens experience; provides useful way of practising problem-solving skills.	Employee may not succeed; finding staff to act as mentors.
Own facilities	Own standards/customs can be promoted; may be more cost effective than external provision.	Perspective may be too parochial; own staff may lack credibility, knowledge or skills.
Guided experience	Authentic setting (on the job); linked firmly to own practices and job requirements.	Subject to all the pressures and distractions of the workplace.

Table 9.1
Training locations –
advantages and
disadvantages

Source: based on Cole 1988.

9.1 Action learning

A very useful development tool, often used with decision-making managers, a group of whom should meet together on a regular basis to act as client and consultants to each other. The group members then work through their own and one another's problems in a supportive way. It is usual for the group to be assisted by a consultant who will work on the group processes. For action learning to work well all group members must be highly committed, for as a method it is not cheap and can consume considerable amounts of managers' valuable time. At its best it is a powerful tool through which managers can learn in a problem-centred manner from each other. The ideas behind action learning were developed by Revans (1972).

9.2 Appraisal (performance management)

Today many organizations, dissatisfied with traditional models of performance appraisal, are developing in their place more comprehensive systems of performance management. This development is discussed in full in chapter 10. Anderson and Evenden (1994: 248) provide a working definition of performance management:

> Performance Management involves having in place systems and methods which translate the goals of strategic management into individual performance terms through HRM. If the selection function's contribution to strategic management involves getting the right people, then performance management and development means getting the people right. This includes appraisal of individuals as well as planning and influencing their future performance through targets and development.

There is little doubt that a well-planned and executed system of performance management can help individuals focus on key targets, on their own development needs with regard to achieving those targets, as well as those needed for longer-term career progression. Some performance management schemes give the responsibility for training to the individual herself. This avoids the HR or Training Manager becoming the gatekeeper to, or the rationer of, training. Each individual (via the appraisal process) is then responsible for ensuring that they know their own deficiencies and take steps to address them, formally or informally, inside or outside of the organization.

9.3 Assignments

An assignment may relate to a particular programme of training, or may be given for more general reasons as a developmental tool for managers. An assignment, in essence, is a specific problem, worked on by a team or an individual with the objective of producing a firm proposal within a given period of time. It should utilize and develop a wide range of skills including time management, problem solving, negotiating and communicating.

9.4 Case studies

The use of case studies is a common technique in management training programmes. A case study is a description and explanation of a real-life event from which the trainee can draw lessons, examples and illustrations. The idea is that lessons learned can then be applied to the trainee's workplace. If in studying the case study the trainee is able to work with other trainees, then it is likely that a range of ideas, solutions and recommendations can be found to the problems highlighted in the case material.

9.5 Coaching

The principle of coaching is very simple, and is based on the notion that an experienced employee is in possession of a range of skills, knowledge and competencies that could help an inexperienced member of staff better do her job. In just the same way that a football coach can teach a young player skills and techniques, so the same principles can be applied to industry and commerce. Coaching needs to be planned, with the 'coach' setting the trainee a series of tasks which are progressively more difficult, in order that he might gain the abilities to perform his job with greater insight and knowledge.

9.6 College/university-based courses

Longer courses based at universities or colleges have the advantage of allowing the employee the opportunity to meet others from similar organizations and of similar ambition who are also course members. The course may be award bearing (such as the DMS or MBA) and may often extend over several years of part-time study. The requirement to please all members of the group will lead the course tutors to set the course material in a strong theoretical context and use practical examples that are general and widely applicable. Such an approach,

while being offensive to none, may also not meet the specific requirements of any of the course members – it may work well at the general
level, but not at the level of the individual course member, concerned
about how the knowledge learned from the course can be applied back
to the workplace. Despite such shortcomings, award-bearing courses
are popular with employees because the qualification gained might
well have considerable currency in the job market.

9.7 Computer-based learning

The use of computer-based technologies has opened up many new
opportunities for trainers to impart information in an efficient and
effective manner. Such opportunities include interactive video, which
allows different solutions to a particular problem to be tested and
explored by the trainee. The higher the degree of interaction, the less the
opportunity for the employee to be passive in the learning process.
Many employers who have numbers of staff who work with computers
have built into their networks training packages which can be accessed
by employees during quiet moments in their working day. The packages might contain information about new products, techniques or procedures, and employees would be expected to work through them in a
progressive and systematic manner.

9.8 Delegation

In this case a boss gives a subordinate specific responsibility and
authority to perform new or additional tasks. It gives the capable junior
employee the chance to learn while still being carefully supervised by
the manager. When undertaken properly, delegation is not abdication,
but rather a planned process for the development of junior employees.

9.9 Demonstration

Commonly referred to as 'sitting next to Nellie', this is probably the
simplest form of training and involves the trainee working alongside an
experienced worker and acquiring her skills. Although simple, the
method is not without its problems. For instance, the experienced
worker may be reluctant to impart her knowledge and skills to the
newcomer, or she may be poor at communicating to others how she
does her job. Alternatively, in addition to passing the required knowledge, she may also pass on bad habits and sloppy work practices.

9.10 Developing teams

Many organizations are today devoting considerable training resources
to team development. Training, focusing on group dynamics, is
designed to allow individuals to explore how they might operate more
effectively as a member of a team. In essence the technique operates by
analysing how team members currently function in the achievement of
the group's task, and how their efforts and contributions can be
developed to produce a more cohesive team in the future. The technique often involves a consultant working closely with a team and its
members over a period of time.

9.11   Job rotation

This involves an employee being seconded to another position or department for a period of time. Knowledge and skills learned in the new position should help her perform her own job better, or prepare him for future career moves.

9.12   Open/distance learning

This is the system by which organizations use their training resource in such a way that employees access technology-assisted instruction at times to suit themselves. Many organizations have designed their own training packages which can be used across a wide geographical area either as a distance-learning or open-learning tool, and which might be supported by tutoring by local managers in periods of off-the-job training.

Alternatively, employers might make use of simpler technologies to help their employees gain knowledge. Such a method might include workbooks containing structured learning activities, exercises and self-test questionnaires.

9.13   Role playing

The use of role plays is common where it is considered essential for the trainee to experience the nature of an interpersonal encounter. This is particularly useful if staff may be exposed to stressful situations, possibly involving contact with angry or upset customers or members of the public. The role play may be tightly or loosely scripted, and if the role play is undertaken in an authentic manner, the participants should be able to feel genuine emotion, and appreciate the need to think on their feet.

9.14   Simulation

Most often used for the training of individuals such as pilots, and cases where a simulation of the work that they are being trained to do enables trainees to acquire some of the requisite skills in a safe and progressive manner. Gradually, as their skills develop, they will be introduced to the 'real thing'. Simulations will also be used for groups such as the fire brigade, divers, all branches of the armed forces and others where training closer to the job could be either dangerous or prone to error.

9.15   Training room instruction

This involves taking the trainees away from the workplace in order that they might receive instruction in a particular technique or knowledge area. The major advantage of such a method is that a number of people can be brought together in one place to receive instruction at the same time. In terms of efficient use of resources, clearly this makes good sense. However, the major drawback of using purely didactic methods is that very little of what is said or demonstrated is retained by the trainee. It is not realistic to expect that simply because a trainee has attended a presentation about a particular policy, technique or procedure that she is able to apply that knowledge in the workplace. Indeed it is likely that she will not.

10. Self-managed Learning

The idea of 'self-managed learning' is worthy of separate consideration, rather than as a part of the above section. The concept is increasingly popular within organizations and is not inconsistent with the ideas of 'development' propounded earlier. Self-managed learning is seen to be consistent with delayering, empowerment and individuals taking greater and greater responsibility in the workplace. It places the responsibility for development firmly with the employee, and can take a number of forms. At its simplest, every part of training is devolved to the employee. That is, it is the employee who is responsible not only for identifying what it is that they should learn, but how and when it should be learnt. Other versions use 'performance management schemes' (see chapter 11) to work with the employee in identifying training and development needs and working towards addressing them. Yet other schemes still use competence-based models (not entirely dissimilar from NVQs) to help the individual identify exactly what it is that is expected of them, and to what extent they are currently deficient. So, assessment against this competency framework can be by the individual, the manager or by peer review. The three models explained here form only a tiny sample of the huge range of alternatives currently being explored by employers. Many are more structured than those outlined here, and work to ensure that the training and development activities and achievements of employees are fully recognized, recorded and used as an aid in career and organization planning.

11. Conclusion

It is apparent that a significant skills shortage exists within the British economy. In other words, the cuts suffered by training budgets during the early 1990s recession were deep enough to ensure an insufficient supply of skilled manpower come the end of the recession. This is a classic British problem, and one that has been repeated on a number of occasions. In essence the training budget is still regarded by many employers as peripheral to the main business of the organization and dispensable in times of economic downturn. The folly of this argument is evident in the continuing low skill levels of many of the workforce and the difficulties that many employers can experience in recruiting, despite the existence of high levels of unemployment. The weak skill base of the British workforce continues to hamper economic development. The situation can and will only be reversed when trainers are able to demonstrate more forcibly that training makes a significant and irreplaceable contribution to the bottom-line performance of the organization. The weakness of senior managers in accepting this point is matched only by the failure of trainers to convey it.

As the world of business becomes ever more competitive the need for a comprehensive and proactive approach to training becomes more necessary. As Connock (1991: 121) has said:

[training and] . . . Development strategies lie at the heart of the organization's ability to implement changing business strategies and the components of the H.R. vision.

However, old approaches to training will not be sufficient. It is not enough to argue that more will mean better. The key to organizational and individual development lies in workers taking responsibility for addressing their own training needs. Failure to do so will spell disaster for the organization and individuals who will find themselves the possessors of redundant sets of skills. Organization training budgets cannot ever stretch to meet both the short-, medium- and long-term needs of the organization and the aspirations of the individual. Likely patterns of future employment will make the concept of lifetime learning a reality, and employers will be only one of a range of training providers accessed by employees – others will include professional associations and educational establishments. Despite this, the role of the employer will still be crucial; and as Victor (1995: 23) has argued:

organizations must play a strong role in people development by establishing a dynamic stability that gives each individual a clear perspective on how and why they need to develop. Having provided this, they must, through line managers and personnel, provide sufficient resources to enable individual employers to take responsibility for their own development.

GODDARD AND ROBERTS ENGINEERING LTD

Goddard and Roberts Engineering Ltd were established in the 1920s and in the Second World War built depth charges, land mines and other incendiary devices for the allied forces. After the war they expanded into missile systems, but because of lack of investment in the appropriate technologies failed to win significant orders with either the Ministry of Defence or overseas governments. As a consequence, the company decided to diversify more widely and went into the manufacture of, first, washing machines, then tumble dryers, and latterly dishwashers. Partly this diversification was managed through acquisition (of a Swindon based tumble dryer manufacturer) and partly through new product development. All defence-related production was ceased in 1970. The company now operates on three sites: one in Chelmsford, where washing machines are made, one in Lincoln, where dishwashers are made, and the Swindon site, which still manufactures tumble dryers. In all 2,000 staff are employed, split roughly equally between the three sites. There are 200 employed at the head office, which manages finance, marketing and corporate planning, and is also located in Chelmsford (but some 5 miles from the factory).

Training and development policies have traditionally been the responsibility of the local factories, and to date each has interpreted their responsibilities in a different way. The company has recently appointed a new HR director and he has undertaken to reassess the organization's training and development, to coordinate it centrally and to attempt to get best value for money.

The HR director has visited all of the company sites and held talks with local senior managers and site training officers. The following issues have emerged:

1. The technology used in the Lincoln plant is nearly obsolete, and while considerable investment has been made in new plant and machinery, many of the older staff are reluctant to operate the new machines, claiming that they de-skill the workforce, and produce poorer quality products. Newer workers have been recruited to operate the new machines. Apart from some teething troubles, no significant problems have been identified with regard to quality.

2. Relations between the central functions and the manufacturing plants are generally poor, with particular problems in the area of marketing. The production managers all claim that the marketing department is making sales promises to customers without first referring to the production schedules in place at the factories. This has resulted in a number of deadlines being missed, and not a little acrimony.

3. Recruitment and selection of all staff is undertaken locally, with differing qualifications, skills and experience expected of staff in different plants to perform what are considered to be similar tasks. Three years ago a graduate recruitment programme was introduced centrally with ten graduates annually allocated to each manufacturing plant and five to head office. Turnover rates for the graduates have been worryingly high – 40 per cent in Swindon, 50 per cent in Lincoln and 30 per cent in Chelmsford and head office. The turnover rate for other staff ranges between 10 and 15 per cent, depending upon the site.

4. In the past each plant has operated more or less independently, with head office setting performance targets and leaving it to the local managers to achieve them as they see fit. The board have now decided to reduce the number of managers in the whole organization and seeks to introduce a flatter, leaner structure. It is envisaged that the number of managers will be reduced from 140 to less than 80. It is intended that those currently employed as supervisors will take on a role of greater significance which will include recruitment, discipline and work management.

5. Many of what are now the senior managers and board members employed at the head office of the organization were initially recruited when the company still saw its future in defence-related manufacture.

6. Several board members consider that the techniques for the manufacture of washing machines, tumble dryers and dishwashers are very similar, and they would hope to rationalize production from three to two sites. The senior managers of each factory site (most recruited since 1970), however, vehemently disagree, and feel that head office managers do not understand their problems.

7. The company is soundly financed. Although it is profitable, the company has struggled to maintain its margins in recent years in the face of strong competition.

TASK

Provide a report for the Board which outlines the major problems as you see them from your HR perspective. Your report should also contain your recommendations for the training and development programme for the organization. It should identify short-, medium- and long-term issues to be covered.

QUESTIONS FOR FURTHER CONSIDERATION

1. How important a role does the trainer play in the training process?

2. Consider the advantages and disadvantages of on-the-job and off-the-job training.

3. How would you go about evaluating an off-the-job training course that you have attended?

4. Consider the training methods described in the chapter. Which methods of training do you consider would be most suitable for the following (be sure to support fully and justify your answers):

   training tele-sales operators

   training traffic wardens

   postal delivery staff

   professional sports men and women

5. Consider the idea of self-managed learning. Are employers simply 'passing the buck' by expecting employees to take responsibility for their own training and development?

6. Consider your own employment, or your course of study. What is the balance between employer- or tutor-managed learning and employee- or student-managed learning? Do you consider the balance to be correct?

•REFERENCES•

Anderson G & Evenden R (1994)
Performance Management: its Role and Methods in Human
Resource Strategy, in **HUMAN RESOURCE MANAGEMENT**
Harrison R (ed.). Wokingham, Addison-Wesley.

Bratton J & Gold J (1994)
**HUMAN RESOURCE MANAGEMENT: THEORY AND
PRACTICE**
Basingstoke, Macmillan.

Buckley R & Caple J (1992)
THE THEORY AND PRACTICE OF TRAINING
London, Kogan Page.

Cole G (1988)
PERSONNEL MANAGEMENT: THEORY AND PRACTICE
London, DPP.

Connock S (1991)
HR VISION: MANAGING A QUALITY WORKFORCE
London, Institute of Personnel Management.

Gode W (1972)
TRAINING YOUR STAFF
London, The Industrial Society.

Hamblin A (1974)
EVALUATION AND CONTROL OF TRAINING
London, McGraw-Hill.

Harrison R (1994)
EMPLOYEE DEVELOPMENT
London, Institute of Personnel Management.

Manpower Services Commission (1981)
GLOSSARY OF TRAINING TERMS
London, MSC.

Molander C & Winterton J (1994)
MANAGING HUMAN RESOURCES
London, Routledge.

Mumford A (1993)
**MANAGEMENT DEVELOPMENT: STRATEGIES FOR
ACTION**
London, Institute of Personnel Management.

Pepper A (1984)
**MANAGING THE TRAINING AND DEVELOPMENT
FUNCTION**
Aldershot, Gower.

Reid M, Barrington H, & Kenney J (1992)
TRAINING INTERVENTIONS
London, Institute of Personnel Management.

Revans R (1972)
ACTION LEARNING
London, Blond and Briggs.

Robinson K (1988)
A HANDBOOK OF TRAINING MANAGEMENT
London, Kogan Page.

Victor P (1995)
Companies Cannot Pass the Buck on Training
People Management, 7 Sept. 1995.

Wood S (1991)
**CONTINUOUS DEVELOPMENT: THE PATH TO
IMPROVED PERFORMANCE.**
London, Institute of Personnel Management.

10

JOB EVALUATION

AS A RESULT OF STUDYING THIS CHAPTER YOU SHOULD BE ABLE TO:

- Appreciate the significant reasons for the introduction and use of job evaluation schemes by employers.

- Comment on the various methods and techniques used for job evaluation.

- Appreciate the part job evaluation plays in equal pay claims (and the supporting legislation and institutions).

- Consider the challenges facing job evaluation systems as they attempt to operate in an environment which is changing rapidly.

1. Introduction

> Job evaluation is the name given to any activity which sets out to make a systematic comparison between jobs and assess their relative worth, for the purpose of establishing a rational pay structure. In essence job evaluation aims to reduce reliance on arbitrary methods of pay determination by introducing an element of objectivity in the way jobs are compared. Every job evaluation method requires some basic job analysis in order to provide factual information about the jobs concerned. Nevertheless, as with many other aspects of personnel management, judgement has to be exercised in the final analysis. (Cole 1988: 118)

Job evaluation attempts to produce a ranking of jobs, and to do so in such a way as can be defended if necessary. From the ranking an equitable pay structure can be developed. In undertaking a job evaluation exercise a number of important factors must be taken into account:

a. It is the *job* that is being evaluated, not the *holder* of the job. This implies that if the holder of the job changed to someone who was more or less 'efficient', the ranking of the job would remain unaltered.

b. Job evaluation cannot ever be, and should not purport to be, an entirely objective exercise. For this reason job evaluation exercises are often managed by a group that will consist of both employer and workforce representatives.

c. Job evaluation does not determine pay or pay-scales, but it does provide a significant piece of evidence upon which pay may be based.

d. Job evaluation will compare jobs against each other, thus providing a relative judgement and not an absolute one. In making such judgements the evaluators will try to act logically, equitably, consistently and fairly.

The reader might be forgiven for thinking that systems of job evaluation belong to a past age and have little to do with what the organizations of today require: flexibility, flattened hierarchies, and pay based on performance and not necessarily on the specific job held. However, recent evidence would, to a degree, contradict this and indicate that job evaluation is still widely used. The 1992 Workplace Industrial Relations Survey (Millward et al. 1992) indicated that over the previous decade the percentage of organizations with job evaluation schemes had risen from 21 per cent to 26 per cent. Moreover Spencer (1990), in a major survey of over 370 organizations, found that the reason why employers were using job evaluation was not only to develop systems for fair pay but also as a basis for achieving performance pay. As Kessler (1995: 264) says:

> job-evaluated grading structures have also had to confront newer pressures relating to the changing character of organizations. The collapse of organizational hierarchies, and the emergence of organic structures responsive to fluctuating circumstances, place a premium upon employee performance beyond the constraints of rigid job descriptions. In short, employee adaptiveness to shifting needs becomes more important than the shape of a job ossified within job-evaluated grades.

It seems, then, that the nature and purpose of job evaluation is changing: it still relates primarily to pay, but it also needs to take account of the developing and emerging needs of organizations and the requirements for flexibility and responsiveness.

> The giant consumer goods company Unilever employs 20,000 managers worldwide, and they are currently categorized into 17 job grades with pay largely determined by length of service and age. By 1997 a new job evaluation scheme should have introduced a new less rigid system with six work levels. One of the features of the scheme will be to pay newly appointed managers only 90 per cent of the base rate for their job, but as they become more proficient in the post it will allow them to earn up to 110 per cent of base salary. Also available will be merit bonuses worth up to 15 per cent of salary. (Reported in *Personnel Today*, 7 Nov. 1995.)

2. Job Evaluation Methods

It must be stated again that job evaluation is not an exact science and, despite the complexity of the schemes sometimes selected for use, it still requires the application of a considerable amount of good judgement and common sense. It is because job evaluation can be seen as an imperfect tool that it is common for the team of evaluators to be chosen by management and unions together. Indeed, it is common for the evaluators to be union and management nominees. The benefits of such a joint approach become apparent when the potential 'problems' highlighted by Armstrong and Murlis (1980: 95) become clear:

> It is not possible to predict the outcome of a study, unless it is rigged, nor is it possible to prove that the results are correct. But the method of job evaluation is logical and is based on a systematic analysis of the facts.

There are a number of methods used to undertake job evaluation, but commonly they are divided into analytical and non-analytical methods. A number of them are considered below. For a more detailed consideration of the alternative methods for job evaluation please see Armstrong and Murlis (1988).

3. Non-analytical Methods

3.1 Job ranking

This method requires that a selection of jobs is used as a benchmark against which others will be compared. In essence the method requires that detailed and comprehensive job descriptions are available for all positions, and each job is compared to these descriptions and 'slotted' into position accordingly. Clearly the selection of the benchmark jobs is crucial, for these should represent a range of jobs at all levels in the organization. Job descriptions should be written in such a way that they are easily understandable by all of those who have to use them. In practice, a number of evaluators, working independently, will place the jobs against the benchmarks and then will come together to consider any over which they do not agree.

The principal weaknesses of this method are that it depends heavily on the benchmark jobs, and on the evaluators having a sufficiently detailed understanding of those jobs and the others which are to be compared against them. It also relies to a great extent on subjective judgements and (arguably) is unlikely to produce radical results.

Its great advantage is that it is cheap and quick to use.

3.2 Paired comparison

This method attempts to compare each job with every other job and decide if it is more or less important. The method is best described by reference to table 10.1.

Using this method the positions of Account Manager and Computer Programmer have jointly received the highest rating. The major advantage of this system is that it does allow each job to be compared against all others, but again it does rely on the application of a considerable amount of subjective judgement.

	Acc Tech	Snr Sec	HR Off	Acc Mgr	Comp Prog	Sales Supvr	Total
Accounting Technician	–	2	2	1	1	2	8
Senior Secretary	2	–	1	1	1	1	6
HR Officer	2	3	–	1	1	2	9
Account Manager	3	3	3	–	2	2	13
Computer Programmer	3	3	3	2	–	2	13
Sales Supervisor	2	3	2	2	2	–	11

Table 10.1
Paired comparison table
for job evaluation

Score 3 if considered to be of greater importance
       2 if considered to be of equal importance
       1 if considered to be of less importance

3.3   Job grading or job classification

This system approaches the problems from the other way – it defines a number of job levels and then 'slots' each position into one of the levels. In practice the evaluators have to agree on the job levels to be used (the list below offers examples), agree a definition of the level of responsibility commensurate with operation at each of the levels, and then compare all job descriptions against the predefined levels. Jobs would then be 'slotted in' at their appropriate grade.

Level 1   Junior member of staff working under close supervision. Little scope for initiative. Performs a range of routine tasks, e.g. data entry, filing.

Level 2   Junior member of staff performing tasks that are mostly of a routine nature and require the application of well-defined rules. Some scope for initiative is called for, as indeed is the use of experience and aptitude. Work is subject to less direct supervision. Tasks performed might include routine administration, word-processor and computer operation, data entry and retrieval.

Level 3   Experienced clerical level, requires the use of initiative and discretion. May be responsible for a small group of junior staff and the allocation and checking of work. Performs a wide range of routine and non-routine tasks within a given area of responsibility. Day-to-day work is not closely monitored, although the accountabilities are clearly defined.

Level 4   The tasks performed require a degree of specialist knowledge or considerable experience. May be responsible for a number of junior members of staff and their supervisors, or may hold a position that requires the application of specialist knowledge and skills to a range of varied and changing situations. May be required to undertake the appraisal of junior staff and contribute to training programmes for junior staff.

Level 5   (and beyond): Additional levels as may be necessary.

Whichever scheme is used for job evaluation it must allow for new positions to be added, for jobs that change significantly to be re-evaluated and for those employees who feel that they have been

FACTOR	DEGREE				
	1	2	3	4	5
Job knowledge and skills	4	8	12	16	20
Responsibility for others' work	3	6	9	12	15
Mental/physical effort	4	8	12	16	20
Complexity of work	6	12	18	24	30
Contact with clients	3	6	9	12	15

Degree definitions (example):

Job knowledge and skills:

First degree   To maintain basic systems (e.g. filing), to operate and maintain a range of office machinery (e.g. word processor, calculator), to undertake (under supervision) a range of routine tasks.

Second degree   To be responsible, under close supervision, for the administration of a routine area of work. This will involve the use of a range of office machinery and liaison with clients.

Third degree   To supervise a small number of staff undertaking a range of tasks of a routine and non-routine nature, to be responsible for the checking of work and ensuring that staff adhere to published guidelines and procedures. Or, to work alone and to be responsible for more complex and non-routine case work.

Fourth degree   Etc.

Figure 10.1
Example of points rating chart for carrying out job evaluation

incorrectly evaluated to appeal, and have their case quickly and speedily reconsidered.

4.   Analytical Methods

4.1   Points rating method

This method attempts to identify within the organization a number of factors that are common to all jobs. Each of the factors is grouped, then awarded a number of points according to their perceived and agreed value to the organization. The factors may also be weighted to emphasize further the importance they are accorded (see figure 10.1 for an example). Each job description is then compared with the rating chart and the appropriate number of points awarded to each job according to the score it achieves against each of the factors. Once all of the jobs descriptions have been compared they can be put into a rank order according to the scores awarded. Once this has been carried out, groups of jobs closely related in terms of points scored can be allocated to pay bands, or indeed according to whichever method of salary determination is used.

The 'success' that a particular job will achieve under the points rating method will depend on a number of elements, but will crucially depend upon, first, the factors that have been chosen, and, secondly, the rating and weighting that is accorded to those factors. The factors chosen must represent all aspects of the jobs under consideration, and no area of significance can be ignored. Moreover the weightings must genuinely reflect the degree to which they are considered important to the organization. It is clear that any change in weightings would advantage some jobs and disadvantage others.

The problem outlined above is rarely solved to the satisfaction of all, and it is for this reason the organizations will often 'buy in' ready-made systems such as the Hay / MSL, or employ a firm of consultants to specially construct one.

> Human resource managers in the university sector are considering a radical overhaul of the sector's job structure. Currently academic, administrative, technical and manual staffs are employed on different terms and conditions with differing job structures. Further, staff employed in the 'old' universities are employed on different conditions to those employed in the 'new' universities (or former polytechnics). The plan under consideration involves putting all 180,000 staff employed in the sector onto a common grading structure based on competencies. In effect it will end the distinction between different categories of staff. It is envisaged that a competence-based approach will be used for the job evaluation, and a range of criteria used: some akin to NVQ competencies, others using older criteria such as qualifications, experience and reliability. (Reported in *Personnel Today*, 1 Aug. 1995.)

5. Job Evaluation – Winners and Losers

It is inevitable that one of the consequences of undertaking a job evaluation exercise will be that some jobs will be 'up-rated' while others will be 'down-rated'. This may be good for the 'winners', less good for those who stand to lose out. In section 2 the importance of employee consultation was highlighted. The benefits of careful groundwork in this area will be felt when the results of the evaluation come to be implemented. It is usual for those whose jobs have been up-rated to receive the appropriate increase in pay. However, more problematic are the holders of those jobs which have been down-rated. In practice it is common for the pay of those affected to be frozen at its current level and to remain frozen until, via the normal process of annual pay increase for other jobs, the down-graded job reaches it new value. This may take a number of years, and for a period of time the holder of the job will be effectively overpaid. This overpayment usually continues until either the person leaves (in which case the new appointee would be paid at the new 'correct' level), or until the rising pay of other jobs allows the overpaid job to reach its new equilibrium.

The holders of the over-rated jobs who find that they will not be in receipt of an annual pay rise for a number of years will not be feeling 'overpaid'. Indeed, most people in such a situation would look on the down-grading of their job in quite personal terms. Many employers will recognize the difficulty that such an employee will experience and would be sympathetic to redeployment or transfer, or other suitable alternatives.

6. Job Evaluation – Changes and Challenges

As suggested earlier, job evaluation, although still a technique in widespread use, is also one that is having to change and adapt as the circumstances within which it operates also change. These changes are numerous, but the most significant of them are:

a. The changing nature of work and work culture, particularly with reference to delayering, performance pay and the changes brought about by new technologies.

b. The pressures on organizations to seek and set pay levels that give more attention to external relativities rather than to job evaluation alone.

c. The general requirement for greater workforce and workplace flexibility makes, to some extent anyway, a number of the tenets upon which many job evaluation schemes were built obsolete.

d. In a number of mainland European countries job evaluation has retained a more traditional form. It is particularly common in those countries which have minimum rates of pay, such as Spain, and countries which are very committed to equality of opportunity, such as Germany.

7. Job Evaluation and Equal Pay

The Equal Pay Act of 1970 says that men and women should receive equal pay if:

the woman (in the same organization) is employed on *like* work with a man; or,

in the same organization, the woman is employed on work rated as *equivalent* with that of a man; or,

where the work is of *equal* value.

The Sex Discrimination Act of 1975 implies in every women's contract of employment an equality clause which in effect means that there is an assumption that when the work performed by a women is like, equivalent or of equal value (as set out above) to a man's employed in the same organization, then the clauses and terms of the contract of employment should be the same, that is, equally beneficial to all workers regardless of their sex.

The Equal Pay (Amendment) Regulations of 1983 further strengthens the law on equality by making provision for equal pay for work of equal value. The law relating to equality need not be observed by an employer who is able to show that the difference in pay or conditions is due to a material difference other than sex, and:

arises as a result of compliance with other laws regulating the employment of women; or, arises as a result of giving special treatment to women concerning pregnancy or childbirth.

When a dispute arises the employee is entitled to take the grievance to an industrial tribunal. The employee can make a claim for arrears of wages and damages. The claim must be based on one of the following criteria:

That she is doing work that is *broadly similar to that of a man* in the same organization.

That she is doing a job *rated the same under a proper job evaluation study*.

That she is doing *work of equal value to a man's* in terms of the demands it makes (e.g. physical, mental, decision-making).

It is important to note that comparisons can only be made with members of the opposite sex, and that the person with whom the employee wishes to compare her / himself must be employed by the same organization.

If a case comes before a tribunal and there exists in that company a job evaluation scheme which has rated a woman's work as equal to that of a man, then the tribunal will award equal pay. The only acceptable defence that the employer could make would be that there was some material difference in the work.

If a woman claims (under the Equal Pay Amendment Regulations) that she should receive equal pay to a man because her work is equal to that of a man in terms of physical or mental effort (or the other demands that it makes) then she must argue that she is doing *work of equal value* to that of the man.

In cases such as these the industrial tribunal will consider, first, whether the work is the same or broadly similar. If it is, then the tribunal's deliberations can be comparatively simple. However, if the work is not the same or similar then the tribunal will appoint an expert (generally one nominated by ACAS, the Advisory, Conciliation, and Arbitration Service) who will undertake a job evaluation exercise. She gathers evidence and carries out investigations before presenting a report to the tribunal, who will award equal pay if they accept that the expert has indeed found the jobs to be of equal value.

8. Job Evaluation and the Minimum Wage Debate

There is no doubt that if a minimum wage is introduced into the United Kingdom the question of differentials between job grades will have to be re-examined, for it is inconceivable that a minimum rate of pay could be introduced for those employed at the bottom without it having a knock-on effect for those employed higher up. The natural tool for this examination would be job evaluation, and out of this urgency to re-examine jobs and their grades would come new methods of job evaluation. What is also likely is that not all jobs will be covered by the minimum wage. Some jobs (for instance, trainees, young workers and apprentices) would still be employed at below minimum-wage levels. If this is the case, job evaluation may also be used to 'prove' that certain categories of employee fall into those groups that need to be paid less than the minimum. Under these circumstances job evaluation could become a very political task, and the opportunities for it to be conducted in an atmosphere of consultation and cooperation greatly reduced.

9. Conclusion

For many organizations job evaluation will, for the foreseeable future at least, play an important part in determining the ranking of jobs and assisting with the determination of pay. That said, it is equally certain that job evaluation, like most areas of human resourcing, is having to change and develop as it is confronted by fresh challenges. Not least among these challenges is the need to ensure that although it develops systems that are fair, it also develops systems that are flexible. Peter Wickens, the former Personnel Director of Nissan UK (quoted in Goss 1994: 90), points to the rigidities of practice and attitude engendered by elaborate job evaluation schemes, and claims:

> The preservation of the system becomes more important than reacting rapidly to change – in short the tail begins to wag the dog.

If job evaluation schemes are to continue to be a significant contributor to the efficient running of organizations they must fully encompass the need to delayer, to accommodate simple and flexible payment structures, to recognize the blurring of lines of demarcation, the moves towards multi- and flexi-skilling, and the increased tendency to base pay on performance. Armstrong and Murlis (1988: 95) contend that soon it may no longer be possible to evaluate the job, not the person; and:

> For this reason, there will be a greater emphasis on salary progression . . . systems . . . which are designed to accommodate people whose contribution develops over a longish period and across several conventional salary grades as they gain experience.

EQUAL PAY

In July 1995 the House of Lords ruled that North Yorkshire County Council had sexually discriminated against school dinner ladies whose pay had been cut to below that of male counterparts such as dustmen, street sweepers and cleaners. The cut had come about because of the government's requirement that councils put up for competitive tender many of the services previously exclusively performed by local authority staff. Among those services going to 'compulsory competitive tendering' were the schools meal service. North Yorkshire County Council's Direct Service Organization successfully bid to run the meals services, and to do so dismissed the 1,300 dinner ladies and offered to reemploy them at £3 per hour rather than the £3.31 per hour at which they had previously been employed. Holidays were also reduced.

The new rate of pay was below that paid to the gardeners, street sweepers and cleaners with whom they had been compared in a major job evaluation exercise in 1987.

The women, backed by the union, appealed to an industrial tribunal, claiming that their treatment amounted to discrimination. They won their case. The Council appealed to the Employment Appeal Tribunal and had the decision of the lower tribunal overturned. The women appealed to the Court of Appeal, who ruled that the wage levels were not discriminatory because they were 'genuinely due to the operation of market forces'.

The women then appealed to the House of Lords, where the five Law Lords ruled unanimously that the action of the Council had been wrong. Lord Slynn of Hadley said:

> I am satisfied that to reduce the women's wages below that of their male comparators was the very kind of discrimination in relation to pay that the Equal Pay Act sought to remove. The women could not have found other suitable work and were obliged to take the wages offered to them if they were to continue with this work. The fact that two men were employed on the same work at the same rate of pay does not detract from the conclusion that there was discrimination between the women involved and their male comparators. It means no more than that the two men were underpaid compared with other men doing work rated as equivalent.
>
> The fact is that the employers re-engaged the women at rates of pay less than those received by their male comparators and no material difference other than the difference of sex has been found to exist between the case of the women and their male comparators.

The decision means that the 1,300 school dinner ladies will receive back-pay of about £1,500 each, while the local authority (and its council-tax payers) face a bill of about £3 million, including legal costs of about £1 million. The ruling will also add about £1 million per year to the wage bill.

It is considered by some that the ruling puts under doubt thousands of contracts awarded by local authorities to privatized direct-service organizations, and will lead to a flood of claims from workers whose pay has been cut. Ultimately it <u>may</u> lead to many thousands of jobs being lost, if councils find they cannot afford to pay the new rates of pay or if contracts are instead awarded to private-sector companies.

TASK

Consider this case and the judgement of the House of Lords. Was the Equal Pay Act intended to protect women in this position and, if yes, how does it stand up to Compulsory Competitive Tendering, when for some low-paid women the options may be a wage cut to a low-paid job, or no job at all?

1. Distinguish between analytical and non-analytical techniques for job evaluation.

2. You have been asked by your Director of Human Resources to introduce job evaluation in your office. Outline the steps you would take to ensure its smooth introduction.

3. 'The underlying principle of job evaluation is the assumption that all jobs within an organization can be ranked hierarchically, relative to one another, based on their value to the organization' (David Goss, *Principles of Human Resource Management*). Consider the validity of the statement for the modern Job Evaluator.

4. Examine the forms of job evaluation discussed in the text and consider the circumstances and/or organization type for which each might be suitable.

5. Consider the advantages and disadvantages for an organization of contracting out responsibility for job evaluation to a firm of independent consultants.

6. Can you *really* compare the content of unlike jobs?

7. Why is it important that jobs are evaluated and not the holders of those jobs? What practical problems do you see with this differentiation?

•REFERENCES•

Armstrong M & Murlis H (1980)
A HANDBOOK OF SALARY ADMINISTRATION
London, Kogan Page.

Armstrong M & Murlis H (1988)
REWARD MANAGEMENT
London, Kogan Page.

Brewster C, Hegeswisch A, Holden L & Lockhart T (1992)
THE EUROPEAN HUMAN RESOURCE MANAGEMENT GUIDE
London, Academic Press.

Cole G C (1988)
PERSONNEL MANAGEMENT: THEORY AND PRACTICE
London, DPP.

Goss D (1994)
PRINCIPLES OF HUMAN RESOURCE MANAGEMENT
London, Routledge.

Institute of Administrative Management (1976)
OFFICE JOB EVALUATION
London, IAM.

Kessler I (1995)
Reward Systems, in **HUMAN RESOURCE MANAGEMENT: A CRITICAL TEXT**
Storey J (ed.). London, Routledge.

Livy B (1975)
JOB EVALUATION: A CRITICAL REVIEW
London, Allen and Unwin.

Livy B (1986)
CORPORATE PERSONNEL MANAGEMENT
London, Pitman.

Millward N, Stevens M, Smart D & Hawes D (1992)
WORKPLACE INDUSTRIAL RELATIONS IN TRANSITION: THE ED/ESRC/PSI/ACAS SURVEY
Aldershot, Dartmouth.

Spencer S (1990)
DEVOLVING JOB EVALUATION
Personnel Management, Jan.

Thierry H (1992)
Pay and Payment Systems, in **EMPLOYMENT RELATIONS**
Hartley J & Stephenson G (eds). Oxford, Blackwell.

Wickens P (1987)
THE ROAD TO NISSAN: FLEXIBILITY, QUALITY, TEAMWORK
Basingstoke, Macmillan.

FROM PERFORMANCE APPRAISAL TO PERFORMANCE MANAGEMENT

•CHAPTER•
11

AS A RESULT OF STUDYING THIS CHAPTER YOU SHOULD BE ABLE TO:

- Consider the reasons for appraising the performance of staff and the techniques used.

- Appreciate the skills needed by both the appraiser and the appraisee for performance appraisal to be undertaken successfully.

- Examine the major weaknesses and criticisms associated with traditional systems of performance appraisal.

- Contrast performance appraisal with performance management as techniques for controlling and developing the individual in the workplace.

- Consider how performance appraisal can contribute to the development of systems of performance management.

1. Introduction

Performance appraisal inevitably takes two major forms: informal and formal. Informally a boss will appraise the performance of a member of staff on a continual *ad hoc* basis. It is a product of constant workplace interaction, and undoubtedly leads to the boss making judgements, conscious or otherwise, about the ability of the employee, the value of her contribution to the organization and her strengths and weaknesses. Formal methods of performance appraisal, meanwhile, seek to set in place more systematic procedures for considering the contribution of the individual employee. It is the formal mechanisms of performance appraisal that this chapter will consider.

Livy (1987: 177) has defined performance appraisal as:

> the name given to procedures which make regular assessment of employee performance. Normally, they are conducted annually. Conventionally, superiors assess, record and discuss performance levels with their subordinates. Performance appraisal enables employees to receive feedback on their performance, identify training needs and make further plans for development. It is a systematic review of progress.

In recent years doubt has been cast on the value of the formal 'set-piece' annual performance appraisal interview, and systems of 'performance management' have been advocated in their place. This chapter will consider this development as well as other trends in the appraisal of workplace performance.

2. Reasons for Appraisal

There are a number of reasons why performance appraisal is carried out by organizations. These include:

a. To identify actual levels of performance.

b. To review performance, giving feedback to the employee, and to set goals for the future.

c. To identify potential performance.

d. To offer counselling and career guidance.

e. To identify training needs.

f. To review salary.

g. To identify employees within the organization who might be considered to have 'potential' to perform at a higher level.

h. To aid to succession planning.

It is this plethora of semi interrelated reasons that is behind many of the criticisms that have been levelled at performance appraisal. Indeed, as Fletcher (1984) points out, 'The different aims of performance appraisal frequently clash.' If performance appraisal schemes are to be successful a number of factors need to be considered, but principally:

a. The objectives of the scheme must be clear.

b. The criteria against which performance is to be appraised must be explicit.

c. Those carrying out the appraisals (the appraisers) must be trained and competent to do the job.

d. Equally, those being appraised must also know what is expected of them.

Thames Valley Police are piloting a scheme which will be used for both uniformed and civilian staff. Currently, no appraisal scheme exists for civilian staff, and the one for uniformed staff is paper based, cumbersome and lengthy. The proposed scheme will be computer based, and it is hoped will aid civilian staff to move jobs by identifying relevant skills, as well as paving the way for the introduction of performance related pay for all staff. (Reported in *Personnel Today*, 29 Aug. 1995.)

3. Performance Appraisal Schemes

Performance appraisal schemes have, over the years, taken a number of approaches to the consideration of employee performance as the focus for appraisal. These are outlined below.

3.1 Results-oriented/judgemental approaches

Under such schemes the focus of appraisal is current performance linked to the achievement of 'results' and often encompassing salary review. 'Results' would include sales, profits, wastage levels, number of complaints, quality of product. The requirement is that performance can be objectively measured and compared, employee against employee or year on year. Drucker (1955: 402) is an advocate of such a method of performance appraisal, arguing that:

> An effective management must direct the vision and efforts of all managers towards a common goal. It must ensure that each manager understands what results are demanded of him. It must ensure that the superior understands what to expect of each of his subordinate managers. It must motivate each manager to maximum effort in the right direction.

Drucker sees performance appraisal as part of a wider scheme of 'management by objectives'. That is, the organization at corporate level sets very clear objectives for a future period of time. Such objectives might be expressed, for instance, in terms of sales growth, profits levels, reductions in cost, etc. The objectives are then passed down to departments and operating divisions who in turn set measurable objectives for each manager. Performance will then be appraised against the achievement of these objectives at the level of individual manager, at department level, at the level of operating division and at corporate level. The key to management by objectives is that the objectives, at whichever level in the organization, are measurable, and generally so in financial terms.

In recent years such schemes have been widened to encompass a number of behavioural aspects of performance. For instance, research by Income Data Services (1989) has produced the following list of factors which are commonly appraised:

Job knowledge – the ability with which the worker can perform all aspects of the job.

Flexibility – the ability of the worker to cope with change.

Productivity.

Quality of work.

Attitude to work.

Interaction with others – how the worker communicates and cooperates with colleagues.

Initiative – the ability to solve problems.

Perception – the degree to which the worker is able to interpret job requirements.

Judgement/use of resources – the ability of the worker to plan and organize his work and set priorities.

Attendance and time-keeping.

Safety awareness.

Need for supervision – the degree to which the worker is able to work independently.

Supervisory ability – leadership, or potential for leadership, abilities.

Performance against set targets – the degree to which previous targets have been met.

Inevitably the assessment of such a wide range of factors can only be undertaken by using a combination of both objective and subjective criteria. This of course goes a long way from Drucker's ideas for management by objectives, but none the less the best schemes do attempt to use objective criteria when available.

3.2   Development-oriented schemes

Such schemes are an attempt to change the purpose of appraisal away from the past and give a stronger focus on the future. Their aim is to be less of a summary of last year's performance and more of a target-setting exercise for next; and more a genuine discussion between supervisor and subordinate which gives attention to the areas in which the employee was successful in her job, as well as those at which she was less successful, and which helps them (supervisor and subordinate) jointly to plot a path for enhanced performance in the future. This 'path' will be arrived at by a process of negotiation and mutual consent. Its aim is to meet both the organization's needs (as articulated by the supervisor) and the employee's needs in terms of career and personal development. Such schemes are rarely linked to pay.

Schemes that focus on the development of the employee attempt to change the style of appraisal in a number of ways. First they attempt to give both the supervisor and the employee a greater sense of owner-ship of the scheme, so that it is not wholly 'personnel' driven but a genuine attempt to review the performance of the individual and allow consideration of her own training needs and ambitions. More-over, such schemes attempt to make the whole process more open and transparent. By removing pay from appraisal the employee no longer needs to feel so defensive about his inadequacies and mistakes. The focus of appraisal is now on 'joint problem-solving', the supervisor and the employee working together to improve the performance of the individual, address the aspirational needs of the individual and give a genuine motivational boost.

Retailer Marks and Spencer has announced a revamp of its performance appraisal scheme following criticisms of the old scheme, which was seen as inflexible and time consuming. The new scheme will shift the emphasis of the appraisal away from past performance to giving greater consideration of future development.

Staff will be expected to prepare for the appraisal by gathering evidence of where they have done well and bringing it to the interview. (Reported in *Personnel Today*, 25 Oct. 1995.)

4. Appraisal Forms and the Measurement of Performance

The type of appraisal adopted will to a large extent determine the form and style of the documentation used. The documentation should be designed so as to support the aims of appraisal. However, for many managers, wary of conducting appraisals, the forms themselves will be the focus of the appraisal, and the objective of the exercise is the successful completion of the paperwork. It is vital then that the paperwork does indeed fully reflect the aims of the scheme and allow even the reluctant manager to conduct appraisals to an acceptable standard.

One of the keys to preparing successful documentation is the adoption and development of suitable scales or criteria for the measurement of performance. A number are available and include the following.

4.1 Rating scales

These require the supervisor to appraise the subordinate according to a number of predetermined criteria and against agreed standards of performance. Figure 11.1 is an extract from a performance appraisal form and illustrates the use of rating scales.

There are a number of disadvantages associated with this method of viewing and recording performance, but principally for some workers it is likely that the descriptors for the A to E classification do not match actual performance. Additionally, there is a perceived tendency for managers to rate most employees at, or close to, the middle

FACTOR	A	B	C	D	E
Performance against targets		x			
Relations with customers	x				
Knowledge of job				x	
Quality of work			x		

Figure 11.1
Performance appraisal using rating scales (extract)

Key: A. In all respects performance exceeds that which is expected.
      B. In some respects performance exceeds that which is expected.
      C. Performance is equal to that which is expected.
      D. In some respects performance is less than that expected.
      E. In many / all respects performance is less than that expected.

Factor: Quality of Employee's Work

High _____ Average _____ Low

Figure 11.2
Graphic rating scale

descriptor. Managers are often reluctant to 'rock the boat' and choose instead to avoid confronting poor performance.

Alternatively, a graphic rating scale may be used (see figure 11.2). This is less precise and indicates the general performance of the individual on a plus/minus scale.

4.2   Behaviourally anchored rating scales

In this example the appraiser has to rate the subordinate against predetermined factors which have been identified as important for success. Performance against these factors is then measured in terms of precisely worded performance variables. Figure 11.3 is an extract from a performance appraisal form, and illustrates the use of behaviourally anchored rating scales.

The use of behaviourally anchored rating scales is also far from simple. First, it is important to ensure that the descriptions of behaviour against which performance is to be assessed are indeed those which reflect desired performance in the organization. If they are incorrectly set it is quite possible for a worker to rate highly on the performance appraisal and yet still be considered deficient in many aspects of their work. This would necessitate a major revision of the scheme. Further, it is important that all managers are able to interpret the scales in the same way. For instance, on the scales illustrated above it might be difficult to differentiate between 'Quite mature' and 'Average; sometimes naive'. Appraisers would need suitable training to ensure that they all take a consistent approach.

4.3   Comment boxes

Under these schemes (and generally following discussion with and with the agreement of the appraisee) the appraiser is required to answer a number questions about the performance of the employee. The appraiser is not required to grade according to any predetermined scale but is allowed instead to describe in her own words how the individual has performed. Figure 11.4 is an extract from a performance appraisal form which uses such a technique.

The use of this method will allow managers to make bland, uncontroversial comments such as 'Over the last year John has made a useful contribution to the work of the department.' This is generally unhelpful and tells us little about what John actually did and how well he did it. It tells us neither his strengths nor his weaknesses and does not offer any judgement upon which decisions about reward or training might be made. In addition to encouraging bland comments, this system also does not allow easy aggregation of comments, nor allow easy comparison, employee against employee or year against year.

QUALITY OF WORK Consider his/her standard of and ability to do good work; the pride he/she takes in his/her achievements	Really good quality work; takes a pride in what he/she produces	Usually good but occasional lapses	Often below standard	Definitely poor, little pride or enthusiasm in his/her work
DEPENDABILITY and COOPERATION Consider his/her reliability and how well he/she works with others	Extremely reliable; very cooperative	Generally reliable and co-operative	Sometimes unreliable and difficult	Extremely unreliable; often a source of friction
INITIATIVE allied to COMMON SENSE Consider his/her attitude to meeting difficulties	Handles problems sensibly; develops his/her opportunities quickly	Seeks help with problems outside his/her own sphere	Slow to seek help	Waits for guidance; does nothing on own initiative
EFFORT and INTEREST	Always energetic and interested; requires no pushing	Generally satisfactory, slackens occasionally	Requires urging	Lazy, shows no interest
MATURITY	Exceptionally mature	Quite mature	Average; sometimes naive	Very immature

Figure 11.3
Performance appraisal using behaviourally anchored rating scales (extract)

4.4   Results-orientated appraisal forms

These require the appraiser to agree with the appraisee measurable targets for the year, and the achievement of these is then reviewed at the end of the year before targets are agreed for the next year. Figure 11.5 is an extract from a performance appraisal form which illustrates the use of key results as a measure of performance.

This scheme, while offering a number of advantages in terms of its focus on achievement, evidence and objectivity, also has some shortfalls. Of major concern is the fact that it focuses only on what is measurable. Significant parts of many employees' work are not easily measurable or quantifiable. This would make target-setting for many employees at best a rather abstract exercise. Additionally, in the process of negotiation that would go on between manager and subordinate there may well be a tendency for subordinates to negotiate for targets that are easily achievable. They would then be rewarded for achieving these targets, while others who had accepted more demanding targets might be penalized for not achieving them, even though what they had achieved might have been considerable.

To what extent has the employee demonstrated:

	COMMENT
Commitment to the aims of the organization?	....
A willingness to take on responsibility over and above the immediate demands of his/her position?	....
The ability to persuade others to take action and achieve results?	....

Figure 11.4
Performance appraisal
using comment boxes
(extract)

KEY AREA	TARGET SET	ACHIEVED YES/NO?	EVIDENCE	COMMENT
Sales	Increase by 15% on current year	Yes	Accounts	Achieved 17%
New customers	Identify 100 potential new customers	No	Call records	Identified 42
Support staff costs	Reduce by 10%	No	Payroll returns	Increased by 2%

Figure 11.5
Results-oriented
performance appraisal
(extract)

5. The Appraisal Interview

The appraisal interview has at its core a periodic (usually annual) discussion between manager and the employee. The success or failure of the performance appraisal scheme can depend crucially on the skill with which the manager is able to conduct the discussion or interview. In essence managers need to be skilled at conducting performance appraisal interviews if full benefit is to be gained; while the employee must also be aware of how she can get the most from the occasion. Many organizations give their managers training on how to conduct appraisals, but far fewer give employees training in the same area. This is surprising bearing in mind that increasingly the appraisal is seen as a two-way discussion with the expectation that both parties will contribute fully.

For appraisals to work best both parties need to prepare beforehand. Many organizations will supply both appraiser and appraisee with documentation to focus their preparation. This will allow both to review what has gone on over the last year and also to consider what it is that they hope to achieve from the appraisal. Adequate time must be set aside for the interview itself: at least one hour for junior staff and considerably longer for more senior staff. The interview should be conducted in a quiet place which is free from interruptions.

Most interviewers choose to start by reviewing the past performance of the employee before going on to consider future work targets, as well as considering the training needs of the employee and her career development aspirations. In style the interview should not consist of the appraiser doing most of the talking but be a genuine two-way exchange of views and ideas. Where targets are set, plans made or agreement reached, the appraiser should be sure that the employee is in agreement with what is recorded.

As a result of the interview a 'programme for action' should be drawn up. This should be in writing and should state in outcome (or results) terms what is to be achieved in the period before the next appraisal. This will place expectations upon the employee but may also require the manager to take action to (for instance) provide training or revise working practices or behaviour.

The appraisal interview should not be an occasion at which the manager, for the first time, brings up the fact that, say, the employee has been late on 22 occasions in the last three months. Issues relating to performance, discipline and behaviour should be addressed when the problem is first identified, and not left to be 'sprung on' the employee at the annual appraisal. It is more appropriate to use the appraisal to review how the employee has performed since the problem of poor time-keeping was first identified. Appraisal should not be seen as a surrogate disciplinary system.

> Research by North West Water has shown that different groups can make very different use of 360-degree appraisal systems. In a study conducted by Personnel Manager Paul Victor, twelve managers were appraised by managers, peers, subordinates and themselves, using 37 competencies. Victor found that subordinates gave the most accurate assessments when guaranteed anonymity. Peers, he found, tended to be most critical of their colleagues, while managers tended to rate most favourably. When the managers were asked to rate themselves Victor found a tendency to overrate their abilities. (Reported in *Personnel Today*, 26 Sept. 1995.)

6. Criticisms of Performance Appraisal

Criticisms of performance appraisal as an idea and in terms of the techniques used are not new. One of the most cogent and well-argued critiques came from Douglas McGregor in the *Harvard Business Review* in 1958. McGregor suggested that many managers disliked conducting performance appraisals because they were unhappy sitting in judgement on their subordinates. He favoured a shift away from appraisal to analysis with a more positive approach:

No longer is the subordinate being examined by the superior so that his weaknesses may be determined; rather he is examining himself in order to define not only his weaknesses but also his strengths and potentials. (1958: 334)

McGregor's criticisms have been followed by those of many others, including Alan Fowler (1990: 12), who claimed that:

Although . . . still used . . . there has never been any hard evidence that [performance appraisal] actually improves performance.

Fowler (1990: 14) is disappointed with the lack of continuity and coherence offered by many performance appraisal schemes. He is also singularly unimpressed with their attachment to the idea that appraisal should be an annual event. He writes:

In today's fast moving world, any idea that effective performance management can be tied to a single event is patently absurd, far more effort is needed to build the principles of goal setting, appraisal and supportive action into an on-going and informal management activity.

Research carried out by the Institute of Personnel Management (1992) indicates that many schemes fail to link the appraisal of performance with the achievement of wider corporate objectives; indeed, the IPM claims that many schemes appraise the performance of individuals and assess their training needs in isolation from wider corporate activity.

For appraisal to work best it must be built on principles of trust and communication. That is, the employer must not only show a commitment to the appraisal scheme but must also be willing to share with the employee information about the scheme, its aims and objectives. Fletcher and Williams (1992) argue that one of the fundamental reasons why some schemes fare so badly is that top management fail to show commitment to the scheme and fail to share information, encourage participation and work to build trust and security among employees.

For many managers (and their staff) the performance appraisal scheme is seen to be 'owned' by the Human Resource Department. This was evidenced in the Institute of Personnel Management's 1992 survey. For many managers the job of completing performance appraisals with their staff is simply another task forced upon them by the organization's bureaucracy. Many see it as having little value, or as interfering with the real business of running the organization. This problem of lack of 'ownership' can often be addressed by better training for managers.

Too many appraisal schemes use criteria that are subjective, allowing for the possibility of discrimination. As Townley (1990: 35) points out:

Subjective criteria based on characteristics such as 'demeanour', 'manner', 'maturity', 'drive', and 'social behaviour' have been dismissed as invalid, as they allow for conscious or unconscious prejudice. Equally assessments based on 'leadership ability', 'experience', 'general intelligence', 'general business acumen', 'personal appearance', 'co-operation', 'dependability', and 'stability' have been judged subjective and inherently open to bias.

The use of such subjective criteria will lead managers to make assessments of employees that depend entirely on instinct, that are not defensible and are likely to vary from manager to manager depending upon their relationship with the employee.

It is often the case that conducting a performance appraisal puts a manager in a number of roles simultaneously. She may be required to assess the previous year's performance, set targets for the coming year, discuss with the employee her training needs and career aspirations, come to a decision about pay and/or bonuses and consider the career potential of the employee. Several of these roles directly contradict one other. For instance, it is difficult for an employee to be open and honest about her weaknesses and possible training needs with an appraiser when the same person might be deciding her annual pay rise. At one and the same time the appraiser is required to be a judge, confidant, counsellor and manager. Arguably it is not possible to be all at the same time.

This debate about the contradictory roles to be played by the manager is seen at its height when the question of the relationship between pay and appraisal is considered. Sanderson (1994) makes the following arguments for not linking pay with appraisal:

- When pay and performance are closely linked, the pay issue may overshadow all other purposes of performance appraisal.

- There may be a tendency for employees to withhold negative information about performance, leading to a less than frank appraisal discussion.

- Employees may try to influence appraisers, and seek to set lower, more conservative goals.

- Employees may adapt their behaviour to target on receiving good ratings, rather than genuinely trying to improve overall performance.

- Appraisers may be encouraged to overrate employees if they think that adverse financial consequences may otherwise result.

Sanderson does, however, see a number of advantages in linking pay to appraisal. Most significantly these are:

- All parties – appraisers, appraisees and reviewers – take performance appraisal more seriously.

- Many individuals feel that for reasons of fairness, there should be a link between performance appraisal and pay.

- Organizations are more likely to develop performance-oriented cultures in which high performers are seen to receive extra rewards, and vice versa.

Most performance appraisal schemes consider the individual, ignoring the fact that for many workers the successful performance of their jobs depends crucially on others performing their jobs well. As Nevling (1992: 32) says:

> No-one works in isolation or a vacuum. We all depend upon the output of others to accomplish our jobs. Our appraisal systems assume that everyone works independently. We know in fact everyone interacts with others.

A very small number of employers have embraced the idea of team appraisal. However, there is little doubt that in the vast majority of organizations many more workers, who are appraised individually, do not have sufficient personal influence over their workplace achievements such that they alone should be held accountable for successes and failures. It is they and their colleagues together who determine workplace output and quality.

Many employers distrust and therefore fail to embrace the potential of self-appraisal. Fletcher (1984) believes that appraisal based on self-assessment can be extremely effective. 'Such appraisals become more development-centred, concentrating on remedying (relative) weaknesses and capitalizing on strengths.'

Despite its many critics performance appraisal has been around a considerable time. It is also the case that in recent years the tendency has been for more and more groups of workers to be covered by schemes of performance appraisal. These include school teachers and many other groups of white-collar professionals traditionally not affected by such schemes. In recent years the trend has also been for appraisal to be extended to more and more groups within organizations: it is now very common for groups of manual workers to find themselves being appraised.

> A 360-degree appraisal system at material manufacturer 3M will allow staff a say in determining their managers' pay rises. It is hoped that the new scheme will help support a cultural shift designed to recognize how staff work together rather than simply the results they achieve. Feedback from appraisals will be used by staff in the construction of their personal development plans. (Reported in *Personnel Today*, 10 Oct. 1995.)

7. Performance Management

Increasing numbers of organizations are recognizing the weaknesses of performance appraisal, and turning to what has become called 'performance management' as a technique to consider and develop staff performance. According to Armstrong (1994: 397),

> The overall aim of performance management is to establish a culture in which individuals and groups take responsibility for the continuous improvement of business processes and of their own skills and contributions.

Harrison (1993: 247) develops the idea, suggesting that:

> The aim of performance management is to control: to control the targets that are set for people, and the standards that they reach; and to control their performance by rewarding what is assessed as up to standard, while withholding rewards from what is judged below standard.

The Institute of Personnel Management in their own research (1992) claimed that 'performance management systems' are in operation when the following conditions are met by the organization:

It communicates a vision of its objectives to all its employees.

It sets departmental and individual performance targets which are related to wider objectives.

It conducts a formal review of progress towards these targets.

It uses the review process to identify training, development and reward outcomes.

It evaluates the effectiveness of the whole process in order to improve effectiveness.

Harrison (1993: 247) sees the aims of performance management as fundamentally different from performance appraisal, in that it is:

> a strategy to prescribe and enforce the values, attitudes and styles of behaviour that top management have decided are desirable in employees in order to ensure their conformity to corporate goals and values.

Armstrong and Murlis (1988) claim that performance management consists of six interrelated activities:

a. performance review

b. performance counselling

c. potential review

d. career counselling

e. performance improvement and career development programmes

f. reward review.

We shall examine each one of these in turn.

7.1 Performance review

Much has been said in the earlier parts of this chapter about this aspect of performance management – the taking stock of what the employee has achieved to date, agreeing what she has done where and also where she has weaknesses that need to be addressed. Performance management is very much concerned with results, and therefore the performance review should confine itself to the key results areas of the employee.

Wherever possible the appraiser should use evidence from the employee's performance to support the points that she wishes to make.

7.2 Performance counselling

One of the aims of performance management is to help employees improve their performance in line with the wider aims of the organization. In this respect the manager must act as counsellor to the subordinate and, using appropriate techniques, either direct the employee to, or jointly work towards the identification of, her weaknesses and how these weaknesses should be addressed. The aim should be towards improved job performance.

7.3 Potential review

Here the aim is to provide information for two purposes. First, for the employer, to identify potential future managers, which should act as an aid to succession planning. Secondly, to assist the individual in identifying her career path within the organization as well as ensuring that the individual knows how she should best aim to develop her skills, knowledge and experience in order to achieve that potential.

Identifying potential is not easy, for it implies that the appraiser is knowledgeable not only about the employee and her skills, attributes and motivations, but also about the future requirements of the organization. In all truth it is difficult, if not fraudulent, to attempt to make predictions about the progress of any one individual beyond the short to medium term.

7.4 Career counselling

Career counselling again is not an exact science, but more an attempt to outline to the employee the range of opportunities offered by the employer and to identify 'best fits' between those opportunities and the employee's talents, ambitions and aspirations. The appraiser will then work with the employee to plot the direction in which she should be heading, and to identify the steps she might take to ease her passage. Such steps might involve gaining additional experience and acquiring new skills.

7.5 Performance improvement and career development programmes

Here the aim is for the appraiser to work with the employee to identify her training needs and outline what the employee should do to address these deficiencies; as well as to explain how the organization can help. The appraiser will also explain what she is able to offer the employee by way of training. It is important that the employee 'owns' her weaknesses and skill deficiencies, and that it is she who primarily has the responsibility for ensuring these deficiencies are addressed.

7.6 Reward review

It is common under performance management schemes to link pay increases to performance. However, it is equally common that in order to allow the activities outlined above to be conducted sensibly and in a comparatively unemotional environment, the pay review is conducted at a different time of the year.

The review should be results orientated: the highest rewards should go to those who achieve (or exceed) their targets, with those who fail to achieve receiving little or no increase in salary.

8. The Implications of Introducing a Performance Management System

A performance management system is fundamentally different from one concerned only with performance appraisal and should be viewed as such. If such a scheme is to be successfully implemented the organization needs to take into account a number of factors. Among these are:

a. Managers must be fully trained not only in the techniques of interviewing and career counselling but, equally as important, they must be conversant with the aims and objectives of the scheme. Performance management tries to develop the idea of a 'shared vision', and it is the task of the manager (the appraiser) to ensure that the employee (the appraisee) is able to see her part in that vision.

b. There must be visible top-management commitment to the system.

c. The performance management system should be tailor-made to the needs of the organization, and it should aim to support, or help develop, a culture of high performance and achievement.

d. The commitment of the organization to the scheme as well as the benefits that will flow from it should be communicated to all employees.

e. The scheme should be designed is such a way as to support the achievement of the organization's mission and the realization of its values.

f. The principal accountabilities of managers and staff must be clear in order that all staff are aware of their objectives, the standards of performance expected of them and the measures that will be used to assess their performance.

g. It is important to develop an integrated approach to achieving better-motivated and more committed employees, through a combination of results-orientated appraisal and performance-related pay, together with policies and procedures to develop within employees the attitudes and behaviours which lead to enhanced performance. This would include career planning, performance counselling and training.

PERFORMANCE APPRAISAL AT THE NATLAND BANK

The Natland Bank performance appraisal scheme was introduced in the late 1960s and has been little revised since. The company has now decided to review its systems and has enlisted you as part of a working group to consider how it can best proceed. The group is to hold its first meeting later today and the members have been asked to consider the existing scheme and identify its major weaknesses. The documentation relating to the scheme is shown in figure 11.6 (in the appendix at the end of this chapter). In essence the manager meets the subordinate and then completes the form in private. Its details are not shared with staff. Once the form has been completed it is forwarded to a senior manager who counter-signs it and can add his own comment if he or she wishes. The appraisal is carried out annually.

TASK

1. Examine the documentation relating to the performance appraisal scheme and identify what you consider to be its major strengths and weaknesses.

2. How would you go about the task of reviewing the value and working of a performance appraisal scheme? In designing a new scheme what factors would you wish to incorporate?

QUESTIONS FOR FURTHER CONSIDERATION

1. Consider the performance appraisal/management system at your place of work (or a scheme with which you are familiar). What are its objectives and to what extent do you feel it achieves them?

2. Explain the steps you would follow if you were asked by an organization to install a system of appraisal.

3. How would you appraise the performance of:

    a police officer?

    a social worker?

    a general practitioner?

    a head teacher?

4. Appraisal schemes are most useful when they consider performance and behaviour rather than personality. Discuss.

5. You are employed as Human Resources Officer by Conduit Ltd. The company has used an appraisal system for the past five years. Your Director has asked you to consider how it might be improved. How would you go about this task?

6. Consider the arguments for and against making pay a formal part of performance appraisal.

•REFERENCES•

Anderson G (1993)
MANAGING PERFORMANCE APPRAISAL SYSTEMS
Oxford, Blackwell.

Armstrong M (1994)
PERFORMANCE MANAGEMENT
London, Kogan Page.

Armstrong M & Murlis H (1988)
REWARD MANAGEMENT
London, Institute of Personnel Management.

Cyr R (1993)
Seven Steps to Better Performance Appraisal
Training and Development, Jan.

Drucker P (1955)
THE PRACTICE OF MANAGEMENT
Maidenhead, McGraw-Hill.

Fletcher C (1984)
What's New in Performance Appraisal?
Personnel Management, Feb.

Fletcher C (1993)
APPRAISAL: ROUTES TO IMPROVED PERFORMANCE
London, Institute of Personnel Management.

Fletcher C & Williams R (1992)
THE ROUTE TO PERFORMANCE MANAGEMENT
Personnel Management, Oct.

Fowler A (1990)
Performance Management: The MBO of the 90s
Personnel Management, July.

Fowler A (1991)
How to Conduct Appraisals
Personnel Management Plus, June.

Harrison R (1993)
HUMAN RESOURCE MANAGEMENT: ISSUES AND STRATEGIES Wokingham, Addison-Wesley.

Income Data Services (1989)
COMMON TO ALL
IDS Study 442, Dec.

Institute of Personnel Management (1992)
PERFORMANCE MANAGEMENT IN THE UNITED KINGDOM: AN ANALYSIS OF THE ISSUES
London, IPM.

Lester S (1993)
Appraising Performance Appraisal
Training and Development, Nov.

Livy B (1987)
CORPORATE PERSONNEL MANAGEMENT
London, Pitman.

McGregor D (1958)
An Uneasy Look at Performance Appraisal
Harvard Business Review, May–June.

Neal F (ed.) (1991)
THE HANDBOOK OF PERFORMANCE MANAGEMENT
London, Institute of Personnel Management.

Nevling H (1992)
Performance Appraisals: Never Mind the Boss, Please the Customer
Health Manpower Management, 18/4 .

Sanderson J (1994)
FROM PERFORMANCE APPRAISAL TO PERFORMANCE MANAGEMENT: A CRITICAL ANALYSIS
Unpublished thesis, Anglia Business School, Anglia Polytechnic University.

Stewart J (1993)
Performance Management
Benefits and Compensation International, July / Aug.

Townley B (1990)
A DISCRIMINATING APPROACH TO APPRAISALS
Performance Management, Dec.

•APPENDIX: NATLAND APPRAISAL DOCUMENTATION•

CONFIDENTIAL

NATLAND BANK PLC PERFORMANCE APPRAISAL SCHEME

SECTION 1   DETAILS OF APPRAISEE

NAME:...

DATE OF BIRTH:............................   MALE / FEMALE..

BRANCH.......................................   PAYROLL NO...

GRADE..   DATE OF APPOINTMENT........................

DATE OF JOINING BANK...................................

DATE OF JOINING BRANCH...

SECTION 2   CURRENT JOB

PRESENT JOB...   DATE APPOINTED.....................................

OUTLINE OF MAIN DUTIES...
....
....
....
....

MAJOR CHANGES SINCE LAST REVIEW
....
....
....
....

SECTION 3   PERFORMANCE OVER LAST YEAR

PLEASE GRADE EACH ELEMENT   1 = EXCELLENT
                                          2 = GOOD
                                          3 = SATISFACTORY
                                          4 = POOR
                                          5 = UNSATISFACTORY

APPEARANCE   _____

ATTITUDE   _____

TIME-KEEPING   _____

COOPERATIVENESS   _____

ENTHUSIASM   _____

USE OF INITIATIVE   _____

AMBITION   _____

RELATIONS WITH CUSTOMERS   _____

RELATIONS WITH COLLEAGUES   _____

JOB KNOWLEDGE   _____

TOTAL   _____

SECTION 4

GENERAL COMMENT

....
....
....
....
....
....

SECTION 5

RECOMMENDED SUITABLE FOR PROMOTION please indicate:

        a.   YES
        b.   WITHIN ONE YEAR
        c.   NEED MORE EXPERIENCE
        d.   NOT IN FORESEEABLE FUTURE

SECTION 6

APPRAISING OFFICER'S SIGNATURE..................................... DATE...........................

APPRAISING OFFICER'S NAME...

COMMENTS BY SENIOR MANAGER

....
....
....
....
....

SENIOR MANAGER'S SIGNATURE.................................... DATE................................

SENIOR OFFICER'S NAME...

Figure 11.6
Natland performance
appraisal form

• CHAPTER •

12

REWARD MANAGEMENT

AS A RESULT OF STUDYING THIS CHAPTER YOU SHOULD BE ABLE TO:

- Appreciate the importance of developing a rewards policy that is congruent with the wider objectives of the organization

- Analyse the component parts of pay and the way in which pay packages, including, fringe benefits, might be put together.

- Consider the merits and demerits of performance-related pay.

- Examine the range of fringe benefits available to organizations to include in the remuneration package.

- Explore the ways in which rewards systems can be seen as part of a wider human resource management strategy.

 I am a young executive, no cuffs than mine are cleaner;
I have a slimline briefcase and I use the firm's Cortina.

From *Executive* by Sir John Betjeman

1. Introduction

the pay package is one of the most obvious and visible expressions of the employment relationship; it is the main issue in the exchange between employer and employee, expressing the connection between the labour market, the individual's work and the performance of the employing organization itself. (Hegeswisch 1991: 145)

Pay is a complex and emotive matter. Large salary increases awarded to senior executives of privatized utilities in the UK has brought the question of fair pay, and the so-called market rate for the job, to the centre of the public arena. What is equally clear is that pay is determined by the interrelationship of a number of factors, and in many respects using the analogy of the market-place to describe the systems by which pay is allocated is both misleading and inappropriate. For most workers pay is determined by both economic and social factors, and many of us judge our pay to be fair or unfair not in terms of crude purchasing power but how it compares to the salaries paid to our friends and contemporaries. It is therefore a relative judgement that we make and not an absolute one. For the employer the question of pay will partly revolve around the relative cost of employing labour compared to capital. Ideas of factor substitution are considered in chapter 2 and will not be reiterated here; however, it is appropriate to say that employing labour will be an attractive proposition when it is cheap in comparison to other factors of production. It will be less attractive when the price of labour is high or if other factors of production can perform the job more efficiently. Internally organizations will wish to consider differentials – the relative differences in salaries received by various levels of staff – while at the same time comparing what is paid internally with what is offered elsewhere in the market-place. Pay policies need to have both an internal and an external logic.

2. The Aims of a Rewards Policy

Any rewards policy will have a number of aims. These will include:

a. Attracting and retaining staff of sufficient calibre to meet the needs of the organization.
b. Providing motivation to employees to perform at their best.
c. Recognizing the relative difference and value of each job and worker.
d. Enabling employees to feel part of the success of the organization and to be adequately rewarded for their contribution.

More recently attention has been given to ensuring that pay policies are consistent with the wider aims of the organization: that is, ensuring that the methods by which employee remuneration is decided and allocated themselves contribute to the achievement of organizational goals.

Pay also forms an essential element of the 'work–wage bargain' in that contractually the payment of wages is the consideration given in return for the work that is put in by the employee. Payment of wages, then, is governed by contractual requirements as well as strategic considerations and social and economic pressures. However, the law of contract has nothing to say about the level at which wages should be paid; we have no statutory minimum wage in the United Kingdom.

3. Wages versus Salaries

Sometimes the terms 'wage' and 'salary' are used almost interchangeably, as though their meanings are similar. In fact this is a long way from the truth. The payment of wages is usually associated with manual workers and goes back to the days when demand and hence production levels were volatile, and consequently the demand for manual labourers also fluctuated – from week to week, and sometimes from day to day. 'Direct' labour, as manual workers were often called, was often regarded as a variable cost of production – that is, a cost that could be varied directly with changes in output or production.

The demand for other categories of staff, clerical, managerial and professional, was seen to fluctuate less than that for their manual counterparts, and such workers were given greater security of tenure, and thus 'salaried'. Salaried labour was often regarded as a fixed or semi-fixed factor of production, and could not therefore be changed as output or production changed.

Direct labour was then paid weekly, while salaried (or indirect) labour was paid monthly, reflecting not only their comparative security of tenure, but also the fact that waged staff were paid according to an hourly rate, and their wages directly reflected the time they had worked. Salaried staff, on the other hand, are paid an annual salary, the monthly transfer of which to their bank account is one-twelfth of that sum, and does not therefore relate directly to hours worked.

Other distinctions are apparent between waged and salaried staff. Waged staff are often expected to 'clock in and out' of work, while salaried staff are required to sign in or sometimes merely turn up on time. Waged staff will be penalized in their pay packet if they clock in late or out early, while salaried staff are seen to be able to bend the strict requirements of the working day without financial penalty. The 'staff' status of salaried staff often gives them access to other benefits not always available to their waged counterparts. Such benefits might include pensions, sick pay or better holidays.

Today many organizations see the benefit of 'single status': that is, employing all staff – be they manual or otherwise – on the same conditions of service. Partly this has come about because of force of law; it is no longer possible to treat manual labour as a commodity to be hired and fired at will (in other words, all labour is equally fixed or variable), but also because of a desire by many employers to introduce greater equity into the workplace. The divisions between waged and salaried staff were perceived by many employers to be a source of great resentment. Many employers have largely abolished the weekly payroll and nearly all workers are paid monthly by money transfer into a bank account. Secondly, many employers have harmonized terms and conditions of employment. This has meant common arrangements for pensions, sick pay and holidays, but also shared canteen facilities and shared washrooms. Many employers have also taken the chance to reexamine the nature of the relationship between management and workers, and used the opportunities presented by single status to promote a unitarist approach to industrial relations, or one which sees the success of the organization as being in the best interests of both the workers and its management, and is directly opposite to the pluralist approach, which saw the interests of labour and capital to be in opposition.

> Royal West Sussex NHS Trust plans to cut its wage bill considerably by putting all staff onto personal contracts. By this method the Trust intends to cut its wage bill – currently 70 per cent of its . . . 40m budget to 65 per cent – by the end of 1996. Placing staff on local contracts will mean that they will move off the nationally agreed contracts that have stood for so long and onto locally negotiated contracts. As an incentive to accept the contracts the Trust will offer higher basic rates of pay, but reduced provision for extra allowances.

> The Trust plans to have all nursing staff on new contracts by September 1996, and all other staff by April 1997. To date 25 per cent of the Trust's 2,000 employees, including all senior managers, have moved to local contracts.
>
> The Trust is keen to involve staff unions in creating the new pay and grading structure and sees consultation as key to its successful introduction. In particular it is keen not to jeopardize the trust it has built up with unions in recent talks to reduce sickness rates and staff turnover.
> Reported in *Personnel Today*, 25 September 1995.

4. Influences on Pay Determination

As mentioned earlier, pay is not determined entirely by economic criteria. Roberts (1994) describes seven major influences on pay determination:

a. Beliefs about the worth of a job – skills requirements, responsibility, etc.

b. Individual characteristics – age, experience, seniority, qualifications, performance, potential, etc.

c. The labour market – the local, national or international demand for and supply of workers, both specific and general.

d. The remuneration policy and strategy of the company.

e. The strength of bargaining groups – legal requirements, collective bargaining, unemployment, job security etc.

f. The cost of living.

g. Government intervention – government may attempt to influence how pay is determined by initiatives such as legislation to promote employee share-option schemes and profit sharing, or it may attempt to influence the general level of pay settlement by pay policies, overt or otherwise.

5. The Components of the Rewards Package

For most workers, pay is made up of a number of component parts. Some are paid regularly, like a monthly salary, others less frequently, like annual bonuses, while others are deferred until some time later, like pensions. For many workers most of their salary is fixed (basic pay), while for others a proportion of their pay will be determined in some measure by their output (bonuses). Some of the possible components of pay are set out in figure 12.1.

The actual composition of pay will be determined by a number of factors, not least of all the policy of the company. Dependent upon the product, culture and management style of the organization, pay policy may be skewed in favour of a large performance-related element, or even away from an emphasis on performance in cases where (for instance) no tangible product is produced or no profit is made or desired. In recent years some organizations have offered their employees so-called

The pay package consists of:	
	Basic pay (calculated, monthly, weekly or hourly)
Plus	Additional payments (shift allowance, unsocial hours allowance, etc.)
Plus	Overtime payments (usually calculated at enhanced rates)
Plus	Fringe benefits (e.g. car, private medical insurance)
Plus	Performance-related element (e.g. bonuses, merit pay, etc.)
Plus	Deferred pay (e.g. pensions)
Plus	Any other pecuniary or non-pecuniary rewards
Equals	TOTAL reward package

Figure 12.1
The components of the
reward package

'cafeteria pay'. This is where the total value of the remuneration package is decided by the employer but the employee is allowed to decide himself how he would wish that pay to be made up. He would be free to choose (cafeteria style) from what is on offer. Employees at different stages in their careers might be attracted to different pay packages – for example, the younger worker might want to have a high proportion of his salary paid as current income, while the older worker might prefer to defer current income in favour of an enhanced pension. Different methods of pay determination are discussed in the following pages.

6. Rewards Strategy

Any reward strategy must be built on an acknowledgement of the following factors:

a. Almost without exception every organization depends for its success on the performance of its staff. The rewards strategy must aim not only to recruit and retain staff of adequate quality, but in addition to inspire those individuals to give of their best.

b. The rewards system must aim to help achieve the strategic aims of the organization. To this end it must give credit to those whose performance contributes to the achievement of those aims, not only to reward past performance but also to cement within individuals the appropriate attitudes and behaviours necessary to ensure long-term success.

c. Rewards strategies should aim to be seen to be fair. That is, those who are seen to benefit by them should be aware of why they have benefited and what it is about their contribution that has caused them to be rewarded. Equally, those who have done less well in terms of financial rewards should be left in no doubt why this is so and what it is they should do to improve their situation. As far as possible, then, a rewards system should be transparent, and should not be arbitrary, biased or unjust.

d. Reward strategies will be most successful when the needs of the organization are shared with the individual, and the individual can see that her efforts are rewarded both in terms of personal gain and organizational success.

7. Reward Payment Systems

The examples of the components that may go into the pay package, illustrated in figure 12.1, demonstrate that pay can be (and often is) a complicated issue. Add to these complexities the need to relate pay to the external market rate, the need to maintain internal relativities between different job grades or levels, and the desire by many employers to provide for their staff some system of annual pay progression within bands or scales, and it quickly becomes evident that reward systems need to be positively managed. Most employers will decide upon the objectives of their rewards systems, taking into account the factors discussed earlier. This is to ensure that pay becomes another tool with which to pursue corporate strategy.

Most employers will view salary and wage levels through job grades. This practice, although common, is not without its critics. For instance, Mahoney (1992) argues that what he calls this 'job-based compensation' is not always in the best interests of either the employee or employer. He offers alternatives, such as 'skills-based pay' in which the employee's skills, not her job title, form the basis for remuneration. The major difficulty with moving to a skills-based system would be the problems of complexity it would bring. Most employers would wish to maintain relative simplicity in their reward systems, often to the detriment of some degree of equity and efficiency.

A number of alternative reward payment systems are available to the employer, and several are discussed below:

7.1 Time rate

This is often known as day rate or hour rate, and is probably the simplest and therefore the most common payment system. In essence workers are paid a predetermined rate for the hours, days or weeks that they work. Rates do not vary with output and so pay is not related to performance in any way. The system's major advantage is that it is simple and cheap to administer, and allows for close cost control of labour. Overtime will also be paid at a time rate, usually an enhancement of the basic rate. Time-rate systems are also common for casual, temporary or part-time workers. The relationship between pay and output is illustrated in figure 12.2.

7.2 Payment by results

Payment by results schemes relate pay, in whole or in part, to output. Such schemes may be split into several sorts. At its simplest the worker's pay is determined entirely by output. This is usually known as piece rate. One industry in which such a system is commonly used is casual farm work, where fruit pickers and vegetable lifters might be paid entirely according to their output. The relationship between pay and output is illustrated in figure 12.3.

In many other cases employers offer a low minimum earnings level to their employees, who can then bolster their earning considerably according to their output. Such a system is illustrated in figure 12.4.

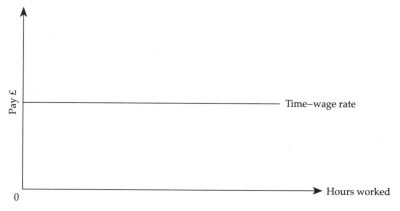

Figure 12.2
Time payment systems –
relationship between
payment and output

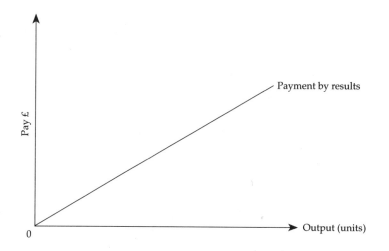

Figure 12.3
Payment by results –
relationship between
payment and output

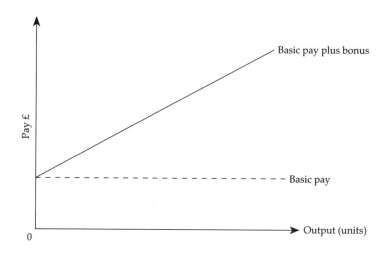

Figure 12.4
Bonus systems –
relationship between pay
and output

Such a system can be seen to have a number of advantages. It guarantees the employee a minimum level of earnings, while also ensuring that in times of business downturn pay can more precisely reflect the level of economic activity in the company.

Payment by results schemes need careful managing, particularly to ensure that they do represent good value for money for the employer. In addition they can be the cause of friction among workers if it is felt that some jobs within the organization are 'easier' than others, and hence offer greater opportunities to earn higher pay. Payment by results schemes can also encourage competition between workers rather than cooperation, and care needs to be taken to ensure that quality is not sacrificed to quantity.

7.3 Measured daywork

Measured daywork payments operate on the assumption that an employee can produce a given level of output per day and it is the production of this output that will justify payment of wages. It is most commonly used in the manufacturing sector where it allows payment to be highly geared: that is, high output can lead to high payments. In effect, it can build bonus payments into base salary calculations. It is designed to maintain a consistently high level of output. It can be straightforward to operate in an environment where the product is simple. Equally, it can be difficult to operate in an environment in which the product is complex, or subject to short and changing production runs, or of an individual nature. Here the output will have to be determined by careful work measurement. If illustrated diagrammatically the relationship between pay and output would also show a very close positive correlation.

7.4 Productivity deals

In these cases, via a process of negotiation between management and workforce representatives, attempts are made to secure the agreement of the workforce to amend working practice in such a way that higher productivity will result. Such working practices might include hours of work, allocation of work, manning levels, the introduction of new technology etc. The benefits of the change in terms of higher productivity can then be divided between the employer and the employees (as an incentive to change).

7.5 Organization-wide incentive schemes

Under such schemes basic pay is usually at a fixed level but will be boosted by the payment of an annual or biannual bonus. This will be paid to all employees, usually as a proportion of pay, and related to the financial success of the organization. Such schemes (as opposed to payment by results schemes) are intended to encourage cooperation between employees towards the achievement of common goals. However, many workers may feel themselves to be remote from any influence on corporate performance and will take the money without feeling that they have been instrumental to the organization's success. Moreover, incentive-scheme payments are often made some time in arrears, distancing the association between work and reward.

7.6   Performance-related pay

Performance-related pay schemes (PRP) relate some proportion of pay to indicators of performance. These might include output, quality, ability to meet predetermined targets, or contribution to organizational success. PRP schemes are increasing in popularity and have spread from the manufacturing sector to the service sector and from the private sector to the public sector. Their growing influence necessitates the dedication of a longer section to them later in this chapter.

7.7   Age-scale systems

This system usually propels the younger employee, via a series of increments to pay made on her birthday, towards the full adult wage for the job. Commonly the adult wage is reached at age 21.

7.8   Annual increment payment systems

This system sets the minimum and maximum pay for each pay band. Employees progress through the various steps within the pay band via annual increments. In some cases (notably the civil service) the number of increments can be large in number causing the employee to wait many years before reaching the top of any scale.

This system is relatively simple to administer – employees who have not reached the top of the scale simply progress one incremental point each year. The system is devised on the assumption that the more experienced employee is more valued to the employer (more skilled, knowledgeable and able to take on a wider range of tasks) than the less experienced, and should be rewarded accordingly. In many organizations such an assumption would not bear close examination. The annual increments are not awarded in return for additional effort, or taking on extra responsibility. They are rarely denied to the less talented employee. In short they do not relate to performance.

7.9   Flexible incremental schemes

Such schemes attempt to overcome the pitfalls identified with the more standard variant, in that they allow increments to be awarded in blocks of more than one, or not be awarded at all. Additionally, with some schemes increments might be awarded to those taking on special responsibilities, or be awarded on a temporary basis to those who, for a period, take on additional work.

7.10   Commission-based payment systems

A relatively small basic pay might be offered to sales staff, with the rest of pay being calculated as a percentage of total sales made. This allows the worker to see a direct correlation between work and reward, but does lead to competition between workers which may, or may not, be seen as healthy. Additionally the onus is on the employee to sell to make a living. There may be little regard for selling the customer the correct product or offering accurate advice. The salesperson's aims are often predatory and his or her instinct to sell the customer the product which pays the best commission, rather than the one which best meets the customer's needs.

7.11 Profit sharing

These schemes have become more popular in recent years, and have an added advantage in that legislation allows them to be set off against corporation tax liabilities. The workforce receive a bonus based directly on the performance of the company and paid in the form of cash and / or shares.

7.12 Cafeteria systems

Such schemes are based on the realization that at different stages in their careers employees may prefer a different balance of rewards. Such schemes therefore allow the employee (within fixed bounds of discretion) to determine the composition, but not the total amount of, their pay package. So within an overall rewards package of £X,000, an employee might make a decisions about additional pension contributions, more (or less) holiday in exchange for less (or more) pay. He may or may not value membership of private health plans, access to company cars, additional life insurance, etc. The overall level of the pay package will be centrally determined but the employee will be free (cafeteria style) to choose the component parts. This is a relatively complex system, and its complexity alone would deter many employers from considering its use. However, within a fixed salary bill it does allow the individual and the organization to maximize the utility of the rewards scheme.

> The future of NHS pay review bodies has been confirmed by Health Minister Gerry Malone. Locally determined pay (pay determined at the NHS Trust level) will be encouraged, and the government is committed to increasing the percentage proportion of pay determined at the local level, although the review bodies, which make national recommendations for medical and nursing staff's pay, will continue for the foreseeable future. The role of the review body is increasingly controversial – some see it as a brake on true local bargaining and flexibility, while others see it as a mechanism to hold back public expenditure. (Reported in *Personnel Today*, 25 Oct. 1995.)

8. Selecting a Payment System

The variety of payment systems on offer is vast – the author has described only a few and in scant detail. It should also be recognized that schemes are not used in isolation. Many organizations will merge the features of several schemes into one. This can complicate matters from the point of view of analysis and comparison, but may make good sense in terms of meeting the needs of the organization. In any consideration of which scheme(s) is / are the most suitable for your organization, it may be useful to keep in mind that Armstrong (1992) claims that over time any payment system will degenerate, hence it will need constant monitoring and review. He argues that to select a payment system the following steps should be followed:

a. Define the objectives and assumptions of the scheme.

b. Analyse the existing scheme and its operation.

c. Evaluate alternative systems.

d. Select from among the alternatives.

e. Monitor the scheme against the objectives and assumptions.

It is also clear that too often in the past reward systems have been corrupted in such a way that they bore little correlation to effort or output, and in many cases allowed wage bills to spiral upwards at times when performance was either flat or in decline. In order for systems to be, and to remain, valid they must be closely related to the aims of the organization and carefully tailored to strategic planning processes. There should be an acceptance that over time the system may begin to fail and require either radical surgery or complete replacement.

9. Salary Bands and Salary Trends

Most systems of salary administration are dependent upon some system of job grading. To a large extent this is obvious, because increased job responsibility is usually associated with increased rewards. Job evaluation schemes attempt to give this association between job responsibility and rewards some structure and legitimacy. When the job evaluation has been completed the jobs considered will have been put into a rank order from which jobs of broadly equal value can be grouped together into grades. The number of grades, their relationship to the organization structure and the ideology of the organization will all have to be carefully considered. While current fashions are to reduce the number of job grades it is still the case that in some large organizations there may still be in excess of ten grades. It will also be necessary to consider how job grades relate to one another. In figure 12.5 the five pay grades are clearly delineated, and there is a gap, in terms of pay between each and the next. Promotion will result in the employee receiving not only a noticeable increase in responsibility, but in pay also.

In figure 12.6 the five pay grades are more closely related and employees on each grade are employed on a pay scale. The top of the scale for grade 1 is paid the same as the bottom of the scale for grade 2. Such a system might (for instance) recognize the enhanced contribution that an employee can make as her length of service increases, and reward accordingly.

Figure 12.7 is a more complex model and uses what are sometimes called 'grade boxes'. This method allows overlaps in pay between grades. An employee on grade 2 could earn more, less or the same as those employed on grades 1 and 3.

While not comprehensive, the three schemes illustrated demonstrate how pay grades can relate to one another. In deciding which is appropriate for her organization a Human Resource Manager will need to take into account a number of factors, but principally:

a. The aims and objectives of the organization.

b. The management culture of the organization.

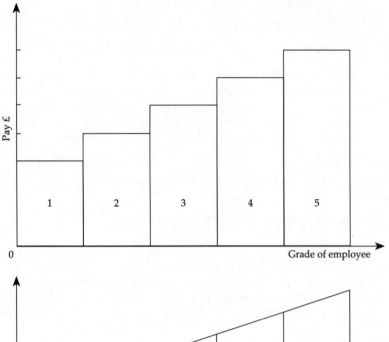

Figure 12.5
Fixed-rate pay grades

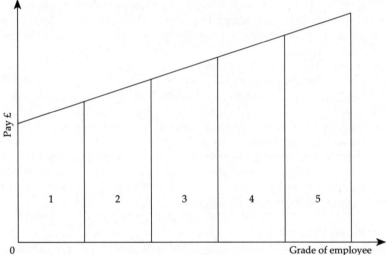

Figure 12.6
Incremental pay grades

    c. The product / service of the organization.

    d. The sorts of staff employed by the organization (e.g. unskilled, skilled, professional, etc.).

    e. The systems used by competitors.

       In recent years many employers have tried to move away from payment systems that encourage the employee to expect a pay rise each year. In particular employers are concerned about the phenomenon known as 'wage drift'. This is the tendency, particularly common where pay scales are used, for the wage bill to continue to increase year by year without any concomitant increase in output or productivity. Increasingly employers are introducing systems that link pay more closely to corporate performance, both as a cost-control measure and as a measure

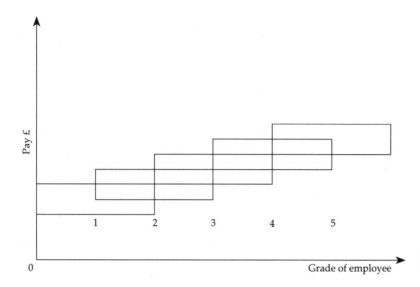

Figure 12.7
Overlapping pay grades

aimed to demonstrate to all staff in the most practical way possible that pay and pay increases must be earned and paid for.

It is also important to consider the impact of the external labour market. For example, if one particular occupation is in short supply, should it attract additional reward? The obvious answer is 'yes', although the occupation itself may not be particularly skilled, and certainly no more skilled than others employed by the same organization. Consideration needs to be given to both the long- and short-term implications of distorting pay systems. An example might be a school that has difficulty recruiting teachers of mathematics. Should the school pay maths teachers a higher salary (to reflect their scarcity), or should it take account of the fact that once employed a maths teacher will perform a job little different from that of any other teacher?

10. Performance-related Pay: The Arguments

Performance-related pay (PRP) is, as mentioned earlier, growing in popularity. However, the evidence of its effectiveness is rather mixed. At the basic level it attempts to apply to more senior and white-collar staff the same principles of incentive that for many years have been used with more junior and manual staff. That is, it attempts to relate some proportion of pay to individual, work-group or organizational performance. PRP can also be seen as a tool of control in that it allows rewards to go to those who most deserve it, to those who have achieved and contributed to the success of the organization. By the same score it will deny rewards to those who have not achieved or whose contribution is deemed to be poor. In this way it can be compared with shop-floor schemes that relate pay to output – if output is poor then pay will respond accordingly, and vice versa.

PRP schemes can work in a number of ways. Commonly they attempt to use performance appraisal to set measurable objectives for the individual employee and then reward him according to the achievement of those objectives. Alternatively, the performance of the work group can be the basis upon which reward is made, in many cases with the whole group sharing the reward.

PRP can offer a number of advantages. It can draw a closer correlation between effort and reward and differentiate between the good and the bad performer. It allows for flexibility within the reward structure and can also, to some extent, allow the overall salary bill to move in line with corporate performance.

But, again, PRP is not without its critics. The major criticisms include the difficulty of setting and measuring the performance of complex jobs when the contribution of one individual cannot be isolated from that of others. It is also claimed that there is little evidence that PRP actually motivates, or even that most managers are actually motivated by reward. Its critics argue that PRP simply gives additional payments to those who are already making a good contribution to the organization, and can militate against the development of teamwork. The award of PRP depends crucially on the objectivity of the senior manager in measuring the performance of individuals. If this is done poorly, or if favouritism is shown, the whole scheme will be discredited in the eyes of the many.

Equally, the senior manager must be able to tell the poor performer that he is not to receive reward from the PRP scheme. There is little evidence to show that managers are prepared to make these judgements; many prefer to 'share the cake more thinly'. If not carefully managed PRP can lead to pay drifting upwards faster than increases in overall performance. This is because the 'poor' and 'satisfactory' performer often receive the pay increase that they might have received had PRP not been in place, while the high achiever receives a higher than average reward. The system can fail if it does not take all or part of the pay increase away from the low achiever and give it to the high achiever.

It is clear that the use of common-sense principles – that is, that individual performance and individual reward should be closely related – is fraught with many difficulties and can lead to a number of unintended consequences. It is also true that PRP, like any other payment system, can almost take on a life and rationale of its own, far removed from the strategic and operational needs of the organization. To be truly successful any PRP system must avoid these pitfall and operate in such a way as to encourage high levels of motivation, output and quality, as well as being, and being seen to be, equitable and fair in its application.

To appreciate fully the context in which performance-related pay would operate, the reader should give due consideration to chapter 11, covering performance appraisal and performance management.

In 1993 the Sheehy Inquiry reported on police pay. One of its recommendations was that performance-related pay should be introduced. A pilot scheme has been tested by 13 police forces. Under the pilot, officers whose performance was deemed to be satisfactory received the pay rise for the year, those whose performance was deemed to be unsatisfactory were denied the increase for the year, and those who were deemed outstanding were given a bonus. Performance was measured against a list of skills requirements and performance levels agreed with managers. (Reported in *Personnel Today*, 10 Oct. 1995.)

11. The Use of Benefits

Many employers have traditionally given their employees a range of other benefits in addition to their wage or salary. In part the form of these benefits will reflect the nature of the industry. For instance, railway employees have received free or subsidized rail travel, employees of motor manufacturers are often offered discount on the purchase of new cars, and employees of clothing retailers have offered staff discounts on the purchase of clothes. Such benefits are offered for a variety of reasons, not all of them entirely altruistic. The reasons include:

a. To encourage certain types of behaviour in employees. Such benefits might include free or subsidized staff uniforms, haircare, subsidizing part-time further education, offering free or discounted use of fitness facilities, offering on-site accommodation (e.g. public houses, farm labourers).

b. To encourage experienced and valued employees to remain with that employer: additional holidays, pension schemes, share ownership.

c. To make employment with that organization seem more attractive: flexi-time, career break schemes, workplace nurseries, subsidized staff restaurant.

d. To encourage consumption of the employer's products: free or discounted products.

e. To demonstrate that the employer cares: sickness benefits, health-care plans, life insurance, pensions, long-service awards.

The use of benefits can be very efficient for the employer, in that some costs can be offset against tax, while those that are produced by the company will be available at only a marginal cost. The advantages of a good package of rewards can be many. The organization might be seen as an attractive employer for which to work. The benefits might also encourage good staff retention, be highly valued by employers and act as a motivator. Used well they will also encourage in the workforce the kinds of attitudes and behaviours that are deemed necessary for organizational success.

12. The Law Relating to Wages and Salaries

The pay of the worker is governed by the terms and conditions set out in the contract of employment, and once that contract has been agreed the employer is legally bound to pay the wage or salary specified. It is important to note that no statutory minimum rate of pay exists in the UK, except for employees covered by the Agricultural Wages Board. Additionally, the employer is not required to increase pay in line with inflation, make periodic reviews of pay, or indeed offer any increase – ever. The employee can, however, expect to be paid his basic pay, in the form agreed, on a regular basis. Factors that could jeopardize the payment would include sickness, holidays (though in practice most employers offer paid holidays), absence through industrial action, or other voluntary or involuntary withdrawal of labour.

A number of items relating to pay must be made explicit in the contract of employment. These are:

a. The rate of pay and the method by which it is calculated.

b. When remuneration is to be paid – weekly, monthly, etc.

c. Any other terms and conditions relating to hours of work and pay; for example, whether or not overtime will be paid or unpaid.

d. Terms and conditions relating to sickness, pensions and holidays.

In addition, most groups of employees are entitled to receive (with their wage or salary) an itemized pay statement. This should state:

a. The gross amount of the wage or salary.

b. The amounts of fixed deductions (trade union subscriptions etc.), and the amount of variable deductions (e.g. income tax and national insurance).

c. The net wage or salary.

Groups of workers who are not legally entitled to receive an itemized pay statement include merchant seamen, police officers, share fishermen, those who normally work outside the UK and those who work for organizations employing less than 20 staff.

The Wages Act of 1986 repealed the Truck Acts and enabled employers to require that new employees be paid in cashless form. This has clear advantages in terms of security. However, those who have been employed by their organizations since before 1986 can still insist on being paid in the form specified in their contract of employment.

13. Conclusion

The increased importance of performance-related pay is one of a number of trends to be seen in the management of reward systems in the United Kingdom. Many of these changes have come about as a result of the deregulation of the labour market that occurred as a result of legislation passed in the 1980s and 1990s. This included the closing down of the Comparability Commission, the repeal of the Fair Wages Resolution, the repeal of parts of the Employment Protection Act and the abolition of Wages Councils. These measures combined to provide an environment in which pay could be more flexible, less rigid and less centrally determined. The past few years has also been a period in which employers (and trades unions) have given greater attention to the overall rewards package – that is, pay, benefits and holidays – and not simply seen rewards in terms of the 'going rate for the job'.

Increasingly pay is seen as a strategic tool which the organization must use in order to help it achieve its aims. The rewards system will be used to promote the appropriate attitudes, behaviours and ambitions within the workforce. It is also recognized that it is unrealistic to expect a rewards system to last forever. In the past it has been common for organizations to employ rewards systems for many years. Today this is less and less common, and as organizations explore the link between individual reward and corporate performance reward systems can be reviewed and either updated or replaced at quite frequent intervals.

There can be no doubt that the successful management of rewards is crucial to successful HRM, and it will remain an ongoing challenge to practitioners to devise and review rewards systems that meet both the needs of the organization and the aspirations of the employee.

PICKING UP THE BILL

In November 1994 the Chairman of British Gas was awarded a pay rise of 75 per cent, taking his salary from £270,000 to £475,000 per year. British Gas is one of Britain's largest companies, making annual profits well in excess of £1 billion per year.

In December 1994 British Gas announced that it was to reduce the number of its retail outlets from 430 to about 240. Additionally their role would change from that of bill payment centres to being more concerned with selling appliances. Staff numbers would be reduced by about 1,700. Alongside this changed role those staff who would remain would face pay cuts (of about 17 per cent) and reduced holidays (down from 33 to 27 days). British Gas argued that they wished to bring pay and conditions down to 'market levels' for the job. They argued that compared with other high street retailers their shop staff were paid above the market rate. Comparisons with other retailers shows that British Gas staff were paid about £6 per hour, Sainsbury's and Tesco's staff slightly under £4 per hour, Dixons staff about £3.50 per hour and Boots staff slightly over £4 per hour. Trade union representatives claimed, however, that the comparison was a poor one because British Gas staff possessed a higher level of skill than staff employed by many other retailers and were trained in energy efficiency, financial skills and the skill to tailor appliances to customers' specific needs.

Sir,

Cedric Brown, the Chief executive of British Gas, must have a pay increase of 75 per cent to make him more competitive. His staff, who created the wealth which he now enjoys, require a pay cut to make them more competitive. The logic is absent and the sentiment stomach-turning. May this be one issue over which rich and poor can unite in protest.

Yours etc.
(Letter to _The Times_, 16 Dec. 1994.)

TASK
Consider the issues raised in this case and the timing of the two announcements. How should the 'market' rate for any job be determined?

QUESTIONS FOR FURTHER CONSIDERATION

1. Consider your own organization, or one with which you are familiar – what are the objectives of the pay strategy? Do you see it to be an appropriate strategy given the objectives of the organization?

2. Why is pay such an important part of the human resource management philosophy?

3. 'Fringe benefits are expensive to devise, costly to administer and of unproved benefit. The clutter should be removed and be replaced by a rewards system that is simple, cheap to run and consistent with the wider objectives of the organization.' Consider the merits of this argument.

4. Does pay act as a motivator?

5. Consider how performance-related pay schemes might be introduced for the following groups of workers: dentists; traffic wardens; social workers; teachers.

• REFERENCES •

Armstrong M (1992)
A HANDBOOK OF PERSONNEL MANAGEMENT
London, Kogan Page.

Armstrong M & Murlis H (1988)
REWARD MANAGEMENT
London, Institute of Personnel Management.

Brewster C & Connock S (1985)
INDUSTRIAL RELATIONS: COST EFFECTIVE STRATEGIES
London, Hutchinson.

Cannell M & Long P (1991)
What's Changed About Incentive Pay?
Personnel Management, Oct.

Casey B, Lakey J & White M (1992)
PAYMENT SYSTEMS: A LOOK AT CURRENT SYSTEMS
London, UK Department of Employment / Policy Studies Institute, Research Series No. 5.

Connock S (1991)
HR VISION: MANAGING A QUALITY WORKFORCE
London, Institute of Personnel Management.

Goodswen M (1988)
Retention and Reward of the High Achiever
Personnel Management, Oct.

Gregg P, Machin S & Szymanski S (1993)
The Disappearing Relationship Between Directors' Pay and
Corporate Performance
British Journal of Industrial Relations, 31 (March).

Hegeswisch A (1991)
The Decentralising of Pay Bargaining: European
Comparisons
Personnel Review, 20 / 6.

Income Data Services (1988)
PERFORMANCE PAY
London, IDS.

Income Data Services (1989)
INCENTIVE BONUS SCHEMES
London, IDS.

Kessler I (1995)
Reward Systems, in **HUMAN RESOURCE MANAGEMENT:
A CRITICAL TEXT**
Storey J (ed.). London, Routledge.

Lupton T (1972)
PAYMENT SYSTEMS
Harmondsworth, Penguin.

Mahoney T (1992)
Multiple Pay Contingencies: Strategic Design of Compensation,
in **HUMAN RESOURCE STRATEGIES**
Salaman, D (ed.). London, Open University.

McGregor D (1970)
THE HUMAN SIDE OF ENTERPRISE
Maidenhead, McGraw-Hill.

Murlis H &Wright V (1993)
Decentralising Pay Decisions: Empowerment or Abdication?
Personnel Management, March.

Roberts I (1994)
Remuneration and Reward, in **HUMAN RESOURCE
MANAGEMENT**
Beardwell I & Holden L (eds). London, Pitman.

Woodley C (1990)
The Cafeteria Route to Compensation
Personnel Management, May.

Wootton B (1962)
THE SOCIAL FOUNDATIONS OF WAGE POLICY
London, Allen and Unwin.

·CHAPTER·

13

RESTRUCTURING THE WORKFORCE: CORPORATE DOWNSIZING

AS A RESULT OF STUDYING THIS CHAPTER YOU SHOULD BE ABLE TO:

- Consider the legal definition of the term redundancy, and the conditions under which an employee might be made redundant.

- Appreciate the reasons why organizations need to reduce staffing levels and hence make staff redundant.

- Consider the rights of the employee under circumstances of redundancy, particularly the right to consultation.

- Evaluate the various criteria for selection for redundancy and how they should be applied.

- Evaluate the role of the outplacement consultant and how an organization might employ such a consultant to assist the process of transition from redundancy into new employment.

> *Efficiency improvements and re-organization have continued throughout the group and all staff have contributed by their understanding of the task and their realism and flexibility. As a result full time equivalent staff numbers were reduced by 576 to 4,567 at the year end, a reduction of some 11 per cent of the workforce. This has been achieved by our continued adherence to a policy of voluntary severance and early retirement with the provision of employee support and counselling for those seeking further employment.*

Extract from the Chief Executive's Review in Yorkshire Electricity Group PLC's annual report and accounts, 1995

1. Introduction

It is probably true to say that one of the most difficult tasks that a human resource manager will be involved with is staff redundancy. This will never be an easy or a pleasant task. Michael Armstrong (1992) recommends five steps that can be taken to make it less painful:

a. Plan ahead to avoid redundancy.

b. Use other methods of reducing numbers or man-hours to avoid or minimize the effects of redundancy.

c. Call for voluntary redundancy.

d. Develop and apply a proper redundancy procedure.

e. Provide help in finding new jobs ('outplacement', as it is now called).

Today, making staff redundant is only one part of the process of change for organizations. The effects of letting staff go can be significant not only for those who leave but also for those who stay, for it is probable that their jobs will not remain the same. Those who stay will have not only a larger workload but also a different workload. That is, the employer will take the opportunity to restructure the work by, for instance, restructuring the organization, introducing new work methods, new technologies, or a more comprehensive business process re-engineering. It is also likely that organizations will attempt to change the culture of work and delayer their structure. This means that it is probable that middle management and supervisory staff will be made redundant as organizations seek to push responsibility for decision-making to junior members of staff.

This chapter takes Armstrong's five points as a guide for the consideration of the development and application of appropriate policies for the reduction of staff numbers.

2. What is Redundancy?

The UK Employment Protection (Consolidation) Act of 1978 states that an employee who is dismissed shall be taken to have been made redundant if the dismissal is attributable wholly or largely to:

a. The employer ceasing or intending to cease carrying on business in the place where the person was employed.

b. The employer has or intends to cease carrying out his business for the purpose for which the employee was employed.

c. The need for employees to carry out a particular kind of work has diminished, ceased or is expected to do so.

d. The need for employees to carry out a particular kind of work at the place where they were employed has diminished, ceased or is expected to do so.

Redundancy occurs when the work done by an employee no longer exists. Under such circumstances an employer can justifiably dismiss the employee. When redundancy occurs an employee is entitled to receive a period of notice relating to her redundancy which will be dependent upon her length of service; or it could be paid in lieu. The employee is also entitled to receive compensation for the loss of her employment based upon her age, salary and length of service.

3. The Causes of Redundancy

There are many reasons why jobs become redundant and no one factor can be easily isolated. However, among the most common factors are:

a. Technological advances such that the same or greater output can be produced with the same or less labour.

b. A reduction in the demand for the product or service which the organization (and employee) is engaged in producing.

c. Cost-reduction programmes – these may be caused by a number of factors, such as increased competition, falling demand, the increase in some costs which must be offset elsewhere to allow price stability, and so forth.

d. Changes in the culture of management – empowerment, delayering, etc.

e. Increases in the cost of labour relative to other raw materials, such that factor substitution takes place, or production is shifted to another location, such as the Far East.

f. Merger and acquisition – requiring the elimination of duplicated services.

g. Reorganization and restructuring the work – that is, the way that the work is done is reorganized such that fewer workers are needed.

h. Contracting the work out. A common feature of the 1980s was the practice of contracting out some tasks previously performed by the employer. Such tasks included catering, security, maintenance and training. However, the European Transfer of Undertakings Directive and recent decisions of the European Court have made this a less attractive option. See chapter 15 for fuller explanation.

i. Closure or collapse of the business, such that the workforce is no longer needed.

The fact that 'work no longer exists' for a variety of reasons, means that the human resource manager cannot take a single approach to redundancy. The selection of staff for redundancy can be both difficult and time consuming and should be approached with considerable care. Additionally, redundancy cannot be seen in simplistic terms. Often it is portrayed as 'cutting out dead wood', 'judicious pruning' or 'stimulating new growth'. However, such gardening metaphors are probably misplaced. The effects on those employees who are left after redundancy must also be considered. It is not uncommon for those who are left to have considerable feelings of guilt because they have retained their jobs at the expense of their friends and former colleagues. This is not an ideal environment in which to 'stimulate new growth'. The period that immediately follows redundancy must be carefully managed if those employees who are left are not to feel angry, disorientated and antipathetic towards their employer.

4. Other Methods of Reducing Manpower

Making employees redundant is only one way to reduce the size of the payroll, and should be seen as the final step – an option to be explored if all else fails. Other possibilities can, and should, be considered. These might include:

a. Reducing or eliminating overtime.

b. Withdrawing work that has been sub-contracted.

c. Laying staff off temporarily.

d. Not renewing temporary contracts.

Such options have the advantage of reducing the impact of cuts in manning levels on full time (or 'core') workers. However, they also fall only on the so-called 'peripheral' workforce. This means that management's scope for flexibility in the use of labour is also reduced. Many organizations would see considerable utility in maintaining the flexible part of the workforce. This would allow them to cope better with problems and shocks that might lie ahead. Such a path of action would be unpopular with the full-time workforce, because it would mean that any job cuts would fall disproportionately onto their heads while the more flexible parts of the workforce would be less affected.

5. The Requirement for Consultation

Employers are required by law to consult workplace representatives about proposed redundancies. This is in order that every opportunity can be taken to explore ways in which the numbers of redundancies involved can be reduced or the effects made less painful. The amount of notice of redundancy to be given is determined by the number of staff the company is proposing to let go. So, if between 10 and 99 employees are to be made redundant at a single site, then at least 30 days' notice must be given. If 100 or more employees are to be made redundant then 90 days' notice must be given. The notification must be given in writing and should lead to consultation. The employer should provide for the workplace representatives the following information:

a. The reasons for the proposed redundancy.

b. The numbers and a description of the employees who are proposed to be made redundant and the total number of employees who could fit that description.

c. The method by which it is proposed that the redundancies take place – for example, procedure, timescale.

d. Details of how the number of those to be made redundant might be reduced, and how the consequence of redundancy might be alleviated.

e. Details of how any redundancy payments to be made will be calculated.

Failure to give such notification can lead to an application to an industrial tribunal for a 'protective award'. This is an award giving employees payment for the period during which consultation should have been taking place. Employers can be excused giving due notification and the 'protective award' if they can show that appropriate 'special circumstances' made it impossible. Such special circumstances might include the fact that the business had to close down suddenly and unexpectedly due to reasons that could not reasonably have been foreseen.

English law gives rights of consultation to the trade unions representing the employees who are the proposed targets of redundancy. In the past, where no unions are recognized, no right of consultation has existed. European law is increasingly giving rights of consultation to *workers or their representatives*, and this is taken to mean the representatives of all workers whether unionized or not. European law also gives a stronger definition of consultation and gives workers, or their representatives, the right to be genuinely consulted about proposed redundancies such that the workers have a right to put forward ideas (and to have them properly evaluated) that might, for instance, result in no workers being made redundant at all.

The European Court of Justice was unimpressed with the UK's implementation of the Transfer of Undertakings Directive (see the European chapters later in the book for a full explanation), and the UK government put amendment regulations before Parliament in November 1995. These regulations will in effect require employers to establish workplace consultation if they plan to make 20 or more staff redundant. To many this seems another step along the way to European-style works councils (again, see the European chapters), while others see the government as taking a minimalist approach. For instance, 96 per cent of businesses employ less than 20 people, and the new regulations will allow employers to bypass recognized trade unions and set up alternative consultation machinery. However, it is recommended that employers set up their new consultation forum before the need for redundancy arises, rather than wait until the middle of a redundancy drive.

6. Rights of the Redundant Employee

When an employee is made redundant he has certain rights. Specifically these are:

6.1 The right to take time off (with pay) to look for another job or to arrange training   The 1978 Act does not specify the amount of time that an employee should be given. However, industrial tribunals have held that two days a week is not unreasonable.

6.2 The right to redundancy pay   This right applies to most workers who have been employed for at least two full years, and includes part-time staff. Some categories of worker are exempt, including share fishermen, apprentices at the end of their apprenticeship, many merchant seamen, employees aged over 65 and employees on fixed-term contracts where the contract contains a term waiving the right to redundancy payment. The amount of redundancy pay to which an employee is entitled will be a function of age, length of service and salary. Many employees will receive only the statutory minimum, but others will receive higher amounts which may have been negotiated through collective agreements. To calculate entitlement to redundancy the following formula should be applied:

a. Ignore all service under the age of 18 and over the age of 65.

b. For each completed year of service between the ages of 18 and 22 the employee is entitled to half a week's pay.

c. For each completed year of service between the ages of 22 and 41 the employee receives one week's pay.

d. For each completed year of service between the ages of 41 and 64 the employee receives one and a half week's pay.

e. The above provisions are limited to a maximum of 20 years reckonable service.

f. The statutory maximum amount of redundancy pay is limited to £210 per week (1995/6). This sum is usually revised annually. However, many employers offer terms which are considerably more generous.

EXAMPLES

1. Stan, aged 36, has worked for his employer for 8 years and earns £450 per week, and should be entitled to the following:

Completed years of service: age 28 to 36 = 8 years

8 years × £210 = £1,680 statutory minimum redundancy payment

2. Mary, aged 50, who has worked for her employer since the age of 16 and earns £200 per week, should be entitled to the following:

Completed years of service: age 16 to 20: 0

Age 20 to 41: 21 years × £200 × 1 = £4,200

Age 41 to 50: 9 years × £200 × 1.5 = £2,700

Total = £6,900

BUT because only 20 years of service are reckonable the amount should be reduced so that:

9 years × 200 × 1.5 = £2,700

11 years × 200 × 1 = £2,200

Revised Total = £4,700

3. Jane has worked for her employer for 10 years. She is 41 and earns £370 per week. Her contract of employment contains a clause to the effect that if she is made redundant she will be entitled to 1.5 weeks pay for each completed year of service.

Completed years of service: age 31 to 41 = 10 years

10 years × 1.5 × £370 = £5,550 redundancy payment

6.3   The right to notice   A person who is to be made redundant is entitled to the appropriate statutory or contractual period of notice (see chapter 7 for details). Compensation may be paid for lack of notice. Where an employer fails to give either adequate notice or suitable compensation for the lack of notice then the dismissal shall be deemed to be unfair. The employee may also apply to an industrial tribunal for a protective award (described above). Even if the employee is not required to attend the workplace during the period of notice, she is still entitled to be paid for that period.

6.4   If the employer is able to offer alternative work then the employee has a right to a trial period without putting at risk her redundancy pay   This right, which stems from the 1978 Act, is designed to allow the employee to see if the new job is suitable and also to allow the employer time to assess the suitability of the employee. It is usual for the trial period to be four weeks but the Act does allow this period to be extended. The Act accepts that for many jobs four weeks is too short a time upon which to make an informed judgement. The length of the trial period should be agreed before the start. If at (or before) the end the employee decides that the job is not suitable then she is still entitled to redundancy pay as described under 6.2 above.

7. Redundancy and the Part-time Worker

Redundancy laws for part-time workers have now been harmonized with their full-time counterparts. This means that those working between 8 and 16 hours a week will no longer have to wait until they have five years' continuous service before they have protection of employment. This ruling in the House of Lords in December 1994 came after a long campaign by the Equal Opportunities Commission, who claimed that Britain's law discriminated against the female workers who made up the vast majority of the part-time workforce. In most respects part-time workers now enjoy the same rights as their full-time counterparts.

8. Selection for Redundancy

To avoid claims for unfair dismissal it is important that proper criteria are devised by the employer and redundancy properly undertaken. It is rare for an industrial tribunal to be critical of the criteria for determining redundancy so long as they can be shown to be fair, objective and based on valid reasoning. Such criteria might include length of service, experience and record of attendance, or indeed involve the use of more sophisticated criteria. Whatever criteria are used it is vital that they can be verified by reference to, for instance, company records, and that they are applied consistently across the whole company. In the case of an individual claiming unfair selection (at an industrial tribunal)

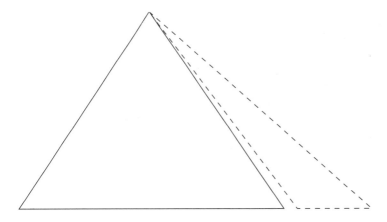

Figure 13.1
Downsizing the
organization

the employer must be able to demonstrate that the employee was selected for redundancy on a basis that is fair and for which evidence is available.

For many years a common basis for selection for redundancy was 'last in first out'. This is a clear and simple way, and employees chosen using this method could be confident that they had indeed been selected 'fairly'. Additionally it would be easy to provide evidence to demonstrate the fairness of the selection. However, many employers realize that using such a method is too crude and simplistic. It is likely that staff chosen using this method would be younger and therefore the employees left would have a higher average age. This could lead to future manpower planning problems as large numbers of the workforce would be retiring in a compressed space of time. Further, there is little evidence to suggest that those employees left would be the 'best'. Many organizations see the benefit of using more complex methods for selection for redundancy. Such methods would have the aim of 'taking a slice off the organization' (see figure 13.1) and yet retaining its integrity in terms of structure, age mix, and so forth.

Today, many employers are concerned to make redundant those members of staff whose contributions are least valuable. They will apply such criteria as the *standard of performance* and *level of skill* as the basis for their selection. Although these might seem to be a clear enough criteria, the expectation that the employer be able to justify its decision by reference to, for instance, company documentation, makes the process far more difficult. Records from past performance appraisals might be used to justify the selection. However, many appraisal schemes are not intended to make such fine discrimination between the levels of performance of individuals. In other words, they were not designed to be used as a basis for selection for redundancy. Unless the employer takes great care, then, it may prove to be very difficult to use existing company records to decide who should be made redundant. Many employers will use the standard of performance and level of skill as only two of the criteria upon which their final decision will be made.

Some employers would wish to consider an employee's *disciplinary or absence record* when deciding who should be made redundant. If such criteria are to be used it is vital that the employer has a clear policy concerning attendance, time-keeping and discipline, and that it has been communicated to the employees. Again it is important that absence or time-keeping is considered over an appropriate period of time. It could be considered unfair to look at only the last three months' time-keeping, when in the case of a long-serving employee, time-keeping had been excellent for the first 12 years of service but had slipped a little in recent weeks. It is clear that by choosing to look at time-keeping over different time-scales the employer will advantage or disadvantage different groups of employees. Where absence is to be used as a criterion all the factors should be considered: for example, the employer should know why staff were absent on any particular occasion, and the frequency of any absence should be considered as well as the total length of time involved. There is also the added problem of deciding which time-scale to take for consideration.

Many employers will choose to use more complex criteria, recognizing the fact that the skills and attitudes previously considered appropriate in the organization are no longer adequate for its new or proposed shape, structure, culture or technology. The 'new' organization that emerges from the redundancies may well need people with different skills and attitudes, and therefore the criteria for redundancy selected may well reflect not only good past performance but more importantly the potential to do well in the future. The employer may then use techniques to match the attributes of the employees against the requirements of the new jobs. This might include interviews or psychological tests, and may involve the use of assessment-centre techniques. The assessors would need to aggregate the information gained from both the analysis of past performance and the assessment of future potential to produce an objective assessment of each employee, and thereby make a decision as to who should be retained and who made redundant.

Employers should avoid the temptation to dismiss part timers first. It is possible that to do so will be indirectly discriminatory. This is because in most organizations by far the majority of part-time employees are women. It is important that employers consider the likely impact of their redundancy criteria on different groups within the workforce: men, women and different ethnic groups. It is also increasingly difficult to justify age as a basis for redundancy. Industrial tribunals are finding in favour of employees who are made redundant because they are close to retirement age. In effect the tribunals are frowning on the practice of age discrimination.

When the criteria for selection have been decided they should be applied fairly, consistently and reasonably. Decisions made should also be transparent, that is, it should be possible for somebody else to apply the same criteria and come up with the same decisions. The employer should also bear in mind the need to ensure that the employees who are left are those who have the talents and skills to ensure the future viability of the organization.

Lambeth Council has used competence tests as an aid to selection for redundancy in its Income Division, which is responsible for the collection of Council Taxes. The tests were designed to test people's ability to perform job-specific tasks such as calculating a council tax bill, and were supplemented by individual interviews. The reorganization of the Income Division has seen a fall in staff numbers from 260 to about 180, and average salaries fall from £19,000 to £14,000. (Reported in *People Management*, 24 Aug. 1995.)

Elida Gibbs, the toiletries manufacturer, has selected staff for redundancy by assessing the degree to which they have certain core skills. The tests, which were agreed with the union USDAW, were designed to test literacy, numeracy and the ability to analyse information. Scores here made up 40 per cent of overall score, with the rest coming from attendance records and length of service. Of 235 staff assessed in this way 46 were made redundant. (Reported in *Personnel Today*, 25 Oct. 1995.)

9. Voluntary Redundancy

In many instances employers will try to meet the requirement for reducing the size of the workforce by inviting staff to volunteer for redundancy. This is likely to be attractive to those employees who are close to the normal age of retirement and would welcome the opportunity to leave early. As an inducement to leave the employer might wish to offer the employee a better than standard redundancy deal plus an enhancement to the employee's pension such that she is not disadvantaged by retiring early. The other major group of workers who might choose to volunteer to be made redundant are those who have the skills and initiative to find other employment. Such employees might welcome the opportunity to receive the lump-sum payment that might be offered to them as an inducement to leave, knowing full well that they are quickly able to return to employment. It is likely, however, that such employees are also those that the employer would wish to retain within the organization, for it is probably they who have the skills most needed to ensure the future success of the company. It is unlikely that the less able employee will volunteer for redundancy knowing that she will find difficulty in obtaining alternative employment. A danger is that those who volunteer for redundancy and are not selected may well become disillusioned and seek alternative employment anyway.

10. Outplacement Consultants

Many organizations employ outplacement consultants to assist redundant staff in finding new employment. Upon finding that they are no longer required by their present employer, many employees suffer considerable loss of confidence and find it difficult to conceive that any other organization would find them suitable for employment. For many employees it will have been a number of years since they last applied for a job, and they may have little or no idea of how to go about the process of finding employment.

It is the task of the outplacement consultant to assist redundant employees to reconsider their career options. For some this will simply involve helping them to identify suitable alternative employers, while others will need help in identifying training needs and how they might be met before they consider rejoining the labour market. For yet others it might involve trying to apply their skills to areas of industry that they had previously not considered. Many employees will need considerable assistance in the techniques of applying for a job and will benefit from advice on how to complete application forms, prepare CVs and write letters of application. If redundant employees are fortunate enough to be called for interview for a position, the outplacement consultant can offer advice on how to prepare for the occasion, perhaps including video-recorded practice interviews which can then be analysed for strengths and weaknesses.

Many employers take great pride in the fact that their employees are well trained and highly skilled. Even though they are no longer required within their organization, with the help of an outplacement consultant they can (hopefully) readily find employment in a new organization elsewhere.

> A report into employment in the banking and finance industry recommended that banks replace job security for their staff with employability: that is, the idea that although banks can no longer guarantee a job for life they can at least make their staff 'employable' when they are faced with redundancy. The report recommends that as job insecurity increases in the sector employers must ensure that staff are better trained and provide learning facilities, career development programmes, open-learning facilities and job rotation. Employees, too, should be encouraged to see the benefits of proactivity and take greater responsibility for their own development. (Create 1995)

BROOKE AND CO. LTD

Brooke and Co. Ltd is a chain of stationers, booksellers and news-agents operating across the eastern counties and the East Midlands of the UK. They have 72 stores, 4 regional offices, 4 distribution depots and a head office. Each store has a manager who reports to a district manager (of which there are 14), and each district is part of a region of which there are 4 of approximately equal geographic size. Each region is managed by a regional manager. The firm is aware that they are operating in an increasingly competitive market, and a report by a firm of management consultants was critical of the organization and management of the company. As a consequence the company has decided to reduce the size of its management workforce by amalgamating the districts and the regions to form new larger sectors. Sector managers would have less of a line management role than their predecessors and be more concerned with groups of products, strategic planning and identifying new business opportunities. Additionally, a number of smaller, less profitable branches are to be closed, while others are to be merged and put under the control of a single manager. In future branch managers will communicate more directly with head office and be more individually responsible for the successful management of their stores. This means that the role of the branch manager would be significantly revised. In total it was estimated that up to 15 branch managers and 4 district or regional managers will lose their jobs.

The senior management of the company recognized that it would be inappropriate simply to make those managers whose stores were to close redundant. They considered that some of their best employees would be lost using this method. Moreover, managers were moved regularly from one store to another, and some have been in their present position for only a few weeks. None stayed in any one store longer than 5 years and sometimes less than 2 years. Instead they decided to retain those employees who were best able to take the new structure forward and make it work successfully.

Brooke decided to use a rigorous selection process to identify the best candidates for the new jobs, and use every piece of information available to them as an aid to selection. The company also decided from the outset that the new structure, its aims and the methods by which those who would manage it would be selected should be communicated to all staff. They were acutely aware that during the period of restructuring normal business would have to continue and all steps possible should be taken to maintain morale at a reasonable level.

First, the company, with the aid of a consultant, produced a person specification which identified the key skills and attributes required to perform the new positions. Information was then sought from employee records of evidence of the possession of such skills and attributes. The company used a very comprehensive performance appraisal system for its managers and 3 years' records were accessed to identify trends and to produce a rank order of managers. The company also tracked the performance of managers from the performance of the stores they managed. Each store was given an annual sales and performance target and performance against target was monitored for each of the last 5 years. Store performance figures were then allocated to each responsible manager. While such methods produced evidence of good past performance the company wanted a closer correlation with predicted future performance before making its final decisions. Here the consultant assisted in the development and validation of a series of specially constructed tests designed to assess the managers against the skills and attributes previously identified.

The tests included a detailed and structured interview with each candidate designed to question the managers' aspirations, motivations, flexibility, training needs and willingness to relocate. The managers were also put through a number of psychological tests designed to assess their intellectual potential and personality type.

The information thus produced was then weighted to produce a rank order of the managers in terms of the skills and attributes required. Those candidates who possessed the required skills and attributes were retained and appointed to the new positions. Those who did not were made redundant. A firm of outplacement consultants were retained to assist those made redundant to find new employment.

TASK

Do you consider that the techniques used by the company would have produced the 'correct' selection for redundancy? Justify your answer. How else might the process have been undertaken?

QUESTIONS FOR FURTHER CONSIDERATION

1. What do you consider to be the true costs of redundancy, and how can they be minimized?

2. You are the personnel manager of MNI Ltd and the board has decided that in order for the company to survive, the payroll must be cut by 25 per cent. This is the equivalent of 275 members of the workforce. The board has asked for advice on how it should proceed. Outline the appropriate methodology for the consideration of the board.

3. Jim is employed as an accounts clerk by ALU Ltd. He is 27 years old and has worked for the company 6 years. Due to economic downturn the management have decided that Jim's section is overstaffed by one; and Jim, as the employee in that section with the shortest length of service, is told that he has been selected for redundancy. He is given a week's notice and two weeks pay by way of compensation. (a) Is the reason for the redundancy fair? (b) Is the calculation for notice and compensation correct? Advise Jim.

4. Redundancy is often seen as a solver of problems (high costs, excess capacity, etc.). However, redundancy can lead to new problems. What do you consider these problems might be and how could they be overcome?

5. 'Last in, first out is always the cleanest, fairest way of selecting staff for redundancy. It gets it over with quickly and minimizes future problems.' Consider this view recently expressed by the HR Manager of a large insurance company.

•REFERENCES•

Advisory, Conciliation, and Arbitration Service
REDUNDANCY HANDLING
London, ACAS.

Armstrong M (1992)
A HANDBOOK OF PERSONNEL MANAGEMENT PRACTICE
London, Kogan Page.

Corby S (1993)
One More Step for the Civil Service
Personnel Management, Aug.

Create (1995)
REDISCOVERING JOB SECURITY: EVOLVING EMPLOYER–EMPLOYEE RELATIONSHIPS IN THE FINANCE SECTOR
Tunbridge Wells, Create.

Goodsir J (1993)
A NEW BEAT IN THE POLICE FORCE
Personnel Management, Dec.

Hogg C (1988)
OUTPLACEMENT (Factsheet 4)
Personnel Management, April.

Lanz K (1988)
HIRING AND FIRING: EMPLOYING AND MANAGING PEOPLE
London, Longman / NatWest.

Pickard J (1993)
OUTPLACEMENT AND THE RUN-UP TO REDUNDANCY
Personnel Management, April.

Thomas M (1994)
WHAT YOU NEED TO KNOW ABOUT BUSINESS PROCESS RE-ENGINEERING
Personnel Management, Jan.

UK Department of Employment booklets:
PROCEDURES FOR HANDLING REDUNDANCIES
FACING REDUNDANCY? – TIME OFF FOR JOB HUNTING OR TO ARRANGE TRAINING
EMPLOYMENT RIGHTS ON THE TRANSFER OF AN UNDERTAKING
REDUNDANCY PAYMENTS

Wood J (1990)
HOW ORGANIZATIONS CAN SURVIVE REDUNDANCY
Personnel Management, Dec.

•CHAPTER•

14

EMPLOYEE WELFARE

AS A RESULT OF STUDYING THIS CHAPTER YOU SHOULD BE ABLE TO:

- Consider the traditional and emerging roles for the welfare function.

- Assess the range of welfare tasks performed within organizations and consider their costs and benefits.

- Appreciate for whom welfare is provided and who stands to benefit from it.

- Evaluate some of the legal, moral and ethical problems that must be considered by organizations as they consider their welfare provision.

1. Introduction

The 'welfare' origins of personnel / HR are explained at some length in chapter 1, and will not be reiterated here. What is important to appreciate, however, is that many employers' perception of welfare has changed radically in recent years, embracing all of the new challenges and stresses of modern working life. Moxon (1943: 64) listed the following as the welfare responsibilities of the personnel manager:

Administration of canteen policy.

Sick club and benevolent and savings scheme.

Long service grants.

Pension or superannuation funds or leaving grants.

Granting of loans.

Legal aid.

Advice on individual problems.

Assistance to employees in transport, housing, billeting, shopping and other problems.

Provision of social and recreation facilities.

Some of the tasks listed above may be familiar to the HR manager of the 1990s, others will not. This is not to imply, however, that the welfare function has diminished, for it has not, and like many other tasks performed by organizations, it has instead altered radically. Today many Employee Welfare Departments (or Welfare Officers or HR Managers with welfare responsibilities) direct their activities towards improving the 'health' of the individual in order that they might improve the 'health' of the organization. The increasing recognition that organizational health is associated with good business performance is leading more and more organizations to reappraise how it is that they can help develop individuals' physical and mental well-being in order that they might perform their duties to the best of their ability.

The traditional role of the welfare worker has been one of independence. That is, although employed by the organization, the welfare worker has worked with individual employees in a confidential manner, not reporting the results of their work except in a general or aggregate manner. An example of this might be that of a counsellor employed by an organization to work with its employees. The counsellor would not be expected to report on conversations held with individual employees; nor should she or he do so if asked. On the other hand, the counsellor might report matters in an aggregate form. For example: 'During 1995 I saw 75 employees who required in total 250 hours of counselling. This represented a 10 per cent increase on the previous year.' The counsellor might also give some form of breakdown of their work. For example: 'Of those employees requiring counselling, 45 per cent were women and 55 per cent were men.' Other ways in which information might be broken down would include common types of problems seen, correlations with workplace events (e.g. redundancy), trends and changes. Such aggregations and breakdowns would be of value to the management of the organization, but should not go against the principle of confidentiality.

More recently, employers have sought to develop a more proactive role for the welfare function; they have seen benefit in putting in place measures, procedures and opportunities for employees to avoid some of the potential pitfalls into which a stressful job might lead them, or to help them cope better should the need arise. Thus many employers will offer their staff advice on time management, healthy eating, drug and alcohol abuse, general health and fitness, and so forth.

This chapter considers the developing role of the welfare function, looking at both the traditional and emergent roles outlined above.

2. The Traditional Welfare Function

An examination of the personnel books of the last fifty years will show that a considerably larger proportion of the space of a book was devoted to welfare issues in the earlier years of the period than has been the case in more recent times. That Personnel (and HR) has been trying to distance itself from welfare there can be no doubt. Armstrong (1992: 773) admits as much:

> the personnel management fraternity has spent many years trying to shake off its association with what it, and others, like to think of as at best peripheral and at worst redundant welfare activities.

Welfare has had a difficult ride in recent years, in which it has had to justify its existence like any other part of a modern organization. The case against it critically depends upon the degree to which it is considered that an organization should be prepared to involve itself in the out-of-work affairs of its staff, or to provide services that are already provided by the state. Additionally, there is little evidence to demonstrate that the provision of welfare services will add to the motivation of the workforce. As Eggert (1990: 172) has said:

> It [welfare] is a topic which is essentially 'soft'. It can be observed, experienced and enjoyed; but its effectiveness may be more difficult to measure. In the world of human resources management there are remuneration systems, succession plans, appraisal techniques, and communication strategies, but where are the welfare systems, plans, techniques or strategies? Welfare is not like that.

Those who advocate welfare provision point to the fact that when an employee has a problem, whether it stems from work or home, it will inevitably impact upon the workplace performance of that individual. That is, the private problems and worries of employees can have a real impact of the quality of workplace performance. Additionally, many individuals' problems arise out of work, or indeed may be directly or indirectly caused by their work – for example, stress or fear of redundancy.

If it is accepted that individuals' problems can affect their work performance, then it can equally be accepted that such problems will also come to the notice of employers, whether via deterioration in performance, increased absence, poor time-keeping or in some other manifestation. Alternatively, an employee might choose to explain to the manager what it is that is causing their worry, and ask for help. Some employers might decide that the management of such situations is best left to the discretion of individual managers, while others will see benefit in a centralized or coordinated response to all such problems. If there is not a coordinated response many managers will look to senior managers to provide guidelines advising them how best to help the individuals concerned. Some managers might feel that they are not adequately trained, or do not have the time, to provide support to their distressed subordinates. The benefits of a coordinated response are that the organization might be able to employ specialists to whom distressed, worried or concerned employees can be referred. This takes the immediate burden off the shoulders of line managers, allowing them to concentrate on their own jobs. Moreover, a relatively small sum of money spent on welfare services might well save money in the longer run, if it allows employees and their managers to give greater concentration to their duties.

Hackett (1991: 72) lists a range of tasks that might quite justifiably be given the 'welfare' tag, and while not exhaustive, this list does provide a very useful indication of the 'rag, tag and bob-tail' assortment of services which sit beneath the welfare umbrella:

- Recognize and help deal with the stresses and strains of employees' lives – through providing personal counselling.

- Ensure that their people have a healthy diet – through providing low-cost, nutritious meals in a well-run staff restaurant or canteen.

- Help keep their people fit – through providing exercise and recreational facilities for employees' use.

- Help keep their people healthy – through regular medical checks, health-care provision and health education, and anti-smoking campaigns – and visit them when they are sick.

- Contribute to the general well-being of their people – through free or subsidized hairdressing, chiropody and other personal services.

- Help people with financial difficulties – through the provision of company loans.

- Help people with particular problems – like ex-offenders, alcoholics, drug abusers, and those who are HIV positive.

- Help people through potentially difficult transitions – like returning to work after having a family, or preparing for retirement.

- Say 'thank you' to people, not just for specific tasks but also for their loyalty and commitment, through long-service awards and leaving gifts.

- Contribute to the well-being of the local community – through allowing company facilities to be used by local residents or by seconding staff to help with community projects.

Given the range and breadth of the tasks listed it is perhaps not surprising that personnel and HR managers have attempted to distance themselves from welfare. It is certainly the case that it is not glamorous, nor is the fact that if done well it is unlikely to elicit praise from senior management, nor often from the recipients. So welfare may not be 'good' for HR people (that may say a lot about the 'baggage' that is carried by personnel and HRM), but there is little doubt that welfare is good for employees, and probably by association, good for the organization in general.

Goss (1994: 124) correctly identifies the reluctance of many HRM commentators to acknowledge the role of welfare within the discipline, citing the reason as being the wish to distance themselves from traditional personnel specialists who too often are caricatured as being 'welfarist' in orientation and hence lacking real business credibility. Often this is also associated with the inability of welfare to relate to wider business and organizational issues. Goss identifies three 'welfare rationales' which he claims limit the ability of welfare to get closer to the realities of business:

Legalistic-reactive: Too often welfare policies have been driven by forces external to the organization (for example, health and safety), and have been seen as an additional cost to be borne by the organization rather than something that is integral to it.

Corporate-conscious: Emerged out of the social reform movement of the nineteenth century, and the welfare workers who were precursors to the Institute of Personnel Management (now of course the IPD). Here welfare played the role of lubricant, working between what was seen as the opposing forces of labour and capital.

Company-paternalistic: Closely identified in the UK with the actions of Quaker companies of the last century, who saw it their duty to provide for their workforce housing, some health care, education for children and other rewards which were often associated with encouraging the 'correct' forms of behaviour in their employees. What was deemed to be 'correct' was often determined by religious or moral considerations.

3. New Models of Welfare

Goss (1994) has identified new trends in welfare which he has summarized in the term 'tough love'. This he sees as a form of welfare driven more by the needs of the organization and less by wider social, religious or moral considerations. Tough love is concerned with promoting appropriate attitudes and behaviour in employees, and is (Goss 1994: 124):

> about the benefits and services which employees want and value and which simultaneously link strategically with the needs of the organization by enhancing performance.

New welfare models must also take account of new forms of work and new work situations: for example, home and tele-working, the growth of temporary and part-time work and the greater emphasis on monitoring the performance of the individual. Welfare, too, must be a proactive and dynamic area of human resource management.

It is clear that new models of welfare cannot entirely supplant what went before. Employers cannot avoid their considerable (and growing) responsibilities for the health and safety of their employees. Nor can welfare be entirely proactive, for it is not possible to envisage or anticipate every possible welfare-type situation to which some rapid response must be made. However, given that, where, how and in what form is this new welfare or 'tough love' making itself felt? A number of examples are given below.

3.1 Time management

Many organizations recognizing the increasing workloads being borne by their employees and are offering them the opportunity to consider carefully their use of time. This so-called 'time management training' is a popular way of re-assessing priorities, objectives and planning. In essence it offers training in self-management. While not always the responsibility of a welfare officer to arrange, it is an excellent example of where roles can overlap. For example, the absence of time management training might lead to an increase in stress, sickness and other symptoms of work overload. The introduction of time management training is an example of proactive welfare.

3.2 Promoting good health

The provision of a staff canteen that offers a range of nutritious meals is a good start, but could be considered to be by itself insufficient to promote the good health of the workforce. Many employers will be proactive in trying to influence their employees to adopt healthier lifestyles. This can take a number of forms:

Healthy eating   Providing employees with not only access to good food via staff canteens and restaurants, but also providing information, education and support for employees to eat a better and more balanced diet generally. The link between poor diet and poor health is well researched and well documented. It is clearly in the economic best interests of the employer to have a well-fed workforce. The results should be seen in lower absence and sickness rates.

Smoking   Many organizations do not permit smoking at work. This is to provide a cleaner, healthier and more pleasant environment for all, not to mention to reduce the risk of fire caused by carelessly discarded cigarettes. The link between smoking and ill health is also well known, and once again employers have a vested interest in encouraging their employees to give up smoking. The costs of ill-health caused by smoking are, after all, often borne by the employer, in terms of sickness and early retirement.

Employers should be aware that non-smokers working in close proximity to smokers can also suffer ill-health. This 'passive-smoking' can lead to court actions for compensation to employees whose health has been damaged by working with smokers in a poorly ventilated environment. This link is well known, well documented and it is unlikely that an employer would be able to avoid liability for such a claim.

Physical fitness   Many of us are employed in sedentary occupations, and within our day-to-day routine take little exercise. Again the benefits of exercise are well known, and even a moderate amount of exercise can, if taken regularly, offer considerable protection against many common and life-threatening ailments. In the past, many employers have offered extensive sports and social facilities for their employees. However, in the main these have been taken up by the young, who might play for the company football team, for instance. While this is not to be discouraged, modern policies concentrate on promoting the fitness of all employees, and not just the young and athletic. To this end gymnasia, fitness suites, aerobics and yoga classes could be beneficial. All are of equal benefit to all age groups and can be enjoyed by both men and women. Not all employers have either the space or resources to provide dedicated fitness facilities for staff. Instead, some are able to purchase their staff free or discounted access to public or private leisure and fitness facilities.

3.3 Drug abuse

In recent years the question of drug and substance misuse has also become a reality for the employer, with many choosing to introduce policies for their control and management. Not least of all because of the problems of definition, there is little hard evidence to indicate how much of a problem drug abuse is to employers, but given trends in society at large it is fair to assume that it is a problem that is growing in significance and as such should warrant positive action. When considering introducing policies to combat drug abuse, employers must consider a number of factors; for example:

What impact is drug or substance misuse likely to have in the workplace? The answer to this question will largely depend upon the sort of business concerned, whether airline, retailer, etc.

Should employees be regularly tested for evidence of drug or alcohol misuse?

If yes, what legal and ethical problems does this present?

If a testing programme is introduced, what is to be done with those employees who fail the tests?

Random drug testing is accepted practice in the world of sport, where the presence of a drug may indicate that a competitor wishes to attempt to enhance performance by foul means. But the presence of traces of drug in the blood or urine of most employees is likely to lead most employers to assume that the employee may well suffer poorer performance and may even be a hazard or danger to him or herself, to colleagues, to customers or the public at large.

The rationale for drug testing employees is that drug abuse can cost employers dear; indeed, employers are likely to be vicariously liable for the actions of an employee who causes an accident while under the influence of drugs. This may be enough for many employers to begin testing programmes. However, the employer should be sure what it is that they are testing for. Are they concerned to penalize the occasional or weekend cannabis user, or are they more concerned with abusers of so-called 'hard' drugs? Do they only wish to penalize those drug users whose use is likely to impair their ability to perform their duty to a satisfactory standard, and who is to be the judge? Can employees legitimately refuse to take a drug test, and what should be the response of the employer to those who do? It should also be remembered that at any one time a significant proportion of the workforce will be taking prescription medicines to address their ailments. A number of commonly used prescription drugs (and over-the-counter medicines) can cause drowsiness or otherwise impair work performance. Are such drug users also to be penalized under the testing regime? This question can be complicated further by the fact that although many people will take their prescription medicine for a short period of time to alleviate or cure a particular illness, many others are long-term users and may well be dependent upon such drugs as valium or mogodon, which are both sedatives, and therefore induce a state of drowsiness within the taker. This is not a simple issue, and faced with the questions outlined here, the employer may choose to leave well alone for fear of what might be discovered! Further, Sigman (1993: 12) warns:

In many cases taking disciplinary action or instigating counselling as a result of a positive result could be highly inappropriate and may have dire industrial relations implications.

What is far more common, probably far more acceptable, and less fraught with legal and other difficulties, is testing after an accident – after all we are all familiar with the idea of the police breathalysing all parties to a road traffic accident. However, for many this is closing the stable door after the horse has bolted, and a carefully planned and regular programme of drug testing is sensible to avoid accidents wherever possible. In reality, however, only a minority of employers need to have such a rigorous policy of testing. Such employers might include airlines, railway operators and others where employees have responsibility for large pieces of machinery which if misused can have severe implications.

3.4   Alcohol misuse

Drug testing has a certain fashionable ring about it but most experts would claim that a far greater problem, affecting many more employees, is often ignored. This of course is alcohol abuse. Alcohol abuse is often overlooked, or simply made a joke of with little account taken of the effects that it may have on workplace performance, absenteeism, or longer-term employee health.

There is evidence that attitudes towards alcohol have hardened over recent years. For example, fewer employers are allowing alcohol to be consumed on their premises, fewer are offering alcoholic drinks in staff restaurants, and more are giving their employees guidelines on social drinking (drinking outside of working time). Some employers also insert a clause in contracts of employment explaining their position on alcohol, its consumption and the risks that employees run in flouting the terms of the contract. Although most common in the contracts of those responsible for the operation of public-use transport vehicles, they are not uncommon in the contracts of white-collar staff.

A concern for some employers has been the state in which some employees arrive for work. This means not only the employee who arrives suffering the ill effects of last night's over-imbibing, but also (for instance) shift workers who arrive for a 2-to-10 shift having consumed a hearty 'liquid lunch' in a nearby hostelry.

Policies towards alcohol abuse tend towards counselling and support, or towards punishment, or a combined 'carrot and stick' approach. Once again the need for a clear, thought-through policy is of paramount importance. It is appropriate to consider drug abuse and alcohol abuse within the same policy – alcohol is after all a drug, with many similar effects to other so-called 'recreational' drugs, and some hard drugs. Introducing such a policy may be difficult, particularly in those organizations which have traditions of tolerance towards heavy consumption of alcohol. Such industries might include journalism, merchant shipping and the City. In industries such as these, introducing new policies will need to be done with consultation, and the policies must be seen to apply equally to all employees regardless of level, grade or length of service. Where a culture of alcohol tolerance has developed and become embedded, reducing or removing it can take some time and cause some pain.

The charity Alcohol Concern and the magazine *Personnel Today* have conducted regular surveys into employers' attitudes to alcohol and the workplace. The results of the most recent survey (reported in *Personnel Today*, 6 June 1995) show that 65 per cent of personnel directors and 70 per cent of personnel managers think alcohol abuse is a problem in their organization. The following were also among the results revealed (all figures taken from the Alcohol Concern/*Personnel Today* 'Alcohol at Work' survey, published in *Personnel Today*, 6 June 1995):

53% of employers have a policy encouraging those employees with an alcohol problem to seek help.

44% of firms offer time off for treatment.

38% of firms refer those employees with a problem to an outside agency.

38% have written guidelines on alcohol abuse.

The major problems caused by alcohol abuse were identified as:

Absenteeism	62%
Poor performance	57%
Lateness	50%
Long-term sickness	20%
Retirement or loss of staff	14%

Among the responses taken by companies to alcohol problems are:

Referral for treatment	59%
Warning on future conduct	48%
Prolonged counselling	42%
Informal approach	42%
Disciplinary action	37%
Dismissal	18%

Employers must think through carefully their response to evidence of alcohol misuse on the part of employees. It is better to have a policy before it is needed than to wait (as so often happens) for a particular event to trigger the review. In considering its policy the organization should decide whether it wishes to punish (use the provisions of the disciplinary procedure) or help (offer the employee guidance and support to enable the problem to be beaten). Most employers choose the latter course of action within a framework of the former. That is, they lay down and communicate to their employees what it is they expect by way of standards of behaviour with regard to alcohol, and offer support to those who consider they might have problems meeting those standards. The support is offered to deter the 'problem' drinker from attempting to keep the problem hidden, and therefore possibly causing greater problems in the longer run. This approach is consistent with the ideas of 'tough love' outlined earlier: the employer sets down clear guidelines as to what is expected of the employee, while at the same time offering support to those who may experience difficulty in meeting the standard. An important point is that the employee is expected to come forward for help and support to address the problem; this might be by individual initiative, or by the recommendation of a colleague or supervisor. Those employees who choose not to benefit from the support offered by the employer will instead be subject to the disciplinary procedure. An employee with a drink problem who falls foul of the disciplinary procedure might find that one of the conditions attached to the disciplinary warning will be a requirement to take full advantage of any support systems offered by the employer. To fail to do so may place the employee's job in jeopardy.

3.5 Stress

Workplace stress has not always received a sympathetic hearing. For instance, Arroba and James (1994: 9) give the example of increased stress being seen as a 'badge of office':

> The idea of stress as a badge of office is caricatured by the image of the 'two-ulcer executive'. Where this idea is prevalent, two ulcers, or some other symptom of stress, have the same sort of status as a larger company car. Suffering from too much pressure is seen as demonstrating to the world the high status of the manager. There is an assumption that as the level in the hierarchy increases, so should the pressure. If this is the case, the implicit argument runs, the manifestations of pressure should also increase.

It is of course often said that some amount of stress is good for us, and as individuals that amount of stress can vary considerably. The focus of much research on stress has looked at the relationship between pressure and stress. Pressure is something we all experience as a result of our everyday lives. It is caused by work, our home life, as well as our social lives and activities. Pressure represents the aggregate of all of these demands made upon us. Stress is our response to the pressures that bear upon us, particularly if the level of pressure is inappropriate. The word 'inappropriate' is used intentionally, instead of (for instance) 'too great'. Research shows that individuals who have too little to do, for example the unemployed, often suffer considerably higher levels of stress than those in comparatively high-pressure employment.

Why is stress a problem that should concern the employer? It is often said that we live in an advanced, high-technology, high-speed world, yet possess the constitutions of our caveman ancestors – to whom stress was an immediate response to imminent danger (for example, being chased by an animal) which heightened our awareness and allowed us to decide quickly whether to 'fight or take flight'. Hence our constitutions are such that stress is essentially there as a short-term measure to help us overcome immediate problems. Today we rarely face 'fight or flight' situations; instead we are faced with a more persistent level of pressure with which our bodies must cope and to which they are responding constantly. In some circumstances the body acts as though it were constantly under attack. This long-term use of what is essentially a short-term response mechanism can be very draining on the body's resources, and can lead to ill health. Some of the longer-term manifestations of stress are: heart disease, ulcers, cancer, backache, respiratory problems, and impaired immune systems. In terms of workplace performance, the individual who was able to thrive at one level of pressure might find that either through long-term exposure to pressure or through an increase in pressure, their performance will deteriorate markedly. This might manifest itself in terms of (for example) reduced concentration, panic attacks, working more slowly or making more mistakes.

The nature of work today is such that we are all expected to work under a greater level of pressure than has ever been the case before. Most aspects of modern business thinking build in greater pressure for the employee: for example, job insecurity, delayering, devolving responsibility, rapid technological change – all contribute to our feeling of being under pressure.

The employer can do much to anticipate the problems which might arise from this situation. For example, policies can be instituted to raise awareness of stress and stress-related problems, individuals can be offered training to help them cope with stress, specialists can be employed to offer individual help with problems. It is even possible for stress levels to be audited and key stressors identified, and if possible reduced to an acceptable level.

Dangerously high or excessive levels of stress do not have to be a feature of modern life. While we will all experience periods of acute anxiety in our working lives, caused by, for instance, temporary work overload, workplace problems and so on, policies can be put in place and techniques can be taught to individuals to make the 'two-ulcer executive' a thing of the past.

Research conducted by an academic at Southampton Institute of Higher Education showed that nearly one in three of health-service staff were taking some kind of medication linked to stress. They were also likely to turn to cigarettes and alcohol as a way of coping with the pressures of work. While most of the symptoms of stress found were similar to other industries, their degree was found to be significantly greater. Among the causes of the stress that were identified were:

The financial situation in the NHS.

Lack of consultation over work methods.

An apparent culture gap between managers and other staff.

Worries about keeping up with new developments.

Having to do things which conflicted with their personal values.

(Reported in D. Currie (1993) *Stress Among Health Service Employees*. Southampton Institute of Higher Education, East Park Terrace, Southampton SO9 4WW, UK.)

3.6 HIV/AIDS

AIDS (or Acquired Immune Deficiency Syndrome) is often perceived as one of the great threats to public health of the late twentieth century. The truth is somewhat different. In fact suicide accounts for considerably in excess of ten times more deaths per year than does AIDS. While the trend in AIDS-related deaths is expected to rise in the next few years, equally suicide is still on an upward trend.

Most would agree that AIDS poses a complex challenge for both society and employers. This is bound up with people's prejudice about sufferers, the sexual and drug-use associations of the disease, the challenges to morality and 'normality' that some see it as presenting, and the fact that it is incurable. What is also the case is that people can be HIV+ for many years before developing AIDS. This may give rise to feelings of unease about some workmates which disrupts normal workplace social intercourse. It may also give rise to homophobia. In amongst all of this employers have to go about their normal business with regard to clients, suppliers, staff and so on. Of some reassurance to employers is the fact that in all probability very few will encounter HIV/AIDS; none the less, some employers feel that they need to have a policy towards this emerging issue.

The Health and Safety Executive/UK Department of Employment's booklet *AIDS and the Workplace* (1990) gives an excellent framework for such policies. The booklet emphasizes the fact that it is very unlikely that an employee could contract HIV/AIDS from the workplace unless they come into contact with the body fluids of a carrier. Those most likely to come into such contact would include health-service workers, prison officers and some members of the emergency services. For most of the rest of the workforce such contact is very unlikely. The HSE/D of E booklet recommends that employers give due weight to education in their policies, for example, by reassuring their employees that HIV cannot be caught from cups, toilet seats, or through sharing an office with a carrier. The booklet recommends the following should be integral to any HIV/AIDS policy:

A commitment to employee education, and informing employees how HIV/AIDS is and is not transmitted.

A commitment to non-discrimination.

Assurance of continued employment.

Medical confidentiality.

Employees also should be encouraged to be accommodating to those who are disabled by AIDS.

So, for many employers and employees the issue of HIV/AIDS is unlikely to be an issue of great significance. For those employers whose staff are at greater risk (health workers, etc.), more proactive policies will be needed. These are beyond the scope of this book, but would include the provision of specialist equipment, and taking particular care with cuts and abrasions.

3.7 Workplace counselling

Many managers, knowingly or unknowingly, will find themselves in the role of 'counsellor' to members of their staff. This is not to imply that they realize that they are in, or willingly take, the role; more it is a recognition that as work becomes more challenging and private lives become more complicated the inevitability of employees turning to their managers for 'counselling' is ever greater. The IPM (now IPD) in their *Statement on Counselling in the Workplace* (1992) define counselling as being:

> any activity in the workplace where one individual uses a set of techniques or skills to help another individual take responsibility for and manage their own decision-making whether it is work related or personal.

The critical aspect of counselling is not to 'solve' the individual's problems for them, or even advise them what to do, more it is acting as a facilitator enabling the employee to recognize their own problems, encouraging them to express and recognize the dimensions of the problem, and, through support and questioning, allowing the employee to explore the range of solutions to the problem. Counselling, then, is not about taking over ownership of the individual's problems, but about helping them explore and define the dimensions of the problem and work through possible solutions – helping the individual to recognize, define, accept, explore, consider alternative solutions to, and hopefully overcome their problem. The manager (or counsellor) is merely the facilitator.

Counselling, in all but a rudimentary way, is a skill that needs training and experience. It is beyond the skills of many managers to do much more than be supportive of their staff. Additionally the manager may be in a difficult position. The employee's 'problem' may be in some part of the manager's making; it may reflect new or emerging policies within the organization (i.e. the problem may be coping with change); the manager may also find that they are unable to disentangle their role as supervisor (and therefore agent of the employer) from that of counsellor working with the individual. Indeed, the potential for moral, legal, administrative, managerial and ethical contradiction is considerable. For instance, the employee may share with the manager information in confidence that could be harmful to the position of the organization. Is the manager to respect the position of confidence in which the employee has placed her or consider her wider loyalties to the employer? For these and many other reasons, a number of organizations employ professional counselling staff for their employees. Such staff might be employed full time, part time or on a consultancy basis, or the organization may instead choose to retain the services of a professional counselling service, who will make members of their staff available either in person, or as is often the case, by telephone or a combination of the two: for instance 24-hour telephone cover plus on-site counselling by arrangement.

External and independent counsellors offer a number of advantages for those employers who can afford their services. Most obviously they are experts, who can bring their knowledge and skills to bear upon the problem. Their degree of independence also gives them a considerable advantage. They may have access to specialist counsellors: those who can deal with debt, outplacement, substance abuse or relationship break-up, to name but a few. Additionally they free up time to allow managers and others to do what it is they are paid for.

It is widely assumed that nursing or medical staff have counselling skills and that company doctors or nurses can act as a surrogate counselling service. Often this is a mistaken assumption – relatively few doctors and nurses are trained counsellors and so their response to an employee would probably be a medical response which may not be at all appropriate.

Where organizations have engaged independent counselling services the take-up by employees has been surprisingly high. Pickard (1993) gives the examples of North West Water, who report a take-up of about 12 per cent of employees, while for Ansells Brewery the figure is nearly 10 per cent. Pickard also claims that of contacts made only about 20 per cent related to workplace issues, while the rest concerned personal matters.

Most anecdotal evidence points to the use of counsellors as being a great success. However, finding hard figures to support this claim is far more difficult. Pickard (1993) gives the example of Glaxo Group Research, who claim that following the introduction of counselling staff turnover dropped from 12 per cent in 1990 to 4 per cent in 1993, although neither Pickard nor Glaxo believed there to be a simple causal relationship. The benefits of counselling are far more likely to be found in the longer term, with the development of a physically and mentally healthier workforce, making a better contribution to their organization. Such long-term benefits may be impossible to measure and impossible to correlate with counselling, but this is not to say that they do not exist.

Some would argue that workplace counselling is a waste of money and of unproven benefit, and indeed that many other organizations (such as the Citizens Advice Bureaux, Relate (Marriage Guidance), etc.) exist to help individuals come to terms with their problems. The second and the third points are undoubtedly true, but the case is far from proven. In this modern age people lead complicated and sometimes difficult lives. Employers expect their staff to not only give of their best at all times, but also be willing to take on rapid change and ever greater responsibility while living with uncertainty. It is not surprising if some of us find the challenge a little too difficult on occasions. The disciplinary code is a blunt instrument and not appropriate for many situations in which employees fail to perform adequately. The sensible and judicious use of employee counselling schemes can act to support those employees whose work and personal problems interfere with what otherwise would be very satisfactory levels of performance. The IPM (1992) in their *Statement on Counselling in the Workplace* claim that counselling can act as 'a maintenance factor in the workplace. People, like other factors, have to be maintained if they are to operate effectively.' It is appropriate to think of counselling as a maintenance activity, working to maintain the psychological health of employees. So while dependence upon voluntary and other agencies is an option that employers might consider, others would argue that this leaves too much to chance, and that it is far better to be proactive in this field, and provide the resources and support systems to allow employees to return quickly to their best.

> The Post Office has introduced trauma counselling for those members of staff who have faced armed robberies. Initial trials over a 3-year period saved more than £100,000 per year in reduced sickness and medical retirements. Following a traumatic incident managers are trained to debrief and counsel staff immediately. Later they are offered extra counselling with a welfare officer, occupational health nurse or specialist trauma counsellor.
>
> The Post Office are confident that the scheme, which had start-up costs of about £90,000, has more than paid for itself in a year, and has made a real contribution to the bottom line. (Reported in *Personnel Today*, 25 Oct. 1995.)

3.8 Private health care

The arguments that surround the provision of private health care for employees (and often their families) are complex and bring together issues of both welfare and reward strategies. In many organizations the provision of private health care is seen as a benefit, that is, it is a constituent part of the overall reward package. For others, the decision to support private health care is more welfare based, and consistent with the arguments made elsewhere in this chapter – it is a rational-economic decision, made in order to enhance the ability of the workforce to perform its job. For other employers it straddles reward and welfare. Whatever the rationale, private health care is not cheap, although the bulk purchasing power of large organizations does allow considerable discounts to be negotiated.

Private health care comes in many forms and can be tailored to suit the needs of individual employers. At one level employers might subsidize the cost of purchasing spectacles, dental care and chiropody, while at the other end they may support (for the employee and family) in- and out-patient medical attention. Such a package might include complete annual health checks, screening for common problems, and advice on health, diet and exercise. Those who benefit from private health care may also be able to get prompt treatment for many medical conditions and hence avoid lengthy NHS waiting lists.

In terms of economic contribution, the employee who is ill or awaiting treatment may be functioning at a sub-optimal level (if they are at work at all). This has a cost for the employer. Once treated they can return to their job and work as expected. Private health care can then exist to compensate for the failure of state provision.

4. Conclusion

The previous section was entitled 'New Models of Welfare'. Whether what is described convinces the reader that welfare has taken on a new form is for the reader to judge. What is beyond question is that human resource managers are asking the same tough questions of their welfare policies that they are asking of every other area of their responsibility and influence: 'is it working?', 'can it be done better?', 'is it needed at all?', 'what contribution is it making to the bottom line?' While the author cannot offer any easy answers to these questions – some of the problems have been discussed in this chapter – the concept of welfare has had to move on. The ideas of 'tough love' described earlier sets one frame of reference for welfare, and one that many employers may find attractive. In essence tough love detaches welfare from moral, social or religious connotations and allies it instead to economic considerations: welfare is provided on economic grounds, to help ensure that the workforce are in the best physical and mental shape to perform their duties. Any spin-offs, such as more general improvements in health, are welcome but of superficial importance. Many may find such a hard-nosed model of welfare distasteful; but in many cases the alternative may be no welfare at all.

SOGGS TRANSPORT SERVICES

Soggs Transport is a distribution company based in East Anglia and employing approximately 100 lorry and van drivers. Six months ago one of the drivers was involved in a serious road traffic accident, which resulted in two pedestrians being killed and three others injured. Police investigations showed that the driver was both over the legal limit for blood alcohol and also a regular user of cannabis.

The management of the company, horrified at the accident, have undertaken a full investigation into its policies and procedures regarding staff conduct and discipline. One of the results of this review is the wish to institute drug and alcohol testing for all new applicants for driver positions, random drug and alcohol testing for those in employment, and immediate testing after any accident or other 'incident' giving cause for concern. It is not proposed that tests will be administered to the ten office staff employed.

These proposals have yet to be presented to the drivers and their union representatives, and before they are the management have decided to meet to discuss the proposal, and consider a number of contentious issues:

1. *What is the legal, moral and ethical position of testing potential or actual employees?*

2. Who is to administer the tests?

3. How random will the tests be? (i.e. if the management are 'concerned' about the behaviour of an employee, should they order a test to be carried out, or ask that the tester 'randomly' select the person).

4. If reliable information came to the firm that an employee was using illegal drugs during non-working hours and yet testing showed no trace – what should the company do?

5. If someone tests positive for (say) cannabis use, what action should be taken, and should the police be informed?

6. What limit on blood alcohol should be permitted – the lowest permitted under the law, or a lower limit? Should any evidence of alcohol in the blood be permitted?

7. What support and education should be offered to employees to help them obey the new rules?

8. Should office staff also be tested (and managers); and if 'yes', would the answers to 2, 3 and 4 be the same?

9. If the tests are carried out by an independent and qualified person, who should 'manage' them: who should select testees, who receive results in what form, who act upon results and how, etc.?

10. What would you do if an employee refused to be tested?

TASK
Consider the above questions.

QUESTIONS FOR FURTHER CONSIDERATION

1. Do employers still have responsibility for the general welfare of their employees? How far does this responsibility extend?

2. Many of the welfare resources provided by employers, and described in this chapter, are also provided by the state or voluntary agencies. What are the arguments for the duplication of services? Would employers not be better advised to refer staff with problems to the Citizens Advice Bureau?

3. Some commentators have accused those employers who use random drug testing of trying to impose their values on their employees private as well as their work lives. Do you agree with this claim, and if yes, what rights do you think employers have to interfere in the employees' private lives? As an example, should employers discourage their staff from engaging in dangerous sports such as rugby, horse-riding or rock climbing?

4. Why have personnel and human resource managers attempted to distance themselves from welfare in recent years?

•REFERENCES•

Armstrong M (1992)
A HANDBOOK OF PERSONNEL MANAGEMENT PRACTICE
London, Kogan Page.

Arroba T & James K (1994)
PRESSURE AT WORK
London, McGraw-Hill.

Cooper C (1989)
A Post Office Initiative to Stamp Out Stress
Personnel Management, Aug.

Eggert M (1990)
Welfare at Work, in **MANAGING HUMAN RESOURCES**
Cowling A & Mailer C (eds). London, Edward Arnold.

Goss D (1994)
PRINCIPLES OF HUMAN RESOURCE MANAGEMENT
London, Routledge.

Hackett P (1991)
PERSONNEL: THE DEPARTMENT AT WORK
London, Institute of Personnel Management.

Health and Safety Executive / UK Department of Education (1990)
AIDS AND THE WORKPLACE
London, HSE / D of E.

Humphrey J & Smith P (1991)
LOOKING AFTER CORPORATE HEALTH
London, Pitman.

Institute of Personnel Management (1992)
STATEMENT ON COUNSELLING IN THE WORKPLACE
London, IPM

Mengranhan M (1989)
COUNSELLING: A PRACTICAL GUIDE FOR MANAGERS
London, Institute of Personnel Management.

Moxon G (1943)
FUNCTIONS OF A PERSONNEL DEPARTMENT
London, Institute of Personnel Management.

Newell S (1995)
THE HEALTHY ORGANIZATION
London, Routledge.

O'Reilly H (1995)
Measure of Concern
Personnel Today, June.

Pickard J (1993)
Helping Staff Over Their Problems
Personnel Management Plus, Feb.

Sigman A (1993)
Testing the Water on Drug Misuse
Personnel Management Plus, Sept.

Useful Addresses

Alcoholics Anonymous
PO Box 1
Stonebow House
Stonebow
York YO 1 2NJ

Terence Higgins Trust
52–54 Gray's Inn Road
London WC 1X 8JU

Narcotics Anonymous
PO Box 417
London SW10 ORP

British Association for Counselling
1 Regent Place
Rugby
Warwickshire CV21 2PJ

• CHAPTER •
15

THE INFLUENCE OF EUROPE: IMPLICATIONS FOR UK HUMAN RESOURCE MANAGERS

AS A RESULT OF STUDYING THIS CHAPTER YOU SHOULD BE ABLE TO:

- Consider the pressures bearing upon HR managers as a result of the Single European Market and the apparent convergence that seems to be under way in social and employment legislation.

- Understand the sources of European law and how that law is enacted into British law.

- Appreciate the particular problems that increasing European social and employment legislation poses for the British government and how British employers are reacting.

- Consider how HR policies and practices must develop as the effects of the Single European Market become more apparent and competition for human resources extends Europe-wide.

- Consider how HR policies can complement other corporate policies to improve the competitive position of the organization.

Please note: those readers not familiar with the workings and procedures of the European Union are advised to consult chapter 19 of this book, which offers a detailed explanation of the development of the EU, its institutions, policies and priorities. Sections 3–9 of this chapter draw heavily on the work of the Institute of Personnel and Development (IPD) as reported in *Personnel and Europe, IPD Executive Brief*.

1. Introduction

For the United Kingdom HR practitioner the issue of Europe may well represent muddle and confusion. The stated opposition of the Conservative government to the European Union extending its influence in social and employment matters may be clear enough, and indeed the resolution of the government is evidenced by its refusal to sign the Social Protocol which was annexed to the Maastricht Treaty. However, almost weekly the decisions of the European Court of Justice, the Council of Ministers and others impact upon the way HR Managers are expected to do their job. The apparent move to a gradual harmonization of employment legislation is taking place, albeit slowly, and Britain has not been able to isolate itself from that movement. Additionally, 1992 brought the opening of the Single Market and with it many challenges and opportunities for those businesses that operate on the international stage – and, indeed, for those who do not, for it is unlikely that they will be able to isolate themselves entirely from its wider ramifications.

The implications of Europe for the UK HR manager are twofold. *First*, it is necessary to be aware of how decisions made in the European Court of Justice and the Council of Ministers will impact upon the workplace conditions of those employed. *Secondly*, the Single Market will bring its own challenges, not least of all the possibility of Europe-wide recruitment policies, greater mobility of staff and the (alleged) age of the 'Euro-manager'. It is argued by some that it will become increasingly common for managers, graduates and technical experts to consider, and take up, employment in countries other than their own. If this trend gathers momentum it may be necessary for pay and wider conditions of service to be competitive on a European and not just a national level.

As more and more of us are employed in organizations that operate across national boundaries the need for training in language and cultural skills grows ever greater. The reluctance of the British to learn languages is legendary, as is the enthusiasm of other nationals to learn English – the international language of business. What is equally apparent is that to be successful, companies must be able to communicate in the language of the customer, be that French, German or Greek. The businessman operating successfully in the Single Market will need to be linguistically competent and culturally aware – neither of these are skills at which Britain has a track record of success.

This chapter will look at the challenges facing United Kingdom HR managers from the two perspectives outlined above.

2. The Impact of European Union Employment Law

The Community shall have as its task . . . to promote a high level of employment and of social protection, the raising of the standard of living and quality of life, and economic and social cohesion and solidarity among Member States. (The Treaty of Rome, 1957)

Readers of chapter 19 will discover that in the main European employment law comes in the form of Directives. These Directives are based on Articles of the Treaty of Rome or the Treaty on European Union. The Directives should then be implemented through the national law of each member state. In principle, then, if you are complying with national law you are also complying with European law. When disputes occur they should be dealt with by national courts. Decisions in such courts will carry the weight of precedent accorded to that court. Such decisions will not have European-wide implications. Disputes will sometimes be referred to the European Court of Justice for interpretation. Decisions made here will be binding on *all* member states, not only in the state where the dispute arose. The HR manager will have to be aware of such Court decisions and the likely implications for his or her organization.

3. Current Directives

The European Union has taken a positive role in developing a framework for employment-related matters within the EU and, at the time of writing (1995), 27 employment-related Directives have been implemented. These cover contracts of employment, health and safety, equality, insolvency and the transfer of undertakings, the protection of employees in the case of collective redundancy, the free movement of workers – including mutual recognition of qualifications and social security rights. Additionally, the law has developed considerably through European Court of Justice case law.

4. Directives Awaiting Implementation

At the present time five further Directives are set for implementation. These include the Directive on Young Workers and the Directive on European Works Councils, to be implemented by all member states (except the UK) by September 1996. The validity of the Directive on Working Time is to be challenged in the European Court of Justice by the UK government. If the challenge is successful the Directive will be annulled, if unsuccessful then it should be implemented by the UK Government.

5. Directives Under Negotiation

The pace of development of new employment-related legislation is unlikely to slow down and the Council of Ministers (in this case made up of the 15 national employment ministers) is currently negotiating a further 11 Directives. Negotiations on some are very slow, others are making steady progress. Directives under current discussion include those to do with Data Protection, a revision of the Transfer of Undertakings Directive, further proposals to do with Health and Safety, and a Directive to ensure rights to employee information and consultation in those organizations employing over 1,000 staff. Details of the progress of Directives can be found by consulting the 'European News' sections of the IPD's fortnightly journal *People Management*.

Once Directives are agreed by the Council of Ministers there is usually a gap of two years before they have to be implemented into national law.

6. The Position of the UK

The aims of the employment-related Directives are to develop a common foundation of good employment practice across Europe. Many countries and employers find no problem with this, and indeed will already be acting within the requirements of a number of Directives. In other cases, however, the cost of implementing a Directive may well be high, and in the short term at least employers may well incur considerable expense.

The position of the United Kingdom is more complex in that as a nation we have a tradition of reliance upon voluntary rather than prescriptive regulation of employment. Directives, by their nature, are both prescriptive and very detailed in their requirements, and many go directly against previous UK practice. For many British employers the cost implications of implementation are quite severe. This, added to British suspicion of the justification for European Union interference in social and employment policy, has led to the development of an uneasy relationship between Britain and her partners.

Matters came to a head in 1991 at the end of the Dutch presidency. At the European Council meeting held in the town of Maastricht to agree and ratify the Treaty on European Union (commonly known as the Maastricht Treaty) the proposal to annex a Social Chapter to the Treaty was rejected by the British government. The Chapter, which was agreed by the other 11 member states (and now adopted by the 3 new members), was designed to provide an additional legal basis for member states to harmonize their employment legislation. The Treaty of Rome lays down the bases upon which employment (and all other) legislation can be passed. In the case of most areas of employment legislation a unanimous vote by the Council of Ministers is required. The Social Chapter would have reduced the requirement for most such legislation to a qualified majority.

The UK will continue to be covered by all existing Directives and all of those passed under the original Treaty of Rome; however, the UK will be exempt from those measures agreed under the Social Protocol of the Treaty on European Union.

The Commission has stated that wherever possible it will still route its proposals via the original Treaty of Rome. However, when agreement cannot be reached the provisions of the Social Protocol will be used.

The UK will come under considerable pressure to end its opt-out when the Treaty on European Union (the Maastricht Treaty) is reviewed at the Inter-Governmental Conference in 1996.

7. European Employment Law in Practice

The implications of European employment law are considered below in the order in which they were listed in section 3 ('Current Directives').

7.1 Contracts of employment

This Directive, introduced via Article 100 in 1991, extends employment rights to more part-time workers. Those working 8 hours a week or more for a continuous period of one month must receive written confirmation of their main terms and conditions within two months of commencing their employment. Changes to those terms and conditions must also be notified within one month. In essence part-time workers should now be treated in a similar way to their full-time counterparts with regard to such matters as protection of employment, equality of opportunity, access to benefits, maternity rights and selection for redundancy.

7.2 Health and safety

Health and safety is without doubt the most regulated area of employment within the European Union. Most legislation is introduced via Article 118A, which was a new Article introduced into the Treaty of Rome with the Single European Act of 1987. Twelve Directives have now been implemented using Article 118A. More are proposed. Proposals can be passed into law under Article 118A via qualified majority voting.

All of the Regulations have been implemented into UK law either via enabling legislation, statutory instruments or acts of Parliament. The range of issues covered by the Directives is too extensive to even list let alone discuss, but some of the significant Directives are considered below.

Display Screen Equipment (VDU) Directive (1990): was implemented by the UK through the Health and Safety (Display Screen Equipment) Regulations 1992. The Directive required employers to provide free eyesight tests and, if necessary, free glasses to regular VDU users. It requires workstations to be designed in such a way as to avoid eye strain, and requires that workers take regular breaks from the screen.

Personal Protective Equipment Directive (1989): requires employers to provide and to maintain correctly personal protective equipment for some jobs. Implemented in the UK via the Personal Protective Equipment at Work Regulations (1992).

Workplace Directive (1989): lays down minimum standards for the design of workplaces. Included is the requirement that rest areas make provisions for non-smokers. Implemented in the UK via the Workplace (Health, Safety and Welfare) Regulations (1992).

Heavy Loads Directive (1990): requires employers to supply lifting equipment or training in proper lifting techniques to avoid the risk of back injuries. Implemented in the UK via the Manual Handling Regulations 1992.

Protection of Pregnant Workers (1992): requires pregnant or breast-feeding women to be removed from workplaces that might be hazardous; employers to make a health and safety risk assessment to protect pregnant women at work; and women to receive a minimum of 14 weeks maternity leave and have the right to return to the job. Prohibits dismissal on the grounds of pregnancy, regardless of length of service. Implemented via the Employment Act 1993.

Working Time Directive (1994): includes measures to limit the working week to 48 hours except by voluntary agreement. It excludes docks, transportation, work at sea and doctors in training, and allows for derogations from its provisions in certain circumstances such as collective agreement arrangements or when there is a need for continuity of production or service. (The UK government has announced a legal challenge to this Directive. The challenge will be heard by the European Court of Justice in 1995 (or early in 1996) and its basis will be that working time is outside the scope of Article 118A (which is strictly concerned with health and safety at work). Britain will argue issues concerning working time should be more properly considered under Article 100, which is the employment matters article and which requires a unanimous vote in order for proposals to be adopted.)

7.3 Equality

The scope of current European Union equality legislation is limited to equality between the sexes. There is no basis under the Treaty of Rome by which the other dimensions to equality can be considered. In many respects the UK is regarded as having among the best provision for equal opportunities of any member state – however, those who have read earlier chapters carefully will have seen examples of the UK none the less falling foul of European Directive requirements (see particularly chapter 6, on equal opportunities).

Currently there are five Equality Directives, all of which have been implemented into UK national law. Additionally, Article 119, one of the founding principles of the European Union, is the right to equal pay for equal work for men and women. The 1975 Equal Pay Directive extends the provision to equal pay for work of *equal value*. The 1976 Equal Treatment Directive legislated against sex discrimination in most areas of employment. The 1978 Equal Treatment Directive (State Social Security) provided for equality in all state benefits except pensions. The 1986 Equal Treatment Directive (Occupational Social Security) provided for equality in all employment-related benefits, except pensions. Finally the Equal Treatment (Self Employed) Directive of 1986 outlawed discrimination on the grounds of sex of self-employed persons.

The main pieces of UK legislation by which the European legislation was implemented include the Equal Pay Act (1970), amended in 1984, the Sex Discrimination Act of 1975, amended in 1976, and the 1989 Employment Act.

Many cases relating to this area have gone before the European Court of Justice, and this has given rise to a considerable body of case law. Some of the more important judgements are outlined below.

Marshall (1986): In this case the Court decided that employers must harmonize retirement ages for male and female employees. The UK has harmonized retirement age – upwards, to age 65 – but with an implementation date of 2015.

Barber (1990): in which the European Court of Justice ruled that under Article 119 pensions are defined as part of pay and therefore occupational pensions must be the same for men and women. It requires employers to equalize their pension scheme rules.

Dekker (1991): the Court held that discrimination on the grounds of pregnancy or during a period of maternity leave constituted direct discrimination under the Equality Directive.

Vroege (1994): the Court ruled that equal treatment legislation applies equally to part-time workers in their access to occupational pension schemes. The Court stated that employees should be allowed to join pension schemes retroactively, but must pay their contributions in full. The right extends back as far as 1976, when the Equal Treatment Directive was passed. (See the case study at the end of the chapter for a full development of this ruling.)

Bilka Kaufhaus (1986), *Rinner Kuhn* (1989), *Kowalska* (1990), *Botel* (1992), *Nimz* (1991): all German cases in which the Court ruled that it is illegal to give part-time staff (when the majority of part-time staff are female) poorer packages of pay and benefits than their full-time counterparts. All aspects of remuneration should be on a pro-rata basis.

Minimum wages: When the UK abolished the Wages Councils in 1993 the Trades Union Congress made a complaint to the Commission which argued that because most workers covered by the Councils were women the likely effect would be a reduction in the pay of many female workers. The UK Equal Opportunities Commission has supported the complaint, but at the time of writing no response has been forthcoming. If the Commission feels that the UK has acted against the principle of equal pay then it can ask for an explanation or challenge the action in the European Court of Justice.

Part-time workers: In the UK until recently a worker employed for less than 16 hours a week had to work for 5 years to gain employment protection, while a full-time colleague was required to work for only two years. The Equal Opportunities Commission challenged this and in March 1994 the House of Lords ruled that such different treatment for part-time workers is contrary to European Union law.

7.4 Insolvency
This Directive, passed in 1980, requires that member states set up a fund to reimburse outstanding pay to workers in the event that their employer becomes insolvent.

7.5 Transfer of undertakings
The Transfer of Undertakings Directive (also known as the Acquired Rights Directive) was introduced to ensure that when a business was sold the employees of that business maintained the same basic terms and conditions of employment and could not be dismissed merely as a result of that transfer.

The Directive was introduced into UK law via the Transfer of Undertaking Regulations. The wording of the Regulations was designed so as to exclude the public sector. The 1980s saw in the UK many tens of thousands of public-sector workers transfer to private-sector employment, for this was a central theme of Conservative government policies of privatization and compulsory competitive tendering. Many transferred on to worse conditions than they has formerly enjoyed in the public sector. The Regulations were challenged in the European Court of Justice in 1992 (the so-called Redmond case) and the Court affirmed that the Directive applied equally to private- and public-sector workers. UK law has therefore been amended via the 1993 Employment Act.

The Redmond case opened the door for thousands of former public-sector workers, who had their terms and conditions of employment cut when they transferred to the private sector, to claim retrospective damages.

7.6 Collective redundancy
The 1975 Collective Redundancy Directive requires (and this is restated in the Transfer of Undertakings Directive) that consultation with the workforce be undertaken in the event of 10 or more redundancies or of a

transfer of undertakings. The UK interpreted the Directives so as to apply only to employers that recognized trade unions. The European Court of Justice has recently ruled (June 1994) that the UK is in breach of both of the Directives and the law will have to be amended to make the following provisions:

a. In the event of an employer wishing to make redundant 10 or more workers proper information is provided and consultation with workforce representatives is undertaken.

b. Proper sanctions should be used against those who do not comply.

c. The requirements of (a) and the sanction of (b) should be available not only for redundancy and transfer of undertaking but also for health and safety directives, which also require information and consultation with workforce representatives.

7.7   Free movement of workers

Principles of free movement of labour and the right of access to benefits in other countries were enshrined in the original Treaty of Rome. Article 48 provides for free movement within the boundaries of the Union. Article 51 gives European citizens the right to the social security benefits available in other member states, and Article 52 provides for the right to provide services without discrimination. The Articles, although apparently clear in their intent, have not been without their problems in implementation. The right to free movement relates to the right to work, live and travel without hindrance anywhere within the boundaries of the Union. The principle is simple, the practice is not – not least of all because national social security systems have great difficulty 'speaking' to one another.

The Schengen Agreement proposed the abolition of all passport controls on passengers travelling between member states. This would mean that the principal point at which passports would be checked would be at the point and place at which the traveller entered the Union. The proposal was agreed by all member states except the UK, Ireland and Denmark, who will keep passport controls for the time being. The agreement was implemented on a trial basis on 1995, with Finland and Sweden deciding to adopt 'observer' status, and Austria wishing to join in 1997.

Work permits are not required to work in other member states. However, member states can limit the length of time that nationals from other Union states can seek work and claim benefit on their territory. Citizens are allowed to move to other member states and join national insurance schemes, with account being taken of the contributions they have made to schemes in other member states.

The principles outlined above seem clear, but the interpretation has been difficult, not least of all because of the vast differences in national insurance schemes and how they are administered and interpreted by officials.

The Union has gradually been moving towards mutual recognition of qualifications. In the 1970s and 1980s the Union tried tackling qualifications one by one and issued Directives covering architecture, general medical practice, dentistry, nursing, veterinary surgery and pharmacy. By the 1980s it was recognized that this qualification-by-qualification approach was too slow and time consuming, and a general Directive was agreed in 1989 requiring that all regulated professional qualifications be mutually recognized across the whole of the Union. This Directive was implemented by the UK in 1991.

The second stage of recognition deals with vocational qualifications. These were covered under the second general Directive, approved in 1992, requiring member states to recognize mutually diplomas and qualifications gained in other member states. Implementation into national law, which should have been completed by June 1994, has been held up in the UK because of delays relating to the higher-level National Vocational Qualifications.

8. Directives Awaiting Implementation

As mentioned earlier (in section 4), many Directives await implementation into national law. This section attempts to cover some of the main provisions of these Directives. The latest date for implementation is given in parentheses.

The UK government mounted a legal challenge to this directive arguing that matters concerning working hours were strictly outside the scope of Article 118A (which is concerned with health and safety at work). The government's argument that such matters should more properly be dealt with under Article 100 (which is the employment matters article) was rejected by the European Court's Advocate General in an interim ruling early in 1996. The full ruling of the court (which is unlikely to overturn the interim judgement) will follow later in 1996.

European Works Councils, adopted under the provisions of the Maastricht Treaty Social Protocol (9/96). The UK is of course exempt from this Directive because of its opt-out. The Directive provides for the establishment of European-level information and consultation systems in all organizations with more than 1,000 employees and employing more than 150 in each of two or more member states. The European Works Council would have rights to meet the management of the employer on at least one occasion each year for information and consultation about the progress of, and the prospects for, the company.

The Directive will apply to UK employers if their operations in the other 14 member states meet that stated threshold, but will not have to extend any information and consultation systems introduced to their UK-based employees. The UK operations of non-UK based employers will also be exempt from the Directive.

> On 9 November 1994 United Biscuits became the first British company to ignore the provisions of Britain's opt-out from the Social Chapter of the Maastricht Treaty by agreeing to establish a Europe-wide works council for its employees. United Biscuits, which has a number of subsidiaries across the European Union and Eastern Europe, has agreed in negotiations with trades unions to establish a works council that will be composed of about 30 employee representatives and will include 4 full-time trade union officials.

> The council will meet once a year, after the annual results have been presented, and will receive a management report, discuss group performance, company strategy, the commercial environment and employment-related matters. It gives employees a role, but not one that involves decision-making.
>
> The Works Council Directive, from which British companies operating only in the UK have an opt-out, came into force in September 1996. However, UK-based multinationals will be required to set up European works councils but will not need to include British employees.
>
> Commenting on United Biscuits actions, the 'Pennington' column of *The Times* said on 10 November 1994:
>
>> the need to explain does impose a discipline on boards. It gives a strong incentive to plan continuously, rather than manage by crisis, or grandly operate as portfolio managers rather than business managers. And that could raise the economic performance of industry as a whole.

The Young Workers Directive (6/96) sets 15 as the minimum working age for young people, except for jobs like newspaper rounds. It also introduces a maximum 40-hour working week for employees aged under 18 and a ban on most forms of night work.

9. Future Developments in European Employment Policy

As well as the Directives awaiting implementation, there are also a number that are passing through the various stages of negotiation. This section will describe a number of such proposals (or draft Directives), as well as giving general consideration to the overall shape and direction of European employment policy.

In December 1989 all member states, with the exception of the UK, signed the Community Charter of the Fundamental Rights of Workers (the Social Charter). It is from the 1989 Social Charter Action Programme that derived from the Social Charter that most social and employment proposals now emanate, although some date back much further. The basic objectives of the Social Charter are considered in detail in chapter 19 and so are not repeated here. Below is an outline of some of the proposals before the Council of Ministers at present and an indication of their progress to date.

The Part Time and Temporary Work Directive is being considered to improve the lot of part-time and temporary workers, such that they should be treated no differently from full-time and permanent employees. This proposal requires a unanimous vote at the Council of Ministers for implementation. The UK has objected to this Directive and it will now be enacted by the fourteen under the provisions of the Social Protocol.

The proposed Reversal of Burden of Proof in Sex Discrimination Cases Directive would make the assumption that employers accused of sex discrimination were guilty unless they could prove to the contrary.

This has run into the opposition of a number of member states and is likely to be withdrawn by the Commission, or seriously delayed.

The proposed Parental Leave Directive would give employed parents the right to three months' leave upon the birth of a child. It applies equally to men as well as women. The UK has indicated that it will not vote in favour of this proposal, so it has been switched for consideration by the other fourteen member states under the Social Protocol.

Many new Directives are under discussion in the field of Health and Safety. Among the provisions included are greater protection for transport workers, greater protection for workers from chemicals and physical agents (e.g. noise) in the workplace, and a requirement for all public and employer-provided transport vehicles to be adapted to accommodate disabled passengers. Progress in most of the five new Directives relating to health and safety is slow.

A number of draft Directives relate to employee involvement. Most are badly bogged down and in some cases opposed by a number of member states. Among the proposals for consideration are the Vredeling Directive, which recommends that all companies with 1,000 or more employees should provide annual information to employees about the progress of, and the prospects for, the company. This Directive was first proposed in 1980 and has been at an impasse since 1986. The so-called Fifth Directive also relates to companies employing 1,000 or more workers and proposes that such companies should establish either worker directors or a works council (or similar arrangements), with the intention that systems be established for informing and consulting employees before major decisions are made that might impact upon the interests of the workforce. This Directive is opposed in its totality by the UK and in parts by other member states.

The future direction of European employment policy will be largely determined by the 1994 Commission White Paper entitled *European Social Policy: A Way Forward for the Union*. The White Paper restated the commitment of the Commission to push ahead with outstanding draft Directives. These include the following areas (which are discussed in detail earlier in this chapter): parental leave, greater protection for part-time and temporary workers, and improving transport for disabled workers. The White Paper also identifies a number of areas for new proposals. These include: social security for workers living in other than their home state, and mobility of occupational pensions. It is also expected that legislation will be developed to prohibit discrimination on the grounds of race, disability, age and religion.

It is likely (and also a stated objective of the Commission) that whenever possible new proposals will be introduced using the provisions of the Treaty of Rome; or if necessary the Social Protocol of the Maastricht will be invoked – from which, of course, the UK is exempt.

Many commentators fear that the eventual aim of the European Union is to force through a common set of employment laws for the whole union, resulting in homogeneity across all member states. However, the leading employment lawyer Olga Aikin, in a presentation to the 1993 IPM Annual Conference (reported in *Personnel Management*

Plus, November 1993), suggests that there will still be considerable scope for national divergence, although common employment laws will be of benefit to pan-European organizations. Notwithstanding this, the judgements of the European Court of Justice in particular lead many to believe that a very closely integrated set of employment regulations is the likely pattern for the future.

10. The Impact of the Single Market

The Single European Act and the removal of barriers to trade will, according to Welford and Prescott (1992: 32):

> initiate greater harmonisation among Member States. By standardising technical regulations and removing competitive bias through unfair practices, there will be a convergence of conditions between European markets.

There is little doubt that the costs of *not* removing barriers to trade would have been immense. The Cecchini report (1988) identified the cost of the inefficiencies of operating 12 separate markets as 12 billion ECUs. The completion of the market should bring about a corresponding reduction in costs. The report identified 4 major areas where the introduction of the Single Market should impact:

1. The exploitation of economies of scale should reduce organization, production and distribution costs.

2. Industrial reorganization, increased competition and increased efficiency should all result in downward pressure on costs.

3. Comparative advantages should be exploited as resources are reallocated giving new patterns of industrial competition.

4. The dynamism that the new market brings should encourage product innovation and process development.

Although the UK government is suspicious of the increase in social and employment regulation emanating from Europe, the same cannot be said of its attitude to the creation of the Single Market. Indeed Pinder (1990: 165) claims:

> There can be no doubt that, in terms of commitment at least, the UK has thrown itself wholeheartedly behind the Single Market Programme. This commitment has generated a significant awareness of many of the broader issues at stake; although it is doubtful whether this awareness has in turn generated a similar level of action to address them in detail. A much quoted survey of companies with sales of over £20 million, carried out in 1989, revealed that 90 per cent were undertaking no market research into Europe, 93 per cent were undertaking no language training and 95 per cent had no sales agents within the EC.

While I would not wish to claim that the situation has not improved since 1989, the HR manager has a vital role in ensuring organizational success in the Single European Market, principally by addressing the following four areas:

a. Considering the varieties of international worker and developing policies to benefit from Europe-wide staff mobility and developing appropriate strategies for management development.

b. Producing policies to benefit from the opportunities offered by, and the threat posed to, the recruitment of professional technical and managerial staffs in the wider market.

c. Ensuring that staff have adequate cultural and language training.

d. Considering executive pay and wider benefits in Europe-wide terms.

Each of these factors will be considered in turn below.

11. Staff Mobility: The International Worker

In his book *International Human Resource Management* (1994) Derek Torrington identifies a number of types of workers operating on the international stage:

a. *The International Worker* – speaks a number of languages, is culturally adept, and although based in one country, is constantly on the move although seldom away for longer than a week. His job is to make deals with the representatives and agents of the companies that he visits. He does not become involved with the operations of those companies, merely arranging deals and developing opportunities.

b. *The Expatriate* – works on assignments in various parts of the world. Typically he will be employed for 2 to 3 years on a contract before being moved on. His task is to become closely involved with the part of the organization where he is placed and articulate the business philosophy of his company. His degree of language acquisition and cultural orientation may be low.

c. *The Engineer* – will be working on assignments in companies for a few months only, installing equipment and training local staff. Considerable periods of the year are spent at headquarters.

d. *The Occasional Parachutist* – makes several overseas trips on business each year. Most involve being away for only a short period.

e. *The Mobile Worker* – has spent a period of time studying in a country and, having enjoyed the experience, returns to work in the same country.

The examples, while not exhaustive, serve to illustrate the range of alternatives by which workers might operate internationally. They also serve to illustrate the range of alternatives that employers must have available to recruit, train, motivate, reward and retain their staff. The terms 'international worker' or 'international manager' are often glibly used with little consideration given to the ways by which people work internationally. The degree of language training required by a worker, or cultural orientation needed, the pay and reward system operated or the methods by which international workers are selected, will vary widely dependent upon the model of international work used by the organization.

12. Recruitment and the Wider Market

The Incomes Data Services / Institute of Personnel Management book *European Management Guide: Recruitment* (1990) offers a good general source of reference for recruitment practices and policies in the member states of the Union. Additionally it offers the warning that:

> Recruitment is an area in which do-it-yourself can be dangerous. In an unfamiliar labour market, decisions must be taken on the basis of local expertise.

Cooper and Giacomello (reported in Sparrow and Hiltrop 1994) illustrate this point with the example of Italy, where the rights of workers are detailed and highly structured and indeed are enshrined in Article 1 of the Italian Constitution. The employer is defined as the provider of work (*datore*) while the employee is the lender of work (*prestatore*). The Italian worker enjoys one of the most comprehensive structures of employment rights anywhere in Europe.

While the IDS / IPM Guide offers ample warning as to various national practices, it does not offer guidance to the personnel manager seeking to develop suitable strategies for Europe-wide recruitment.

In essence a Europe-wide recruitment strategy is little different from any other recruitment strategy. It is simply 'fishing in a bigger and more complex pond' and therefore requires a greater number of variables to be taken into account. For general information on developing recruitment strategies the reader is recommended to refer to the chapters covering manpower planning and recruitment. However, additional variables will need to be fed into the equations, and these will include:

a. Educational, professional and vocational qualifications and their cross-Europe comparabilities.

b. Competition from other employers (Europe-wide).

c. National and regional (un)employment rates.

d. The supply and availability of staff with particular skills.

e. The packages that might be offered to non-national staff (relocation expenses, language training, etc.).

f. Salary levels and conditions of service (e.g. holidays) in relation to major competitors (both national and international).

g. The grades of staff for which international recruitment might be considered. There is evidence to suggest that managerial, technical and professional staff are more likely to be attracted by the prospect of working abroad.

h. International recruitment is likely to be more common (and therefore more competitive) in those industries that are labour intensive. These would include teaching, nursing and construction.

i. Many EU nationals will see the opportunity to work in another EU country as an chance to gain experience before returning to their own state to develop their careers. This possible lack of long-term commitment will need to be accommodated.

j. Careful consideration of the sort of occupations that would be suitable for international recruitment should be undertaken. Casual observation of the classified advertisement sections of major national newspapers indicates that to date it is sales, marketing, data-processing, finance and, to an extent, electrical/mechanical engineering positions that are most widely advertised across Europe. Many of the positions advertised are for people to operate at the strategic level within pan-European organizations.

It is difficult to predict the extent to which in years to come recruitment will take place on a Europe-wide scale. Of little doubt is the fact that competition for the most able employees will increase at the local, national and international levels, and that often it is such people that hold the key to an organization's success. Younger workers are generally more receptive to the whole idea of the European Union and the ideals for which it stands, and it is they who are inevitably the most mobile members of the workforce. British qualifications are generally well regarded within Europe and well qualified and linguistically competent young people from this country will be well received by a wide cross-section of employers. Evidence also shows that nationals of many other member states are linguistically more competent in our language than we are in theirs. Many citizens of Europe see Britain as an attractive place to live and work or study, and it is not unlikely that the current trend of more non-UK nationals being attracted to work in Britain than British nationals attracted to work abroad will continue. This may result in more competition for jobs for UK workers and more choice for British employers.

13. Cultural and Language Training

The weaknesses of the UK industrial training system are well documented elsewhere and also are covered in other chapters of this book; however, it has been estimated that the expansion in trade created by the Single Market will result in between two and five million new jobs being created. It is expected that those jobs will go to countries with the most highly trained workforces. Not least among the skills that the UK lacks are proficiency in other European languages and an awareness of cultures other than our own. Quite clearly the two are linked, and those managers who are able to gain a knowledge of a language will by the same process begin to understand how the people who use that language think. Our language is one of the most obvious manifestations of our culture.

There are some stark comparisons to be drawn between ourselves and our principal European partners. In most mainland European countries English is taught from nursery school level and a high proportion of school leavers have a good command of the language. In the UK the proportion of pupils taking a second European language at GCSE and A-level has fallen over the past decade, while the number of qualified language teachers has also fallen sharply. At university level the emphasis of many modern language degrees in the UK is on literature, not on language. Many British language graduates find employment difficult to obtain.

Despite the lack of second-language skills produced by the education system, there is no doubt that proficiency in the languages of our customers is going to be vital if trade is to be further developed. Many TECs (Training and Enterprise Councils) have made this a priority area and many companies are acting to develop their staff accordingly. To gain a worthwhile degree of proficiency from traditional methods of study can take a long time, and so many organizations have gone for a total immersion approach – that is, totally immersing trainees for a short period of time in the language and culture being studied. This can give a valuable kick-start to language acquisition, or a useful polish to skills that are rusty or infrequently used.

As important as proficiency in language skills is appreciating the customs and rituals of business practice in your customer's country. There are many commercially available guides illustrating the differences between aspects of business practice across Europe. Gibbs, in his 1993 guide *Doing Business in the European Community*, tells us how to (among other things) make a business appointment, the correct style for business letters, the role of business entertaining, the correct protocol for business meetings and the role of women in business, for each of the member states.

An awareness of the business culture of your customer will enable you to use the correct degree of formality, to know whether to suggest breakfast meetings or business lunches, to appreciate the degree to which haggling and negotiation is an accepted business custom and to what extent details should be near finalized before the first meeting. Gifts and hospitality can be a minefield for the unwary, and correct procedure should always be observed. It is important to know at what stage in a relationship it is appropriate to use first names. It is as well not to confuse the Danes with other Scandinavians (or the Scots with the English). It is of value to know that the Dutch are considered to have a very similar sense of humour to the British and are well informed about British current affairs. It is as well to know that Germans are very suspicious of the products of other nations and take some convincing that anything could be superior to a German-made product. This may lead them in any contract to demand tight delivery dates and long warranties, though these requirements may be relaxed once the product has proved itself. It is important to know that formal dressing is not always necessary in Greece, but in Italy those who are expensively and stylishly dressed will impress.

The preceding paragraph offers but a taste or the infinite variety of business practices and customs that need to be observed by business-people abroad. To add confusion to a difficult situation, it is important to note that business culture is not constant over time. Younger managers in all countries are developing a culture that is more relaxed and informal, so to an extent your behaviour towards your customer could depend upon their age as much as their nationality.

14. Pay and Benefits

Many surveys comparing executive pay and benefits across Europe show that British executives are quite badly paid in comparison with their mainland counterparts. This 'evidence' often carries with it a warning that unless British executives' pay is brought into line with the European average the inevitable result will be a migration of British staff to more lucrative positions abroad. The evidence, however, has to be viewed with some caution. The effects of tax rates on gross pay must be considered, as must the cost of living in each country. Additionally, the packages of other benefits offered to executives must be investigated, as must state-provided benefits such as health care and education. The method by which the comparison is made should also be examined. Most surveys compare the rewards given to similar occupations in a range of countries. What is less understood is that in many cases it is difficult to compare occupations across national boundaries. For instance, accountants in Germany and in Britain perform very different roles; also, there are far more accountants in Britain than in Germany. Both of these points could serve to make any crude comparison invalid.

Employers need only take account of Europe-wide levels of pay if the organization intends to recruit from across the Union or if their own employees are likely to be attracted by job opportunities in other countries, or affected in some other way by movements in labour or income. It is likely that these two considerations will apply (in the short to medium term, at least) only to those professional, managerial and technical staff who find that their skills are in Europe-wide demand.

Notwithstanding what is said above, the aim of any remuneration policy is to recruit, to retain, to motivate and to reward. In considering the appropriate reward for the international worker, organizations should consider the varieties of international work outlined earlier. A pay policy appropriate for one variety will not be appropriate for another. Many pay policies for staff working abroad will attempt to give the employee a 'pay plus incentive' package. The 'pay' would give comparable purchasing power with her home salary; the 'plus' would be the incentive to take the job. Considerations will be complicated if a worker is to be transferred to a country where the cost of living is higher than in her own. If the cost of living is higher it would be equitable to compensate the employee for the lost purchasing power of her salary. However, if the cost of living is lower is it equally fair to reduce her pay accordingly? In practice most employers (and employees) would say no!

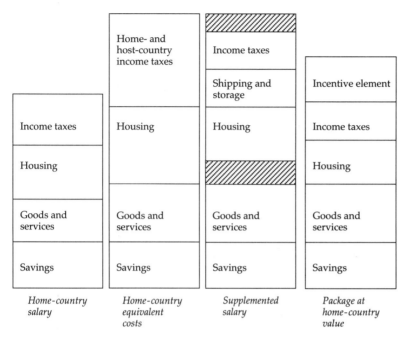

Home-country salary	Home-country equivalent costs	Supplemented salary	Package at home-country value
	Home- and host-country income taxes	Income taxes	
			Incentive element
		Shipping and storage	
Income taxes	Housing	Housing	Income taxes
Housing			Housing
Goods and services	Goods and services	Goods and services	Goods and services
Savings	Savings	Savings	Savings

▨ additional company costs

Source: Torrington 1994.

Figure 15.1
Paying the international worker

Torrington (1994) suggests that a balance sheet approach to pay could be considered (see figure 15.1). This model considers the home-country salary as being made up of the four components indicated. The equivalent cost of buying those four components in the host country is shown in the second column. The third column indicates the degree to which the home-country salary will have to be supplemented and the final column indicates the package at home country value. Note the incentive element to the package.

This package has many advantages but will not be an adequate formula for all the examples of international worker discussed at the beginning of this section. The personnel practitioner will need to be aware of competitor practice, industry norms and employee expectations if suitable remuneration packages are to be devised and updated to keep in line with changing patterns of employment.

15. Conclusion

This chapter should serve to illustrate that international considerations will impact upon the work of all HR professionals. The increasing weight of EU law will influence the workplace practice of almost all employers, and despite the best efforts of the UK government many aspects of the Social Chapter will fall equally onto British companies as onto mainland European employers. Even the 'dreaded' works council, the pillar of the German system of industrial relations and employee involvement, and the butt of much ridicule by UK politicians, is creeping up on us. Already employers are required to consult workplace representatives on matters such as health and safety, and the European Works Council Directive will extend the requirement from mere consultation to full-blown works councils for many organizations operating internationally.

The HR manager must also be aware of other influences and pressures, not least of all the fact that for many professions recruitment now takes place within an international market-place, and this has implications for all aspects of HR practice, from pay to training and development. In this new internationalist world HR professionals will be expected to play their part proactively to ensure that their organizations have the cultural and linguistic equipment necessary to survive and prosper.

It is beyond the confines of this book to look beyond Europe. However, the HR manager cannot afford to be so complacent. Increasingly the growth in world economic activity is becoming centred around the Pacific rim and the so-called tiger economies of south-east Asia. This will bring new challenges to established HR practices as the regulated world of Europe meets the very unregulated new economies in competition for established and new markets.

In September 1994 the UK Institute of Directors called for a ban on European Court of Justice rulings that allowed people to claim rights retrospectively. The call followed a Court ruling in which part-time workers were given the right to join employers' pension schemes and receive backdated benefits. The ruling allows part-time employees to join pension schemes retroactively, from the day they started work at a company to as far back as 1976.

The judgement, which fuelled suspicions that the UK's objection to harmonized social legislation would be overcome by 'back door' methods, came about as a result of a case brought by a Dutch part-time worker against her employer NCV Institut.

The European Court ruled on six cases in the same day (28 September 1994), all to do with sex discrimination in company pension schemes. The rulings were designed to put to an end the confusion brought about as a result of an earlier ruling by the same Court. In May 1990 in <u>Barber</u> v. <u>Guardian Royal Exchange</u> the Court ruled that pensions were part of pay and male and female employees had to receive the same benefits. This left many questions unanswered and left employers and pension fund trustees with the problem of deciding how they must restructure schemes to give men and women equal benefits. Additionally a number of test cases were brought forward by European Union member states in order to clarify certain points of contention. A number of the cases were British. As a result of the test cases the trustees of the home furnishing and fabric company Coloroll, which went into receivership in 1989, are now able to proceed with paying 5,000 former employees £50 million from the defunct company's pension scheme.

The Court decided in the Dutch cases of <u>Vroege</u> and <u>Fisscher</u> that part-time workers have the right to join pension schemes. In practice most part-time workers are women, so their exclusion is deemed to be indirectly discriminatory in terms of pay and benefits. No time limit has been fixed on backdated claims, so in theory they could be made back as far as 1976, the year that the principle of equal pay was enshrined in the Treaty of Rome. The Institute of Directors have claimed that this ruling could cost industry up to £10 billion. However, many actuaries dispute the figure, stating that as most pension funds are contributory it is unlikely that many part-time workers could afford to pay backdated contributions. Those who stand to benefit are those who work (or worked) for employers who operate non-contributory schemes. It is also argued that, as the ruling was made principally on the grounds of sex discrimination, employers could still effectively exclude part-time workers from pension schemes if they were prepared to argue (at industrial tribunals) that they had an 'objective' reason for that exclusion. Such an objective reason might include the complexity and administration costs when turnover of part-time staff is high. This would have nothing to do with whether an employee was a man or a woman, and so would not be covered by the judgement.

The Court rulings, although potentially benefiting women part-time workers, were less generous to their full-time counterparts. The Court ruled that so long as pension ages were equal, women could be disadvantaged by having to work 5 years longer for a full pension in the future.

TASKS

1. You are employed as personnel officer to Tennyson plc, a medium-sized retail chain. Your boss has called you in to consider the implications of the court decisions described above. Consider the steps you would take and the questions you would ask in deciding your recommended course of action.

2. Consider the arguments for and against allowing backdating of claims for access to pension funds to 1976.

(<u>Note</u>: When the Court decision was implemented into UK law, backdating was restricted to two years only.)

1. Consider the reasons why it is deemed necessary for the European Union to have pan-European laws and policies relating to employment and social matters. Couldn't the 'Single Market' work perfectly well without this additional layer of regulation?

2. By refusing to sign the Social Protocol of the Maastricht Treaty the UK has, and in the future will be able to, effectively avoid much of the European law relating to social and employment matters. Discuss.

3. It has been argued by some that eventually all European Union member states will have common laws and regulations relating to employment. Consider the merits of this argument.

4. Consider your own organization, or one with which you are familiar. How has European employment law influenced the way HR policies are either devised or enacted?

5. 'In the UK the part-time and the female worker has benefited considerably from both European law and decisions made in the European Court of Justice. Their full-time and male counterparts, however, have not always fared so well.' Consider the validity of this statement.

6. You are employed as a Trainee HR Officer in a large manufacturing company. You have been asked to prepare for the company's strategic planning group a paper that identifies the role that HR can perform as the company considers opening another production facility in Spain.

7. 'In the years to come the HR manager will need to be as knowledgeable about the culture of other nations, and the requirements of the European Union, as he or she is about performance appraisal and recruitment'. Discuss.

•REFERENCES•

Brewster C, Hegeswisch A, Holden L & Lockhart T (1992)
THE EUROPEAN HUMAN RESOURCE MANAGEMENT GUIDE
London, Academic Press.

Cecchini P (1988)
THE COST OF NON-EUROPE
Brussels, European Commission.

Deal T & Kennedy A (1982)
CORPORATE CULTURE: THE RITES AND RITUALS OF CORPORATE LIFE
Reading, Mass., Addison-Wesley.

Gibbs P (1993)
DOING BUSINESS IN THE EUROPEAN COMMUNITY
London, Kogan Page.

Hollinshead G & Leat M (1995)
HUMAN RESOURCE MANAGEMENT: AN INTERNATIONAL AND COMPARATIVE PERSPECTIVE
London, Pitman.

Kakabadse A & Tyson S (eds) (1994)
CASES IN EUROPEAN HUMAN RESOURCE MANAGEMENT
London, Routledge.

Income Data Services / Institute of Personnel Management (1990–3)
EUROPEAN MANAGEMENT GUIDES. Titles include:
TRAINING AND DEVELOPMENT
RECRUITMENT
TERMS AND CONDITIONS OF EMPLOYMENT
INDUSTRIAL RELATIONS
PAY AND BENEFITS
London, IPM.

Institute of Personnel and Development (Oct. 1995)
PERSONNEL AND EUROPE: EXECUTIVE BRIEF
London, IPD.

Pinder M (1990)
PERSONNEL MANAGEMENT FOR THE SINGLE EUROPEAN MARKET
London, Pitman.

Preston G (ed.) (1992)
CASES IN EUROPEAN BUSINESS
London, Pitman.

Sparrow P & Hiltrop J.-M. (1994)
EUROPEAN HUMAN RESOURCE MANAGEMENT IN TRANSITION
London, Prentice-Hall.

Torrington D (1994)
INTERNATIONAL HUMAN RESOURCE MANAGEMENT
London, Prentice-Hall.

Welford R & Prescott K (1992)
EUROPEAN BUSINESS: AN ISSUE-BASED APPROACH
London, Pitman.

Other Useful Sources of Information

People Management, the twice-monthly journal of the Institute of Personnel and Development, contains a very useful section covering current EU and European issues.

See also the references at the end of chapter 19.

THE MANAGEMENT OF HUMAN RESOURCES: SOME EUROPEAN COMPARISONS – GERMANY AND SPAIN

•CHAPTER•

16

AS A RESULT OF STUDYING THIS CHAPTER YOU SHOULD BE ABLE TO:

- Appreciate the variety of approaches to HR management taken in various European Union member states.

- Compare HR practices in the United Kingdom with those of other states.

- Appreciate the reasons for the diversity in HR management practice, and the source and origins of that diversity.

- Consider the current issues facing personnel practitioners in other European countries.

- Consider the lessons that United Kingdom practitioners might learn from their counterparts in other countries.

Please note: it is intended that this chapter be read following consideration of chapters 15 and 19.

1. Introduction

After consideration of the previous two chapters the reader might be forgiven for forming the opinion that a convergence of national human resource management systems is underway, largely as a result of the European Union, its treaties and directives. Although the Union is attempting to set minimum standards for the employment and treatment of workers, it would be very wrong to believe that this is leading to the emergence of pan-European human resource management systems and procedures. Nothing could be further from the truth. Each of the member states retains much that is individual and unique in the way that human resource practice is conducted. National laws vary widely from one state to the next, as does the culture of work. Of no less significance is the state of economic development – a major determinant of human resource practice and policies is the degree to which a particular economy is 'developed'. Human resource policy and practice does vary greatly from country to country, and despite the fears of many, it is unlikely that the efforts of the European Union will (or indeed are intended to) change this in the foreseeable future.

1.1 Differences and comparisons

In France and Belgium the State Manpower Service has to be informed of all vacancies, while in Portugal and Denmark, for instance, no such requirement exists. In Italy (theoretically at least) all employment should be approved by the State Placement Service. In the United Kingdom, for the vast majority of positions, employers can recruit who they wish. A number of countries require consultation with the workforce (as represented by a works council) before employment takes place, while in other countries no such requirement exists. Similarly, the methods used in recruitment vary widely. In some countries the use of recruitment consultants is common, in others it is banned (e.g. Spain and Germany) for anything other than advising on the development of recruitment methods and assistance in selection: they cannot actually place staff. The degree to which newspapers are used to advertise positions is also variable from country to country, so too with informal and speculative forms of recruitment and letters of introduction.

The extent to which anti-discrimination legislation exists also varies. In Portugal it is illegal to discriminate on religious grounds and in Italy on political beliefs. Many countries employ quota systems for the employment of disabled workers. However, the size of the quota, together with the definition of disability, vary widely. In Italy the quota is 15 per cent, in Germany it is 6 per cent, while in the UK it is only 3 per cent.

Across Europe interest in flexible systems of pay is common. However, what is less common is the method by which flexibility is explored and developed. In the United Kingdom share schemes (supported by tax relief) are common; they are rare elsewhere. In Sweden the use of group bonuses is the norm, profit sharing is popular in France and Germany, while performance-related pay is common in Italy and in the United Kingdom.

1.2 A comparison: Germany and Spain

This chapter attempts to discuss some of the differences between EU national HR systems by taking two member states as examples. Germany and Spain present an interesting contrast. Germany, a founder member of the Union, is also the wealthiest and has the largest economy as well as the largest population. Spain, a recent joiner, has one of the highest rates of unemployment in the Union and, in the 1980s, one of the fastest growing economies.

The direct comparison of any aspect of national economic or social activity with practice in another country is fraught with difficulty. For true and valid comparison to be made, consideration should be given to the legal and social systems, the historical development of the nation and its culture. In a book of this sort such consideration can only be minimal. Here, then, I can only offer the briefest insight into practice in Spain and Germany, and highlight some of the major differences between HR practice.

Consideration of each country will be prefaced by a brief introduction which will act as a 'pen portrait' and attempt to give the reader, in a nutshell, a picture of the nation, its recent development and some of its current problems.

2. Germany

❝❝*Some of these (costs) will have to be sorted out very soon, otherwise companies like Daimler-Benz will slowly but surely move out of this country.* ❞❞

Edzard Reuter, Chairman of Daimler-Benz, referring to the burden of social costs imposed on business in Germany; quoted in the *Daily Telegraph*, 31 Jan. 1995

2.1 Introduction

That the German economy has been the most successful in the European Union there can be no doubt. It has also proved to be the locomotive economy for many other countries. The country is politically stable, has a well-educated and trained workforce, and generally enjoys excellent industrial relations. However, in more recent years, particularly since the unification of East and West, the economy has slowed somewhat and many detect considerable structural problems within the system. The strength of the older industries (iron and steel, coal and engineering), have diminished considerably, and newer industries (such as micro-electronics) do not always exist in a size and form to replace them. The traditional German strengths in such industries as car manufacturing, which used to employ directly nearly three-quarters of a million people, are now on the wane, partly as a result of over-capacity in the European car industry and partly as a result of fierce competition from the newer players in the market – the Japanese, among others.

The strength of small and medium-sized engineering companies has been a feature of the German economy. The so-called *Mittelstand* companies, often family owned, often very conservative in outlook and practice, have found the going tough as the economy has suffered. This has led to a wave of (officially encouraged) mergers and acquisitions as companies tried to achieve economies of scale and, as importantly, a synergy between traditional engineering skills and the so-called new technologies.

Inward investment has also been a feature of recent years. Many large international companies see Germany as the heart of Europe and an ideal base from which to expand both throughout the Union and into the former Soviet Bloc countries. Bavaria in the South has received a large share of inward investment because many multinationals such as Hitachi and Motorola have chosen to locate there. Bavaria, the home of BMW, and Baden-Württemberg are the two strongest areas economically. In Baden-Wurttemberg the major employers include Bosch, Daimler-Benz, Porsche and IBM.

Many German companies, concerned by high labour costs at home, have invested heavily abroad. Popular locations for outward investment include the Czech Republic, Hungary and Spain. All offer the advantage of both a comparatively highly skilled workforce and

```
┌─────────────────────────────────────────────────────────────────┐
│                  GERMANY: KEY STATISTICS (1993)                    │
│                                                                     │
│  Population:          81 m.        Land area:       356,732 km²    │
│                                                                     │
│  Gross national product: DM2820 bn.  Per capita income:  DM21,153  │
│                                                                     │
│  Workforce:           30.5 m.      Unemployment:    8%             │
│                                                                     │
│  Significant industries:           Major employers/companies:      │
│      Manufacturing/General             Daimler Benz, Veba,         │
│      engineering                       Siemans, DBP Telekom,       │
│      Motor vehicle manufacture         Volkswagen, Metro-Gruppe    │
│      Coal, steel                                                   │
│                                                                     │
│  Source: Handelsblatt (1994).                                      │
└─────────────────────────────────────────────────────────────────┘
```

Figure 16.1

comparatively low unit labour costs. The key statistics are presented in figure 16.1.

2.2 Human resource management in Germany

The British HR manager looking at the German model would find little that appears familiar. In almost every respect the German system is more codified, more regulated, more bureaucratic and, some would say, more ordered. By comparison the British system seems wild and chaotic.

The German system is built upon a number of foundations that were laid down in the 1950s. These include an industrial relations system that has only 16 trade unions (compared to the over 70 in the UK that are affiliated to the TUC). Additionally, German trade unions are organized along industry wide lines rather than the more complex and to some extent contradictory system that exists in the UK. German trade unions are open to all people employed in an industry regardless of occupation or rank. German unions are affiliated to the Deutsche *Gewerkschaftsbund* (DGD), the equivalent of the TUC.

Wage negotiation in Germany is equally simple. Each union negotiates with representatives of the employers federation on a *Land* (or state) basis. So, for instance, the metal workers union *IG-Metall* would negotiate with the employers association Gesamtmetall. This means that the German HR manager (even at senior levels) will have nothing at all to do with the negotiation of pay. He or she would be concerned with the implementation of the agreement at a local level. It is important to note that not all *Länder* are 'equal', and the relative prosperity of each is incorporated into the calculation for determining pay. For example, *Baden-Wurttemberg* is the richest, closely followed by Bavaria, and these two will tend to come out best in pay negotiations. The poorer *Länder*, such as *Niedersachsen* and *Schleswig-Holstein*, would be awarded proportionately lower pay increases. Most, but by no means all, employers are members of the employers association. Those who are not, are not bound by the results of the negotiations. One notable company who stand outside of their trade association is the vehicle manufacturer *Volkswagen*, who choose instead to negotiate separately with the appropriate trade union.

Of equal importance to the system of trade union organization and operation is the system of industrial democracy that is commonly known as 'co-determination', dating from the 1951 *Montanmitbestimmungsgesetz* (Co-determination Act) and extended by the 1952 *Betriebsverfassungsgesetz* (Workplace Labour Relations Act), and further in 1972 with the passing of the Works Constitution Act (*Betriebsverfassungsgesetz*). The application and scope of the acts depends upon the size and ownership of the company, but those companies with a sole proprietor, or where the proprietor carries some personal liability, can be exempt. These are known as *Offene Handelsgesellschaften* (OHGs) and *Kommanditgesellschaften* (KGs).

The German public company (identified by the initials AG at the end of its name) has a two-tier board system. At the top is the *Aufsichstrat*, which is also known as the supervisory board. It is composed of non-executive directors largely made up of the representatives of shareholders. The co-determination laws make provision for inclusion of between one-third and one-half of the members of the *Aufsichstrat* to come from representatives of the workforce. The employee members of the supervisory board are shared between members of the trade unions who are represented at the company, and representative of different levels of employee from the company, typically shop floor, supervisory and managerial in proportion to their numbers in the workforce.

The *Aufsichstrat* has no executive powers of its own but has the right of veto and must appoint the *Vorstand*, or executive committee, which will consist of the senior managers of the company. The task of the *Vorstand* is actually to run the company on both an executive and day-to-day basis. One member of the *Vorstand*, called the *Arbeitsdirektor* (or labour director), is elected by the workforce representatives on the *Aufsichstrat*. The labour director is often a career manager with responsibility for HR and industrial relations. The way that he or she is appointed helps to ensure that they genuinely represent the interests of the workforce.

2.3 The works council

At plant level there is the works council or *Betriebsrat*. Its members are elected by the employees to serve for a period of 4 years. The size of the council is determined by the size of the company. Its composition – the ratio of manual to non-manual and male to female staff – should be in line with employment in the organization. Employers should give council members time off work with full pay to attend to their duties. In larger organizations some council members will be excused work duties entirely. The employer is expected to bear the cost of the works council entirely and council members enjoy considerable legal protection, to avoid possible victimization.

The works council has rights of consultation and co-determination. Specifically:

2.3.1 Consultation Although the employer is not obliged to consult the works council extensively, the latter has the right to receive information about the following matters, and also to make suggestions:

a. The organization of work, the work environment and employment.

b. The hiring of senior staff (i.e. executives).

c. Where planned changes in the organization could have consequences for the workforce.

d. Health and safety.

Although the employer must take note of the comments and suggestions made by the works council, particularly with regard to apprenticeship and training matters, it is not obliged to heed them. The works council must be consulted prior to the dismissal of an employee. If the employer fails to do so, then the dismissal is considered to be unfair. The employer can still dismiss the employee even if the works council disagrees with the decision.

2.3.2   Co-determination   The right to co-determination operates at two levels. First, the works council genuinely has the right (as an equal partner) to co-determine the policy of the company. The areas concerned here include:

a. How wages and salaries are to be paid (i.e. method, time, etc.), plus the use of or introduction of bonus schemes, piece work, performance pay, and so forth.

b. The working day: start and finish times, breaks, shift working, flexi-time, part-time workers, rosters.

c. Overtime and short-time working.

d. Matters relating to employee conduct: smoking bans, clocking on/off arrangements, employee/locker searches, the introduction of CCTV to monitor employees, tachographs, and so on.

e. Leave and its scheduling.

f. Changes to contracts of employment.

g. In the case of transfer of the undertaking.

Secondly, the right to co-determination gives the works council the right to block or veto some measures proposed by the employer. These include:

a. Decisions on the appointment or transfer of employees.

b. In many cases, the summary dismissal of a member of the works council. However, the veto of the works council can be overturned by the Labour Court.

The scope of the works council is determined by the *Betriebsverfassungsgesetz* (the 1952 Workplace Labour Relations Act). This Act also makes provision for cooperation at company level. It places an obligation on both the employer and the council to work to achieve harmonious workplace industrial relations. It also forbids the works council to call for industrial action, and in the event that industrial action occurs, the council is obliged to take a neutral stance and work to resolve the dispute.

2.4 Hours of work and holidays

There is a statutory minimum entitlement to 18 working days holiday per year. However, for the majority of employees this has been pushed up by local plant-level bargaining to 30 days per year. Additionally there are 9 national statutory public holidays as well as a number of others that are particular to only one, or only a few *Länder*. These are often days of religious significance and so would be celebrated according to the religious allegiance of each *Land*. Thus, for instance, *Reformationstag* (31 October) would be a public holiday in Protestant areas (predominately in the north of the country), while 15 August (Ascension of the Virgin Mary) would be celebrated in Catholic areas (predominately the southern *Länder*).

There is a legal maximum working hours of 48 per week. However, in many cases plant-level bargaining has reduced this down to between 37 and 40 hours per week. Employees are allowed to work beyond the statutory maximum working hours for up to 30 days per year. In return for doing so many collective agreements stipulate that the employee should be given time off in lieu, or allowed to receive payment at an enhanced rate; or be able to choose between the two. Overtime rates are often high and can vary from between 25 per cent for overtime worked on a normal day, up to 200 per cent for working on a public holiday.

2.5 Pay

There is no statutory minimum wage in Germany, but for those companies who ally themselves to the employers associations described above collective agreements are binding, and many such agreements do prescribe minimum levels of pay.

Labour costs in Germany are among the highest in the world, both in the service and in the manufacturing sectors. This caused real problems as the country struggled to get to grips with the recession of the early 1990s, particularly with the on-going need for huge investment in the East of the country (largely paid for out of increased taxes) and the continued strength of the *Deutschmark* in the international currency markets.

The works council has the right of co-determination over how bonuses or other enhancements to basic pay are made. This has led to the establishment of a number of traditional bonuses and 'bonus points', such as at Christmas or other holidays, or in recognition of years of service. Equally popular (and suitably remunerated) are company suggestion schemes.

Popular methods of providing an incentive element to pay include profit sharing (which is common among managerial staff), employee share-ownership schemes (which have received the 'blessing' of the state, and hence tax allowances), incentive, or merit, pay is common for manual grades who meet targets of quality or output, and performance-related pay is increasingly common for professional, technical and managerial staff.

2.6 Equal opportunities

Legislation provides for equality of provision on grounds of sex, origin and political orientation. Despite the clarity of the law, in practice women still tend to earn less than men: about 20 per cent less on aver-age. Works councils have the right to challenge the grading of particular jobs, and many have been particularly vigilant in considering cases in which many women have been employed on the bottom grade of the scale.

The German constitution makes discrimination on ground of race illegal, but there is no additional law to back this up and it is often seen as a weak area.

Employers are required to employ 6 per cent of their workforce from among the disabled community. Generous assistance is available to help with the adaption of the workplace to take disabled workers. Disabled workers enjoy special rights to protection of employment and cannot easily be dismissed. Those employers who choose to flout the requirement to employ 6 per cent disabled workers must instead pay a levy of several hundred marks per month for each disabled worker that they are below quota.

Maternity provision allows for 14 weeks off on normal salary, of which 6 should be taken before the child is born and the rest after. Locally negotiated agreements commonly extend this provision. Parental leave (known as *Erziehungsurlaub*) is also a feature of German law. This allows a parent time off work once the period of maternity leave has expired. It applies only where both partners are working. Parental leave may be taken by either the father or mother, or shared. Employees taking advantage of this opportunity do not receive pay-ment from their employers but are entitled to state benefits.

2.7 Trade unions

The number, size and role of German trade unions was considered earlier in this chapter; however, it bears repeating that Germany has only 16 large industrial unions and they represent all grades and occupations in a particular industry (far fewer than is the case in the United Kingdom). Additionally, there is a union for civil servants and one for white-collar workers. There are also 17 Christian trade unions who are affiliated to the Christian Trade Union Federation. Trade union membership is about 11 million and generally considered to be falling. The largest union is *IG-Metall*, with in excess of 3 million members. With reunification, many former West German trade unions began to recruit in the East. Here union density was (and is still) much higher, with up to 90 per cent of the workforce belonging to unions, compared to 30–40 per cent in the former West. This gave a much-needed boost to recruitment.

The rights to form and to join a trade union are enshrined in the constitution. However, closed shops are illegal, as is discrimination against workers who are, or who are not, union members. The right to strike is not regulated by law, but both employers and employees (and their representatives) are expected to behave by a closely regulated code of conduct during disputes. The code has been established largely as a result of decisions made in the German Labour Court. The code describes the conduct to be followed regarding areas such as collective bargaining, disagreements and strikes. Civil servants are forbidden to strike – to do so is illegal.

It is expected (and generally is the case) that the majority of work-place disputes will be resolved via the system of industrial democracy, or co-determination, described earlier in the chapter. However, the costs of co-determination are borne entirely by the employer. These costs can include time off work for works council members to perform their duties, providing administrative and support services – in large companies (more than 300 hundred employees) this would include paying for full-time council officials, and the costs of training the council members.

2.8   Current issues

The recession of the early 1990s, the effects of unification and the Single European Market have led some to question the continued wisdom of the highly structured system of industrial democracy that exists in Germany. There has been a call in some places for a more flexible and responsive approach to ensure that the competitiveness of German industry continues. But German unions see their primary goals to be cuts in the working week without loss of pay, and the complete convergence of the former East with the West, so that levels of pay and conditions of service are in line.

Unemployment is high, particularly in the east, and pressure to cut public-sector expenditure is considerable. However, the state sector supports many people – not only public servants, but also many students, those undertaking national service, the unemployed, and the retired. Significant cuts in the public sector will, according to many, simply increase unemployment.

In October 1994 the German engineering employers federation Gesamtmetall condemned the call by the leaders of the I-G Metall trade union for a 6 per cent increase in pay. Representatives of Gesamtmetall argued that if forced to honour such a deal many companies would be brought to the brink of collapse, and in future pay settlements would have to be governed by the employer's ability to pay. The union side claimed that the pay increase would give a much-needed boost to domestic demand, helping to secure jobs and create new ones.

Employers also face a struggle to renegotiate a 1984 agreement to cut from 40 to 36 the number of hours worked per week. Currently hours worked are 37 – this number has been falling steadily since the 1984 agreement. The cut, which was agreed following a 7-week strike in 1984, is causing considerable *concern for employers, who claim that it will add to costs. They are keen to stick with the present 36 hours and may prove to be unwilling to budge. Union leaders claim that the cut (and the trend to shorter working hours) should be maintained in order to promote job creation.*

TASK

Consider the issues highlighted in the case, and the German system of pay bargaining as detailed earlier in the chapter. Could such a system be implemented in the United Kingdom? If your answer is 'yes', what practical problems would it bring? If your answer is 'no', why has it worked so well in Germany, and for so long?

3. Spain

3.1 Introduction

The accession of Spain to the European Union and the gradual reduction of its protective tariffs between 1986 and 1993 marked the end of a long period of transition – from Franco's dictatorship to democracy, to membership of the mainstream of Europe, and to a modern advanced economy.

Spain has enjoyed high rates of growth in the years since membership of the Union. This has been complemented by high rates of inward investment. Despite this, Spain still suffers the highest rate of unemployment in Europe and persistently high inflation. The traditional industries of Spain remain strong and these include agriculture and tourism.

In recent years Spain has been trying to modernize its economic and social infrastructure. To date, however, the quality of roads, telecommunications, health care and education all remain very patchy. In truth in the last thirty years Spain has undergone the kind of industrial revolution, and all that entails, which many other countries experienced over a period of a century.

When Spain joined the European Union in 1986 the majority of significant industries were state owned and held by the state holding company Instituto Nacional de Industria (INI). Since 1984 the government has followed a policy of restructuring and modernization. This has involved heavy loss of jobs and many organizations being transferred to the private sector or into another holding company called Teneo, which is seen as a half-way house to full privatization. At its peak INI was among the 50 largest trading companies in the world, with interests as diverse as airlines (Iberia), aluminium manufacture (Inespal) and electricity production (Endesa). European Union law forbids the state subsidies once enjoyed by the INI companies and hence the government has followed the path of rationalization and privatization.

Spain has been very successful in attracting inward investment by using such showcases as EXPO '92 in Seville and the Barcelona Olympic

Figure 16.2

```
┌─────────────────────────────────────────────────────────────────────┐
│                   SPAIN: KEY STATISTICS (1993)                        │
│                                                                       │
│  Population:          39 m.        Land area:      504,750 km²         │
│                                                                       │
│  Gross national product: Sp. pta. 60tr.  Per capita income: US$12,252 │
│                                                                       │
│  Workforce:           15 m.        Unemployment:   22%                │
│                                                                       │
│  Significant industries:           Major Employers/ Industries:       │
│       Fresh Produce                    Bayer AG (German owned), Repsol,│
│       Tourism                          Telefonica, Endesa, Banco de    │
│       Car Manufacture                  Santander,                      │
│                                        Volkswagen (German owned)       │
│                                                                       │
│  Source: Nielson (1994).                                              │
└─────────────────────────────────────────────────────────────────────┘
```

Games as a springboard to develop the sort of infrastructure needed to modernize and develop the economy. The public exposure enjoyed as a result of these events has created great interest in the country and investment has followed. Information technology firms are expanding in Spain (Rank Zerox, IBM, Olivetti, Fujitsu and Siemens to name a few); Spain is Europe's third largest manufacturer of cars; many large banking and insurance companies (including British companies) have invested heavily in the country (indigenous banks are seen as slow and expensive); while many manufacturers see Spain as an excellent location. Britain's fastest growing insurance company, Direct Line, made Spain their first venture into Europe when it announced expansion plans in November 1994. Spain's key statistics appear in figure 16.2.

3.2 Human resource management in Spain

The influence of HR management in Spain can perhaps be judged by two facts: that Spain has a smaller number of qualified HR practitioners than most other European Union member states, and most companies employ fewer HR managers than is the case elsewhere. Given that, many commentators still believe that the influence of HR is in the ascendant, and claim that 'today few would question the need for a strong, well organized and properly staffed personnel department' (Filella 1992: 29).

The Spanish working population number some 15 million with approximately 20 per cent self-employed and of the remainder about half working in the private sector and half in public service. Women make up about one-third of the workforce.

Many employee rights are embedded in the Spanish constitution, including the right to form unions and the right to strike.

Historically, one of the major weaknesses of the Spanish labour market has been the interventionist role played by the government. Partly this is a hangover from the Franco days, and partly the inclination of more recent administrations (for instance the Worker Statute of 1980, amended in 1984). The consequence has been that the government has been at the heart of such matters as regulating and managing pay, redundancy and employee mobility. The other key influences have been the 1959 Stabilization Plan, which aimed to promote a greater degree of integration between the Spanish and the world economy, and the

Moncloa Plan of 1977, an agreement between government, industry and unions aimed at promoting steady economic growth coupled with fiscal reforms and cuts in government expenditure. The agreements worked to a degree but membership of the Single European Market and the Maastricht Treaty exposed further weaknesses in the system. In 1993 the Spanish government proposed a plan to reduce the role of the state, extend free collective bargaining and transform the labour market. The plan was eventually introduced in 1984 without full agreement and accompanied by a wave of strikes. Details are discussed further on in the chapter.

The British employer would be aghast at the degree of regulation surrounding employment in Spain. In principle there are five main Acts that are of major significance, discussed below.

a. *Ley de Contrato de Trabajo* (1944) is the major law regulating work contracts. The state defines a number of forms of employment contract. The 'standard' contract assumes work to be full time and for an indefinite period. The other types of employment contract available include:

For the employment of physically handicapped persons.

For workers over the age of 45.

For temporary workers.

For apprentices or trainees.

For home workers.

For the creation of jobs designed to reduce unemployment.

And a number of other categories.

The regulation is designed to allow employee and employer to decide which is the most suitable form of relationship between them. Each form of contract then contains standard terms and conditions appropriate to that form of employment.

b. *Ordenanza General de Seguridad e Higiene en el Trabajo* (1971) refers to health and safety at work. It requires employers to safeguard the physical integrity of workers in the course of their employment. It puts a concomitant duty on employees to observe workplace rules.

c. *Ley General de Seguridad Social* (1974) regulates the social aspect of employment, from the time of employment to retirement. It includes details of entitlement to social security and retirement and death (widows) benefits.

d. *Ley Basica de Empleo* (1980) refers to regulations governing the commencement and termination of employment. This particular area has been the cause of much frustration and strife in recent years. Trade unions have tried to make it almost impossible to dismiss employees, while employers have sought ever more imaginative methods to rid themselves of problem or superfluous employees. Breaches of contract can result in the dismissal of the employee, and if the dismissal is by reason of redundancy or if the breach is by the employer, then compensation should be paid to the employee. Probationary periods vary from 15 days for non-qualified workers to 6 months for graduates. Either party can terminate the contract during this probationary period.

e. *Ley Organica de Libertad Sindical* (1985) codifies the right to form trade unions, to join and to participate in industrial action, including strikes.

Additionally the state has attempted to maintain a monopoly over employment by requiring all employers to register all employment contracts and dismissals with the state employment agency (INEM).

3.3 Hours of work and holidays

All employees are entitled to a minimum of 30 days' annual leave per year. This is in addition to 13 public holidays. It is not uncommon for many firms / industries to close down for practically most of the month of August. The 13 public holidays are not 'national' but vary, as is the case in England and Scotland. In Spain they vary between the regions but should be set before the start of the calendar year.

The maximum working hours allowed per week is 40, and in no case should the actual working day exceed 9 hours. Additionally there should always be a break of 12 hours before the end of one shift and the start of the next. Overtime should not exceed 80 hours per year. However, those companies involved in the provision of services to the general public, or commercial sales and distribution, can set their hours of work as they wish. Those employed on night shifts should receive a premium equivalent to 25 per cent of the normal rate of pay.

All employees are entitled to one and a half days rest a week, although the 5-day week is increasingly common. If necessary the weekly rest period can be accumulated over a 4-week period.

3.4 Pay

Spain has a national minimum wage which is set, and periodically reviewed, by the government. It is called 'the minimum interprofessional salary', and is set in consultation with employers and trade unions, and takes into account a number of economic factors. It is graduated according to age. Overtime is not permitted for employees who are under the age of 18. Those working overtime are often given additional time off as an alternative to enhanced pay.

The use of job evaluation is very common in Spain as employers seek to establish and define the relative differences between jobs. This is particularly important because pay is often sectorially negotiated and relative levels of pay need to be anchored to different jobs according to the content of those jobs.

The use of flexible pay systems has attracted much attention in Spain in recent years, with systems of merit pay and performance-related pay being particularly common. In general such benefits are only offered to managerial and professional staff.

3.5 Equal opportunities

Essentially the law provides for equal opportunity for all regardless of sex, race or creed, and indeed the rights of women as workers are enshrined into the 1978 Constitution. Female participation in the workplace (about 30 per cent) is low in comparison to European Union norms, as is female participation in the professions and in management.

Statutory maternity leave is 16 weeks (18 weeks in the case of multiple births). Six of the weeks should be taken before the birth. The state social security system pays 75 per cent of a woman's salary during this period. In order to qualify for maternity benefits a woman must have contributed to the social security fund for at least 180 days in the year prior to the birth. In an increasing number of cases contracts of employment will also give the right to paternity leave.

Financial incentives are available for employers to meet the quota requirement that 4 per cent of workers should be drawn from the disabled community; also, help may be given to firms who need to adapt aspects of a workplace to accommodate a disabled worker. Despite this, the quota is still often ignored.

3.6 Trade unions

All workers have a constitutional right to belong to a trade union, although actual membership is very low – estimated to be about 15 per cent of the workforce. Trade unions in Spain (like several other southern European countries) are intensely political animals and have great powers of worker mobilization, as exemplified in the general strike of 1988, and widespread unrest caused by the government's proposed reforms of 1993–4. There are two major unions in Spain, the CCO (Comisiones Obreras) and the UGT (Union General de Trabajadores). The only other sizeable union is particular only to the Basque region and is known as the ELA/STV (Euzko Langillen Alkartasuna/Solidaridad de Trabajadores Vascos).

Spanish trade unions are generally democratic in their practices and representatives are elected by their members. Unions have a legal right to strike and a strike may be called in any of three ways:

a. By the members themselves holding a secret ballot.

b. By the legal representatives of the workers and the work's council.

c. By the trade union organizations themselves.

Any decision to strike must be notified to the employer in advance (5 days). The notice must not only contain the objectives of the strike but also the measures that should be taken to avoid it. It must also contain details of the strike committee, which should be elected by the strikers. The committee has the task of negotiating to end the strike, and ensuring that essential services are maintained.

3.7 The works council

In all firms employing 50 workers or more, 'workers committees' should exist. The workers committee is elected (by law), and all workers, be they temporary or permanent, have a right to participate in the elections. The size of the committee is determined using the scale set out below:

from 50 to 100 workers: 5 members

from 100 to 250 workers: 9 members

from 251 to 500 workers: 13 members

from 501 to 750 workers: 17 members

from 751 to 1,000 workers: 21 members

above 1,000: 2 members per 1,000, up to a maximum of 75

The committee should elect its own officials, such as president and secretary, and meet twice a month. Decisions are made by a simple majority. The committee has the right to receive from the employer a considerable amount of information. This includes the following rights to consultation, negotiation and information:

- The right to three-monthly reports on the industry in which the employer operates, to include trends, employment, sales figures and production.
- The right to at least three-monthly notification of plans for new employment contracts or extensions of employment contracts, and the right to be informed of absence statistics and accidents at work.
- The right to receive reports on any plans to restructure the workplace which affect the workforce. This might include job evaluation, shift changes, new machinery, new methods of working.
- The right to be informed of all sanctions against workers.
- The committee has the right to collective negotiation.

Committee members also have the right to protection against dismissal over and above normal protection of employment. This is in order to prevent victimization of committee members going about their lawful business. Committee members are also entitled to time off work to carry out their duties.

3.8   Current issues

To Spanish HR managers three major problems have been evident in recent years:

1. The inability of the supply side of the labour market to react to changes in the demand side – hence persistent and on-going labour shortages of many key skills.
2. The lack of flexibility in the labour market with regard to terms and contracts of employment and dismissal.
3. The absence of a real 'work ethic' in Spain. Many people are keen to make money but fewer recognize that employment and enterprise is a legitimate way to make it. Many have expressed alarm at the rate at which indigenous Spanish companies have been sold by their owners to foreign investors.

Following the elections of June 1993 the government invited the two main labour unions (the CCO and UGT) to talks to negotiate a new social agreement. The talks were to be held without precondition. No agreement was reached and on 17 January 1994 the unions called a national strike. The government did not give in to the objections of the strikers, and on 13 July 1994 the new reforms came into effect.

Many aspects of employment were affected by the new laws, but principally the government was concerned to open up to negotiation between employer and employee dozens of areas that had formerly been fixed by the state. Such areas included work schedules, contracts of employment, wage increases and pay structures, occupational and geographical mobility. Additionally, no longer are employers required to register employment contracts and dismissal with INEM (the state employment agency). Far more flexibility of employment contract is now allowed, with some offering pay below the national minimum wage if they are accompanied by a guaranteed minimum level of training. From recruitment to redundancy almost every area of employment is affected by the reforms. Some commentators fear that the reforms have still not gone far enough in throwing off the restrictions that hinder the working of the labour market.

In November 1994 the Board of the Spanish national airline Iberia announced that it was to shed over 20 per cent of its 25,000 workforce. The airline, which is owned by the state holding company INI, had previously suggested a cut of up to 15 per cent in pay and the loss of 2,000 jobs. This had been rejected by the unions. Iberia has been heavily subsidized by the Spanish government over the years, most recently in 1992, with a Brussels-authorized injection of pta.20 billion. However, the expected losses for 1994 together with the accumulated loss from previous years means that this sum has been effectively wiped out. Without drastic action there is a real risk that the company will be forced into liquidation. The action proposed by the board involves the sale of Iberia's subsidiaries to INI for subsequent disposal. Currently Iberia has a stake in Aerrolineas Argentinas, Chile's Ladeco, Venezuela's Viasa as well as three domestic airlines. Disposal of these holdings will effectively end Iberia's ambition to be a global carrier. INI has also sought authorization from Europe for additional public subsidies valued at pta.130 billion, approximately £640 million. It is likely that this further subsidy will be opposed by other governments and their national carriers.

The scale of the changes is such that it is envisaged that the company would be segregated into a number of areas, most probably handling, marketing, information systems and maintenance, each of which would eventually be sold off, leaving a rump of about 5,000 staff (mainly aircrew) and a reduced fleet of airliners.

The changes being experienced at Iberia are typical of the problems faced by many of Spain's largest companies as INI attempt to manage large sections of its holdings on a more commercial basis.

TASK

Is it possible to reconcile the need for the deregulation of the Spanish economy with the wish for employees to maintain their jobs? What role can human resource managers play in this process, in both the long and short terms?

4. Conclusions: Lessons for the UK

1. The personnel management systems in Germany and Spain are, as illustrated, very different. This is not surprising given their different histories, economic structures, cultures and legal and social systems. However, what is also evident is that despite their differences they have more in common with each other than they have with UK practice.

2. Both place great store by their respective systems of workplace democracy and employee participation. No such system exists in the UK.

3. Both the German and Spanish systems are closer than is the UK to the emerging European model of personnel management that is gradually developing in Brussels (see the previous chapter). Although both Spain and Germany have their differences with what is proposed by the European Commission, these are minor in comparison with the root and branch opposition taken to so much by the UK government.

4. The level of investment by British industry in Europe is at high and growing levels. Research indicates that British companies are less fearful than our politicians of European personnel practices.

5. That there are moves towards greater workplace flexibility across the whole of Europe there can be no doubt. Indeed, some European HR practitioners might eye with envy the degree of flexibility accorded to their counterparts in the UK. However, the degree to which industrial democracy, consultation and cooperation are embedded into the workplace culture of so many of our partner countries makes it inconceivable that they will come to do things in a way that does not in some way embrace the ideas of the workforce.

QUESTIONS FOR FURTHER CONSIDERATION

1. Consider the factors that determine a nation's system of HR management. What factors are likely to influence its development and change?

2. Consider the major strengths and weaknesses of the German and Spanish systems as described. Are there aspects that could be introduced into the UK? If yes, which ones and how should they be introduced?

3. To what extent do you consider that individual employers should be left to determine their own relationship with their employees, and to what extent does the state have a legitimate interest in promoting good practice, either by legislation or by other methods?

4. The position of the British government has been consistently to oppose many of the moves towards legislated greater worker participation and consultation. Many major British employers have no objection to more formalized employee participation and consultation. Does this indicate that the British government is out of touch with the British business community?

•REFERENCES•

General

Beardwell I & Holden L (1994)
**HUMAN RESOURCE MANAGEMENT: A
CONTEMPORARY PERSPECTIVE**
London, Pitman.

Brewster C, Hegeswisch A, Holden L & Lockhart T (eds) (1992)
**THE EUROPEAN HUMAN RESOURCE MANAGEMENT
GUIDE**
London, Academic Press.

Brewster C & Tyson S (1991)
**INTERNATIONAL COMPARISONS IN HUMAN
RESOURCE MANAGEMENT**
London, Pitman.

Gluc E (1994)
The European Response to HRD
Training and Development, Dec.

Graham H & Bennett R (1995)
HUMAN RESOURCES MANAGEMENT
8th edn. London, McDonald and Evans.

Income Data Services / Institute of Personnel Management
(1990–3)
EUROPEAN MANAGEMENT GUIDES. Titles include:
**TRAINING AND DEVELOPMENT
RECRUITMENT
TERMS AND CONDITIONS OF EMPLOYMENT
INDUSTRIAL RELATIONS
PAY AND BENEFITS**
London, IPM.

Hollinshead G & Leat M (1995)
**HUMAN RESOURCES MANAGEMENT: AN
INTERNATIONAL AND COMPARATIVE PERSPECTIVE**
London, Pitman.

Perry K (1994)
BUSINESS IN THE EUROPEAN COMMUNITY
London, Butterworth Heinemann.

Personnel Management (Feb. 1992–)
Personnel Management in . . .
Series covering personnel management in the European Union
member states. London, Institute of Personnel Management.

Pinder M (1990)
**PERSONNEL MANAGEMENT FOR THE SINGLE
EUROPEAN MARKET**
London, Pitman.

Torrington D (1994)
INTERNATIONAL HUMAN RESOURCE MANAGEMENT
London, Prentice-Hall.

Germany

Arkin A (1992)
At Work in the Powerhouse of Europe
Personnel Management, Feb.

Conrad P & Rudiger P (1990)
**HUMAN RESOURCE MANAGEMENT IN THE FEDERAL
REPUBLIC OF GERMANY**
Berlin, Walter de Gruyter.

Financial Times Survey (1993)
Baden-Wurttemberg
29 April.

Financial Times Survey (1993)
Germany
25 Oct.

Gaugler E & Wiltz S (1992)
Federal Republic of Germany, in **THE EUROPEAN HUMAN
RESOURCE MANAGEMENT GUIDE**
Brewster C et al. (eds). London, Academic Press.

Spain

Bruton S (1994)
THE BUSINESS CULTURE IN SPAIN
London, Butterworth Heinemann.

Crabb S (1994)
Death Knell of Spanish Customs
Personnel Management, Aug.

Filella J (1992)
Waiting to Join the Mainstream
Personnel Management, July.

Filella J & Solar C (1992)
Spain, in **THE EUROPEAN HUMAN RESOURCE
MANAGEMENT GUIDE**
Brewster C et al. (eds). London, Academic Press.

Income Data Services (1994)
Reforms Herald New Era for Industrial Relations
European Report no. 391, July, IDS.

Salmon K (1991)
THE MODERN SPANISH ECONOMY
London, Pinter.

Walker A (1994)
Training Assessment in a Spanish Company
Training and Development, Dec.

·CHAPTER·

17

TRAINING IN EUROPE: A BRIEF CONSIDERATION

AS A RESULT OF STUDYING THIS CHAPTER YOU SHOULD BE ABLE TO:

- Consider the importance given to, and the approach taken to, training and development in a range of European Union member countries.

- Offer comment on the relationship between training and the wider framework within which the management of staff is undertaken.

- Appreciate the role that the European Union and its agencies have played in promoting training.

- Draw comparison between the approach to training and development in other states and that in the United Kingdom.

Please note: in order to get full value from this chapter it is recommended that the reader should first consider those covering training in the UK (chapters 8 and 9) and the chapters on Europe (15 and 16).

1. Introduction

The aim of this chapter is to outline the variety of approaches taken to industrial, commercial and management training within different member countries of the European Union. The reader should not be surprised to discover that practice is very different from country to country. It is outside the scope of a book such as this to give consideration to the education systems of the countries examined. However, the reader should be aware that one of the key factors influencing any national system of training will be the compulsory education system, in terms of its quality, the way in which it prepares young people for the world of work, and the degree to which it offers vocational pathways to those pupils who are not inclined to follow traditional academic routes. Also beyond the scope of this book is consideration of the culture of the various nations – in this context culture is taken to mean the degree to which education and training is seen as a valuable thing. The chapter is comparative in nature, highlighting significant differences between the structure and processes of training and development in the member states of the European Union. The chapter does not consider all member states; instead it focuses on a number of larger states and those where practice is most different from that in the UK.

2. Training Compared: A Cross-section of Practice in European Union Countries

2.1 Vocational training

In *Denmark* the system for initial vocational training is very closely regulated by the state and operates with close cooperation between employers and technical and commercial schools. The training system, which grew out of the guilds, is organized into approximately 90 specialisms. However, the system encourages flexibility and late specialization. This initial training (which comprises both practical and theoretical work) leads to the award of a nationally recognized training certificate which, according to the European Union comparability tables, is equivalent to a UK Level 3 National Vocational Qualification (NVQ). In any one year approximately half of the nation's school leavers will follow this route.

The courses, curricula and assessment are developed in close liaison between the Vocational Education and Training Council, local Trades Committees (which are joint employer–union bodies) and the schools and colleges themselves.

In *France* most initial vocational training takes place in schools and follows the completion of compulsory education at age 16. However, in some cases young people may leave school at 14 or 15 in order to go on to a vocational training college. It takes 3 years to acquire the initial vocational training certificate. This combines both practical and theoretical aspects and is the equivalent of a UK NVQ at level 2. Such qualifications are available for both the technical and administrative worker and are generally regarded as being a necessary prerequisite for skilled or even semi-skilled employment. The higher training certificate, which is available from specialist colleges, is rated at NVQ 3. Approximately 30–40 per cent of the population of school leavers will follow this route.

Running alongside the vocational training certificates is the apprenticeship system, which had up until recent years fallen into disrepute. It had become regarded by many as a source of cheap labour for employers, with no guarantee of employment for the apprentice at the end of his / her indentureship. Lately the system has been overhauled to raise the standard of the training given (both practical and theoretical) and to guarantee that payment will be made at the appropriate proportion of the adult rate.

In *Germany* the falling birth rate meant that typically in the period of the 1980s employers were able to offer many more initial training places than there were young people to fill them. The situation has deteriorated somewhat in recent years, but many firms see the advantage of offering training places to young people. This is because traditionally geographical and occupational mobility is much lower in Germany than it is, for instance, in the UK. Employers then see the importance of attracting young people into their company, often employing and training many more than they themselves need, allowing them the opportunity to retain the best while releasing the rest into the labour market. Approximately 70 per cent of young people enter employment this way. Typically their training lasts between 2 and 3.5 years, dependent upon occupation.

The *German* system, known as the 'dual system', provides for the on-the-job training under the supervision of skilled employees and attendance at special vocational training colleges. The college provides general as well as occupationally specific education. In the old West Germany there are in excess of 1,500 vocational training colleges. In order to employ young trainees employers must register with the Federal Employment Institute (the state job placement and training authority). As an accredited firm the employer agrees to abide by the terms and conditions laid down by the Federal Employment Institute for the employment and training of young people. The implication of this is that firms are unable to employ young people to work in any of the recognized occupations unless they are prepared to offer the training that is required.

Successful completion of the training gives the young person a qualification which is deemed to be the equivalent of NVQ 3. This qualification is also seen as ideal preparation for the those who wish to go on to become master craftsmen (*Meister*). Such people will fill the ranks of supervisors and foremen in their employing organizations. Those employers who wish to be accredited training organizations must, as one of the terms of qualification, have workplace instructors who fulfil certain qualifications. These qualifications include the require-ment for all workplace instructors to have passed a master craftsman examination.

In *Italy* vocational training is generally considered to be weak and of variable quality. Some people blame this weakness on the lack of influence of guilds or similar organizations, while the variable quality is often put down to the lack of central coordination of qualifications. There are *no* national standards for vocational training, and *no* institu-tional network to deliver national qualifications to a national standard. Additionally, vocational training is delivered in both the public sector and by a variety of providers and methods. The state supports provi-sion through three outlets:

1. State-run technical and vocational training colleges are funded and regulated by the Ministry of Education. These are financed centrally and are part of the general system of education. They train about 1.25 million people annually. They have a better reputation than the regional training centres (described below), and trainees typically leave with a qualification equivalent to an NVQ 3.

2. Regional training centres provide training services in three main areas: agriculture, industry and services. The standard is variable, the curriculum varies from region to region and from centre to centre, However, they do have an annual intake of approximately 400,000 trainees. The standard of the courses is considered to be low, with the first-level course (which lasts 2 years) at the level of about NVQ 2, while the second-level course (which lasts one 1 year) is located between NVQ 2 and 3.

3. The apprenticeship system is considered to be weak and is generally used to allow young people access to the workplace. Employers taking on apprentices are given special concessions on national insurance contributions. In total there are in excess of a half million apprentices who, although their employment is regulated by law, are often considered to be given a bad deal by their employers. This is because of the failure of the system to guarantee that apprentices be given the right to attend the prescribed 8 hours' school instruction per week that should accompany the practical element. Generally apprenticeships last 5 years; most young people being taken on at age 14. The vast majority of apprenticeships are in craft areas.

In *Spain* vocational training is overseen by the Vocational Training Council, which has 13 members drawn from industry, the unions and government. Its terms of reference were laid down by the 1990 amendment to the 1985 National Training and Development Plan.

The National Training Plan, developed by the National Employment Institute (known as INEM), categorizes training into 7 main areas:

1. Vocational training for the young and long-term unemployed.

2. Retraining schemes, sandwich courses for vocational training students, university courses and training schemes for military personnel.

3. Training for industries or companies undergoing restructuring.

4. Training for women returners.

5. Training schemes for students.

6. Training for the disabled and for migrants.

7. Sandwich courses for those aged under 25.

INEM sponsors training in a number of different forms. Young people may be employed on a fixed-term training contract which can last between 3 months and 3 years. INEM will sponsor such an arrangement if the employee spends at least 25 per cent (and sometimes up to 50 per cent) of their time receiving formal training. It would be expected that such a contract would culminate in the employee achieving a vocational training certificate. The INEM subsidy can be as high as 50 per cent. Employers may also apply for subsidies to take on graduates in order that they might receive work experience. Again, contracts may be for between 3 months and 3 years. The unemployed have access to INEM-sponsored training, particularly if they wish to be trained in those areas in which skills are in short supply.

INEM will subsidize the cost of workplace trainers, and will also support their training. Employers can apply to become approved INEM Collaborative Centres, which will allow them to apply to have the costs of their trainers subsidized and to take on additional (sponsored) trainees.

2.2 Management training

The typical manager in *Denmark* will have an engineering qualification – usually a degree – while others will have business degrees. There is little use made of business schools in Denmark, most training undertaken will be in-house, or for smaller firms in particular the employers association (the DA) and the personnel managers association, provides some management training. Such training generally consists of short courses and is not certificated.

The role of the manager and supervisor in *France* is unusual in that it has legal status: the former is known as a *cadre* and the latter as an *agent de maitrise*. Their status is recognized in collective agreements with the expectation that to achieve such a position the employee should be properly qualified. Often such qualification is gained through a combination of technical study and several years' appropriate experience. Alternatively, a graduate from a *grande école* (a technical university) might be deemed to be a cadre upon graduation. These technical universities, which offer an education of the highest standard, provide many of the future leaders of French commerce and industry. Generally speaking most French managers are well educated, with many having attended a *grande école*, of which there are over 160 across the country. Graduates of *grandes écoles* account for only 10 per cent of the number of traditional university graduates, but are sought out and prized by many of the largest and most successful companies in France. The emphasis of the curricula at most *grandes écoles* is biased towards analytical and theoretical studies, and although some contain a practical element and, to an increasing degree, emphasis on wider interpersonal skills, there still exists concern that the curriculum is too narrow.

A number of private business schools exist in France. The best-known is INSEAD. They offer MBAs along American lines, and are considered to provide graduates mainly for consultancy companies. In general, an MBA is not regarded as an essential business qualification for general managers in France. Many business schools also provide an extensive consultancy and short-course service.

The average *German* manager is well qualified: given that he or she will probably have completed military service and a degree that may have taken 6 years of study, it is not uncommon for them to enter industry or commerce in their mid to late twenties. Those who have ambitions to reach senior levels in their field commonly hold a doctorate, making the age of entry to work still later. As well as traditional universities Germany also has a strong network of *fachhochschule* (technical universities). Typically these are smaller than traditional universities and provide qualifications that are closely related to the needs of industry and commerce. This would include, for instance, mechanical engineering, electrical engineering, business administration and social work. Graduates of *fachhochschulen* generally study for a shorter period than university students (4 years) and this period would typically include two periods of work placement known as *praktikum*.

Typically German employers recruit on the basis of sound academic performance in a vocationally relevant subject. Once recruited promotion is usually internal and geographical, and occupational mobility is less common than it is in, say, the United Kingdom. There are few schools of management in German universities or *fachhochschulen*, and those employees seeking postgraduate qualification in business often study abroad. However, there are many private training providers that offer a multitude of management development courses, and these will be used by those employers who do not offer such provision in-house. Most larger organizations offer extensive management training opportunities themselves, and managers receive continuous and on-going development throughout their careers.

The typical *Italian* manager is also a graduate, with degrees in engineering, law or business being the most popular. Additionally, many universities have postgraduate business schools which offer MBA degrees. A master's degree is not a legally recognized qualification in Italy, but MBAs are increasingly popular. This increase in popularity is widely thought to have gone hand in hand with the increased tendency for Italian employees to change employers in search of personal and professional advancement – hence their need for a transferable qualification. Most of the MBAs offered fall along traditional American lines, and many are closely linked to an American business school.

Traditionally management development in Italy has been undertaken in-house via company training departments and the extensive use of consultants. This system has diminished a little in recent years as the MBA has taken hold, but it is still the form in which the vast majority of managers will receive their post-entry training. Management training and development is given great importance in Italy and considerable resources are devoted to it.

It has been widely recognized that the *Spanish* university system has been unable to keep up with the demand for graduates. The period of the 1980s saw a huge increase in the demand for trained managers and for MBAs. The shortfalls of the state sector have been in part met by the private sector, which consists of many hundreds of companies of varying size and quality. This sector is largely unregulated and most of the companies within it survive or fall on their reputation alone. MBAs are offered in about 100 private-sector colleges. As well as MBAs the private sector offers many other services – mostly, however, short courses and consultancy.

Although not regulated, private training providers (like other businesses) must be registered. There are estimated to be total something over 1,000 in all. Industry and commerce make extensive use of their services and buy in a large number of training courses. Most are only of short duration and are generally uncertificated.

The Spanish university system is gradually responding to the increased demand for management development and training, However, its response is still small-scale in comparison to the private-sector provision which has so flourished in recent times.

2.3 Continuing and on-going training

In *Denmark* the right to on-going training is enshrined in law, and government supports and sponsors vocationally relevant further education and in-service training. In particular the government is keen to encourage training for the identification of new market opportunities, the application of new technologies and the improvement of quality and productivity. The grants given by government may be applied for by public- and private-sector training providers. Generally the courses are run locally and with the support of both employers and trades unions. Many courses are aimed at unskilled and semi-skilled workers. The state has made a point of emphasizing its support for the continual training and development of all employees, and the provision of occupationally relevant skills for the young and long-term unemployed. The importance attached to training by the government is underlined by its willingness to give employers wage compensation for employees who are taking courses.

The tripartite nature of training in Denmark is impressive, with the government giving broad direction to, plus financial support and sponsorship for, training that is locally provided to meet locally identified needs. The system has the full support of employers and their associations and trades unions.

In *France* the importance of training is such that employers are required, in consultation with their works councils, to prepare annual training plans. Generally such plans are drawn up on a rolling 5-year basis with annual updating. They must include:

An identification of training needs and how they will be met.

A commitment to equality of access for both men and women.

A consideration of the particular training needs of young people.

The recognition and value of any qualifications gained.

In drawing up the plan, account should be taken of investment levels, technology, economic factors and work (re)organization.

Meetings should be held at least three times a year to discuss the progress made in implementing the training plan.

The right to continuing vocational training is available to all, and each year in excess of 25 per cent of the workforce receive training. The emphasis of this training is on maintaining and improving existing skills, and/or adapting skills to accommodate technological change. The minimum level of expenditure on training is governed by statute. In addition, all employers pay a levy on the wage bill to fund national and regional training initiatives. The government has signalled its wish to increase the amount spent on training, and there are many organizations able to supply industry with its needs. These include:

Both technical and traditional universities.

Engineering schools.

The national correspondence college (CNED).

The *lycées* and *lycées techniques* – the approximately 6,000 general and technical post-16 colleges.

Many Chambers of Commerce act as registered training providers.

In *Germany* much of the development and coordination of the training effort is undertaken by the Federal Labour Institute – known as the BfA – which is based in Nuremberg. It is the official job placement service: it runs job creation schemes, provides careers advice and offers numerous training opportunities to employers and employees.

At the company level the 1972 Works Constitution Act requires employers and works councils to cooperate in the promotion and development of training. Additionally, works councils have co-determination rights in a number of areas of training. Essentially both parties should ensure that full access to training is given to all workers, and in particular give attention to the needs of the older worker. The works councils have the right to put forward proposals as to who they consider should be given training. They can demand the non-appointment of any person who they feel does not have adequate qualifications for the job. Employers must consult works councils on training and training facilities, while works councils have the right of co-determination on the implementation of training.

On-going training is taken very seriously in Germany, where about one in five of the workforce receive training in any one year. The more senior the employee the more training they are likely to receive. Most supervisors and managers will be engaged in some form of training activity on a regular basis.

Many collective agreements have provisions written in stating that in order for an employee to be promoted to a certain pay grade a formal qualification must be achieved. Further, some agreements expect an employer to provide an employee faced with redundancy further training, and possible redeployment, before the decision to let them go is finally made. It is common for collective agreements to contain reference to training and the expectation is that the employer will provide regular opportunities for employee training.

In most *Lander* employees are now entitled to up to 5 days a year off work to participate in vocational education. This should be taken at a recognized educational or training institution and the cost should be borne by the employer.

On-going training takes place in a number of ways. Many larger companies have their own extensive training centres and staff. There also are a number of public training facilities and many private-sector providers. Most training that occurs is uncertificated.

The BfA has set up schemes to monitor the quality of training provision and has written-down guidelines for what it considers to be good practice. This has helped to ensure that private providers of training adhere to recognized standards.

The *Italian* approach to training is more mixed and more fragmented. At its best it is excellent, and many of the larger companies show great commitment to training. Many have their own training centres; the best have even established them as independent entities able to provide training for other employers. At the other end of the scale training can be patchy or even non-existent. There is no legal requirement to train, and many smaller companies see it as a luxury they can ill afford. The single largest part of the training budget is spent on management training, and this and other parts of the budget are increasingly going to private-sector providers. The best of these are often supported or funded directly by trade associations. Elsewhere the standard can be very variable.

The provision of continuing training in *Spain* is also mixed. Evidence, in the form of the Spanish Education Ministry's Annual Training Survey, suggests that foreign companies operating in Spain seem to provide more training than their Spanish-owned counterparts. It has been estimated that despite the unevenness of provision approximately 3 per cent of working hours are devoted to training at a cost of over 1 per cent of the total wages bill. Many collective agreements include provision for training, and joint management–works council training committees are not uncommon. Many agreements make provision for financial assistance and paid leave for study. Also, employees have statutory rights to unpaid time off work to attend vocational training examinations and the right to work shift patterns that will support their studies.

The Spanish government is keen to see the training effort given greater resources. INEM (the National Employment Institute) has considerable funds to support the efforts of training and of trainers.

3. European Union Interventions

The European Union has always recognized the importance of training as a vital ingredient necessary to achieve its wider economic and social aims. It has pursued a number of policies which support training, fund training, and recognize the value of training in all member states, including the mutual recognition of qualifications and awards.

Training is at the heart of the European Union's 1993 White Paper on Growth, Competitiveness and Employment. The White Paper, which was agreed at the end of the Dutch presidency in 1993, was aimed at addressing the economic problems facing the whole of Europe, but particularly unemployment. The White paper identified three causes of unemployment, namely low growth, technological change and structural change. The proposals, which were taken up by subsequent presidencies, included the promotion of life-long vocational training, and the promotion of labour market flexibility through retraining, and increased labour mobility and flexible working hours.

The European Union also sponsors a considerable amount of training itself. The funding for these programmes is put through a number of projects, which are outlined below:

ARION: supports the exchange of strategic-level national education and training personnel.

COMETT: promotes cross-border cooperation between industry and education on issues of new technology.

ERASMUS: provides funds for the exchange of teaching staff and students.

EUROTECHNET: encourages and supports cross-border cooperation on high-tech. programmes.

FORCE: supports occupational vocational training.

IRIS: applies specifically to the training and retraining of women.

LEONARDO: introduced in 1995 to support and further the work of FORCE, COMETT, EUROTECHNET and PETRA.

LINGUA: promotes language training.

PETRA: supports the initial training of young workers.

PHARE: is designed to boost the training and development of organizations in central and eastern Europe.

SOCRATES: introduced in 1995 to support the work initiated under ERASMUS and LINGUA and extend it to school-level students.

TACIS: provides technical assistance to the Commonwealth of Independent States, Georgia and Mongolia.

TEMPUS: offers support for the development of higher education in central and eastern Europe.

In addition, the European Training Foundation, which is based in Turin, is charged with trying to develop a vocational and training system in the states of central and eastern Europe.

Generally speaking, all the funds described are allocated through national Employment Departments and the criteria to access them are often strict. Usually the funds will provide up to 50 per cent of the monies necessary for a particular project. Because they often involve TECs, higher education institutions or local authorities they will require the partner to find the rest of the funds. Notwithstanding this requirement, most funds are heavily over-subscribed.

The European Commission has a training agency, known as CEDEFOP (originally based in Berlin, but now moved to Thessaloniki in Greece). The agency has carried out a great deal of research on drawing up comparabilities between national qualifications in an attempt to draw up an 'international qualification map'. To date it has concentrated its efforts on such industries as agriculture, construction, hotels and catering, textiles, electronics, banking and commerce, and metal working. It has focused in particular on the skilled worker and has managed to draw up in excess of 200 occupational profiles.

◼4. Mutual Recognition of Qualifications

The European Union has spent a great deal of time and effort considering how the qualifications awarded in member states could and should be recognized in other states. Originally this was tackled on a profession-by-profession basis but, not surprisingly, the rate of progress was very slow. Over a period of about 15 years only 7 professions had been covered and Directives were passed requiring all member states to recognize qualifications gained elsewhere in the Union. The professions upon which agreement was reached were architecture, dentistry, general medical practice, pharmacy, midwifery, nursing and veterinary surgery.

Not surprisingly, the profession-by-profession approach was eventually considered to be too slow, and in 1989 a general Directive was adopted requiring all member states to recognize all regulated professional qualifications gained in other member states.

In practice this meant that practitioners have only to fill in gaps in their knowledge between that required in their own state and that required in the country in which they wish to work and carry on their profession. The Directive places a duty upon professional and chartered bodies to provide advice and assistance as required.

The second general Directive passed in 1992 paved the way for the mutual recognition of regulated diplomas, certificates and vocational qualifications. This Directive covers qualifications up to and including NVQ level 4 and its equivalents.

5. Conclusion

The United Kingdom can learn a great deal from how our partners approach training. In a number of countries initial vocational training has been given, and is recognized as being worthy of, parity with traditional academic routes. This is particularly the case in the northern European countries. The UK has tried to raise the value of vocational training, but today it is true to say that it is still regarded as a route to be followed by the academically less able. This may change with the GNVQ (also known as Vocational A-level).

A feature of working lives in Britain is the expectation that we will regularly change our employer. This high degree of mobility is not present in all other European countries. In a number of countries workforces are more stable, and promotion is awarded internally. This stability is reflected in training policies: employers can see real benefit in investing in training because they will, in all probability, reap the rewards.

A feature of training in Britain has been the increasingly non-interventionist stance taken by the government. This is in stark contrast to elsewhere in Europe, where government has seen its role to be ensuring that training needs are identified and met to satisfy both current and future requirements. In some countries this has led to a high degree of government sponsorship for training, in some it has meant that training standards are carefully regulated and providers carefully monitored, while in nearly all countries the workforce is given a considerable say in determining training priorities at both the strategic and operational levels. It is fair to say that Britain is almost unique in considering that employers and employers alone should be given the responsibility for ensuring that the workforce is properly trained. In recent years the UK has set national training targets and instituted awards such as Investors in People and the National Training Awards for organizations deemed to be good trainers. However, these represent the minimum level of intervention by government and fall far short of what is to be found elsewhere, where statutory rights to training and national training plans are the norm.

Formal management qualifications are only really considered to be important in the UK, where the MBA degree has become very popular. Elsewhere, although there is much management training, little of it is award bearing and most is undertaken in-house and close to the place of work.

It is also worthy of note that the systems of workplace cooperation and consultation present in many parts of Europe work in such a way as to make training a shared responsibility between the management and the workforce. The representatives of the workforce work closely with the employer to identify training needs. It requires real cooperation and trust on the part of management if training must address not only short-term needs but also the longer-term strategic needs of the organization.

GEORG HERDER GMBH

The German engineering firm of Georg Herder GmbH is currently poised at an interesting and probably crucial stage of development. Founded in 1956 by Georg Herder himself, the firm has concentrated on doing what it can really do well: manufacturing high-quality products, many of which have been exported to neighbouring European companies. The company has also prided itself on the quality and training of its workforce.

After a long career Herder has now retired and left the firm in the hands of his son. Herder junior is conscious of both the strength of the firm and its vulnerability. Strengths are:

Reputation for quality.

Well established customer base.

Excellent financial position.

Weak points are:

Rather conservative and slow moving.

Management all German.

Turnover has plateaued in recent years.

Japanese competition increasing.

High wage and social costs.

Herder junior is keen to move into another country, either by acquisition or by cementing a strategic alliance with a suitable partner. In recent months the company has held exploratory talks with D.S. House Ltd., a UK-based small engineering company, which has a product range complementary to that produced by Herder. House is also a family-owned business and Herder perceive that the owners are keen to sell.

Before making an offer Herder have asked House's management team each to make a presentation on their area of responsibility, outlining policies, procedures, targets and achievements.

TASK
You are the training manager for House and have been asked to prepare a presentation on the UK system of industrial training, drawing out major points of similarity and difference with the German system.

QUESTIONS FOR FURTHER CONSIDERATION

1. Which of the national training systems considered is most like the British model and which the least? Support your answers with evidence.

2. Several of the governments of the countries considered in the chapter take a far more interventionist approach to training than UK, where in essence firms are free to decide for themselves the value they put on training, and indeed if they choose to train at all. What do you consider to be the appropriate role of government in directing the training effort of individual companies or industries?

3. The French *grande école* and the German *fachhochschule* attempt to put vocational education and training on a par with the more traditional academic routes offered in the university system. Does vocational education and training carry parity of esteem with traditional academic routes in the UK, and if not why not?

4. In the UK many institutions (possibly 100) offer MBA degrees for actual and aspiring managers. In the countries examined in the chapter the MBA is generally less common. Consider the reasons for this.

• REFERENCES •

Brewster C & Tyson S (1991)
INTERNATIONAL COMPARISONS IN HUMAN RESOURCE MANAGEMENT
London, Pitman.

Brewster C, Hegeswisch A, Holden L & Lockhart T (eds) (1992)
THE EUROPEAN HUMAN RESOURCE MANAGEMENT GUIDE
London, Academic Press.

Crabb S (1993)
Training in the Community
Personnel Management, Feb.

Johnson R (1990)
Are the British Qualified to Join Europe?
Personnel Management, May.

Johnson R (1991)
Europe Finds its True Vocation
Personnel Management, Aug.

Johnson R (1992)
TOWARDS 1992: VOCATIONAL QUALIFICATIONS IN THE MEMBER STATES OF THE EUROPEAN COMMUNITY AND MOVES TOWARDS AN OPEN MARKET
London, National Council for Vocational Qualifications, R&D Report No. 2.

Income Data Services / Institute of Personnel Management (1993)
EUROPEAN MANAGEMENT GUIDE: TRAINING
London, IPM.

Organization for Economic Cooperation and Development (1992)
EDUCATION AT A GLANCE: OECD INDICATORS
Paris, OECD.

Personnel Management (Feb. 1992–)
Personnel Management in . . .
Series covering personnel management in the European Union member states. London, Institute of Personnel Management.

Sparrow P & Hiltrop J-M (1994)
EUROPEAN HUMAN RESOURCE MANAGEMENT IN TRANSITION
Hemel Hempstead, Prentice-Hall.

Thurley K (1990)
Towards a European Approach to Personnel Management
Personnel Management, Oct.

UK Department of Education and Science (1991)
ASPECTS OF VOCATIONAL EDUCATION AND TRAINING IN THE FEDERAL REPUBLIC OF GERMANY
London, HMSO.

Van Resandt A W (ed.) (1991)
A GUIDE TO HIGHER EDUCATION SYSTEMS AND QUALIFICATIONS IN THE EUROPEAN COMMUNITY
London, Kogan Page.

•CHAPTER•

18

CONCLUSION

AS A RESULT OF STUDYING THIS CHAPTER YOU SHOULD BE ABLE TO:

- Consider some of the weaknesses of the HRM philosophy as it develops in organizations.

- Appreciate the range of challenges facing organizations (and hence HR practitioners).

- Identify the need for HR practitioners to work to develop their own skills, and be proactive in accepting the need for continuing professional development.

 If marketing is the business, people are the organization.

Alan Anderson, *Effective Personnel Management*

A cursory glance at the HR literature will reveal a profession that is not always confident in its role in the modern business organization. The stinging rebukes delivered by Drucker (1955), Tyson and Fell (1986) and Kuijpers (1995) (all detailed in chapter 1) and many others have hit home and exposed the difficulty that HR people have in demonstrating the bottom-line contribution that they are able to make. For many it is no longer sufficient to claim that the benefits of HR are intangible, or come in the longer term, or in ways that cannot easily be measured. More and more, line managers are being held accountable for their own actions, and not surprisingly also wish to take credit for the achievements of their staff. All this is consistent with the principles of HRM (and developed in chapter 1), but none the less makes the clear identification of the contribution of the HR professional more difficult.

More than ever the HR professional must develop expert skills, and must be able to demonstrate clearly how the use of those skills can contribute to the bottom-line performance of the organization. Throughout this book an attempt has been made to demonstrate how the various aspects of HR can be developed and evaluated – be it recruitment, training and development, performance management or welfare, all must be directed to the strategic objectives of the organization.

The HRM paradigm presents for many a new dynamic through which those concerned with making the best use of the human resources of an organization can work. However, criticisms of whether or not HRM presents a coherent vision for HR practitioners are commonplace. Among the criticisms are that HRM is not a coherent body of thought with predictive qualities that can be tested in a rigorous scientific way. This is of course a criticism often levelled at the social and behavioural sciences, and one within which such scientists have still been able to do much valid and reliable work. HRM, though, is neither a social nor behavioural science, it is a philosophy for workplace behaviour, attitude and practice, which utilizes and draws upon aspects of social and behavioural science. As such it is bound to fall foul of the next most commonly made criticism, that HRM manifests itself in different ways in different organizations and in different situations. It is unlikely that organizations in different sectors of the economy (private, public, not-for-profit), operating at different stages of production (primary, secondary, tertiary), at different stages of development (new businesses, mature businesses, declining businesses), employing very different mixes of employees (unskilled, semi-skilled, skilled, professional, etc.) could reasonably be expected to adopt a philosophy in a uniform manner. HRM must be seen as 'broad church', encompassing a wide range of interpretations and views, and yet still holding allegiance to what Harrison (1993: 35) argues is the core:

> HRM can be defined as the overall and coherent long-term planning and shorter term management, control and monitoring of an organization's human resources so as to gain from them the maximum added value and to best position them to achieve the organization's corporate goals and mission.

Harrison (1993: 67) illustrates and expands her definition with reference to MacKay and Torrington (1986) – HRM may well be:

> Directed towards the management needs for human resources to be provided and deployed, with a greater emphasis on planning, control and monitoring rather than on problem solving and mediation. It is totally identified with management interests and is relatively distant from the workforce as a whole.

Within these broad definitions there is much scope for local interpretation and adaption. A point of adaption that has caused some interest among the literature (see Legge 1989, for instance) is the tendency for some employers to take on only the 'hard' side of HRM – for instance, performance management and performance-related pay – while others focus more particularly on the 'softer' side of HRM – for instance, developing employees. To the purist, HRM in its truest sense requires the application of both the hard and soft sides of practice if the needs of the organization are to be congruent with the needs of the employee. An imbalance on one side or the other will not be sustainable in the long term, nor will it be compatible with the definitions provided by Harrison, MacKay and Torrington.

At the philosophical level HRM may offer more questions than answers for the HR manager who is charged with devising strategies to solve current problems as well as having an eye to the longer term. It is the hope that this text offers to actual or aspiring practitioners ready access to a range of techniques consistent with the HR philosophy and yet also consistent with the day-to-day needs of practice. While it is essential for HR practice to be developed and undertaken within a well-defined and thought-through policy, many of the ideas offered here can be adapted to a wide range of business situations. None the less, I still recommend that the practitioner takes time to explore the debates within HR, many of which are introduced at a basic level in this text.

In going about their business HR practitioners must be prepared more than ever to justify the value of their work, and this must involve applying to themselves many of the ideas explored here. Ideas of lifelong learning and on-going professional development must be actively explored and undertaken – indeed the Institute of Personnel and Development (IPD) requires (as a condition for on-going membership) that all members undertake, and keep a record of, at least 35 hours of 'continuing professional development' (CPD) each year. The IPD even supplies a computer package to all members to assist them in identifying their training needs, recording their achievements, and planning for the future. This practice is not inconsistent with those of other professional bodies.

Proactivity in personal development must translate to proactivity in professional activity. Kanter (1985: 142) identifies some of the qualities necessary in any manager who wishes to be 'innovative' or proactive in their work:

- Comfortable with change.
- Clarity of direction.
- Thoroughness.
- Participative management style.
- Persuasiveness, persistence and discretion.

These are clearly qualities that any HR manager would do well to develop and use in their work. Too often personnel / HR policies have lacked clarity, personnel / HR people have not been comfortable with change and have failed to persuade others.

The pressures on HR managers will not diminish, as elsewhere they are likely to grow, and the challenge to be innovative, participative and thorough to become ever greater. It is equally likely that pressures will come from new and unforeseen directions – this book has given considerable attention to Europe, but has singularly failed to address the challenges from elsewhere in the world, most notably the 'tiger' economies of the Pacific rim. These challenges are well-documented elsewhere, and cannot be ignored (*The Economist* regularly contains articles extolling the achievements of emerging far-eastern economies).

HRM developed out of the changing conditions and business environment of the 1970s (although some would trace its antecedents back to the 1950s). The changing business environment of the future will undoubtedly mean that HRM will also have to grow and develop. Amongst these ever-growing factors will be the greater need for flexibility of response, the casualization of the workforce and the concomitant need to incorporate such employees back into processes of consultation and planning, the challenge to develop innovative reward strategies to ensure that those whose contribution is most valued are best rewarded. International pressures will be ever greater, as will the expectations from the workforce for more challenging and demanding employment, particularly as we begin to see the results of a 30 per cent participation rate in higher education feed through into the workplace.

It is beyond doubt that the challenges offered by a better-educated workforce, less stability in employment and greater than ever levels of competition will keep HR issues, and therefore HR practitioners, to the fore for many years to come.

•REFERENCES•

Anderson A (1994)
EFFECTIVE PERSONNEL MANAGEMENT
Oxford, Blackwell.

Harrison R (1993)
HUMAN RESOURCE MANAGEMENT: ISSUES AND STRATEGIES
Wokingham, Addison Wesley.

Legge K (1989)
Human Resource Management: A Critical Analysis, in **NEW PERSPECTIVES ON HUMAN RESOURCE MANAGEMENT**
Storey J (ed.). London, Routledge.

MacKay L & Torrington D (1986)
THE CHANGING NATURE OF PERSONNEL MANAGEMENT
London, Institute of Personnel Management.

Kanter R Moss (1985)
THE CHANGE MASTERS: CORPORATE ENTREPRENEURS AT WORK
London, Allen & Unwin.

• CHAPTER •

19

APPENDIX: THE INFLUENCE OF THE EUROPEAN UNION

AS A RESULT OF STUDYING THIS CHAPTER YOU SHOULD BE ABLE TO:

- Appreciate the development of, and background to, what is now the European Union.

- Be aware of European legal institutions and legislative processes, their respective roles and their relationships to each other.

- Consider how decisions are made in Europe, and the influences and pressures that are brought to bear on the process of decision-making.

- Understand the implications for UK national law of European Directives and other forms of

- European law and regulation, as well as decisions made in the European Court of Justice.

- Appreciate the social dimension of the European Union, how social policy is formulated, how it impacts on the UK and how it relates to other aspects of the Union.

- Understand the major components of the Maastricht Treaty and the controversies that surround it, particularly the Social Protocol.

- Consider the likely future growth and development of the EU and the pressures that bear upon it and its institutions.

Note: this chapter draws heavily on the work of the Institute of Personnel and Development (IPD) as reported in *Personnel in Europe: Executive Brief*.

> *That Europe is nothin' on earth but a great big auction.*
>
> Tennessee Williams, *Cat on a Hot Tin Roof*

1. Introduction

The European Union which came about as a result of the 1991 Maastricht Treaty has its origins in the Treaty of Rome (1957) in which six countries – West Germany, France, Italy, the Netherlands, Belgium and Luxembourg – came together to form the European Economic Community. This provided for the creation of a common market by bringing down barriers to the movement of labour, goods, capital and services between member states. The Community was enlarged in 1973 when the United Kingdom, Ireland and Denmark joined, and expanded further in 1981 when Greece joined, followed in 1986 by Spain and Portugal. In 1995 Austria, Finland and Sweden joined, bringing the total membership to 15.

The early years of the Community were characterized by high rates of economic growth and close cooperation between the member states. But it is difficult to ascertain how much of this growth was a direct result of the Treaty and how much was due to Marshall Aid and the boom created by the need for post-war reconstruction. Certainly by the early 1980s many of the Community founder nations were of the opinion that progress towards economic union was slow and being hampered by the (then) requirement to achieve a unanimous agreement between all members for new proposals to be enacted. The expansion of the Community in the 1970s and 1980s served only to make this requirement for unanimity more difficult to achieve.

In 1985 a report produced by one of the then British Commissioners, Lord Cockfield, and subsequently adopted by the Commission, recommended that in order to speed up the creation of the single market the member states should adopt 282 specific measures designed to free up movement of goods, services, capital and people. The report was well received and became the Single European Act (SEA) in 1987. It was implemented in 1992. The SEA amended the original EEC Treaty and introduced several new legal bases into the Treaty – for example, Articles 100 and 118A, which relate, respectively, to employment matters and health and safety at work. The new legal bases introduced the idea of allowing the Community to introduce proposals by a qualified majority vote (70 per cent), rather than, as in the past, requiring unanimity.

The Single European Act and the measures that flowed from it (well over 500 to date) have promoted harmonization or mutual recognition of the laws of member states. This included the removal of many non-tariff barriers in areas such as food, hygiene, telecommunications and broadcasting, product manufacture, information technology, intellectual property, competition policy, consumer protection and external trade. Still more needs to be done to open up the market, particularly in the areas of research and development, foreign policy, agriculture, the environment, energy and social policy.

Many of the developments listed above will not have resulted in obvious changes for the consumer. Those which have, include the reduction of border checks on the movement of goods and people, revisions of the old VAT system that existed between states, the reduction of government curbs on airfares and opening up of competition in the skies, and the ability of banks to set up operations in any member state.

The Maastricht Treaty widened the scope of the Community to include inter-governmental cooperation between the 12 states on common foreign and security policy, justice and home affairs. It also paved the way for closer economic and political cooperation with the plan to introduce a single European currency by 1999. The United Kingdom, of course, has an opt-out from this particular proposal.

Today the European Union is the largest trading bloc in the world. It accounts for nearly 40 per cent of world trade. It has a population in excess of 370 million and a workforce that approaches 165 million.

2. The European Union Legislative Process

European law and policies are developed through its four main institutions, namely:

the Council of the European Union

the European Commission

the European Parliament

the European Court of Justice.

The four bodies do not exist in complete harmony. The Parliament, as the only elected body, wishes to have a wider role and often seeks to stretch its (democratic) wings. Currently its major role is to be consulted on proposals put forward by the Commission and then to scrutinize their implementation. Many would like to see the Commission reduce its role as the policy developer and concentrate on its role as the Union's Civil Service (in other words, concentrate more on implementation and monitoring). The European Court of Justice is the ultimate interpreter of the treaties on which Europe is based and the final arbiter of disputes concerning secondary legislation. Judgements made by the Court can have a considerable impact on the national policies of member states. (The UK government has fallen foul of the Court on a number of occasions.) The Council, meanwhile, has the real power but it has to be expressed through the rigid rules on voting. This rigidity (it is argued) has often been used to promote national interest at the expense of the interests of the Union.

2.1 The Council of the European Union
The Council is the Union's decision-making body and the most powerful of the four institutions. Its main task is to approve measures proposed by the Commission. Once approved the measure should be adopted by all member countries. The Council is multi-layered with each layer taking a different but complementary role.

The European Council – meets twice a year to discuss major issues and decide broad areas of policy. Its membership is made up of the heads of the 15 member states.

The Council of Ministers – is the occasion for national ministers holding common portfolios to come together to discuss and decide upon matters of common interest. The composition of the Council will depend upon the matter under discussion. When agriculture is the issue the 15 agriculture ministers will attend, when employment matters are under consideration the employment ministers will be present, and so on.

COREPER – Each member state has in Brussels a Committee of Permanent Representatives. This is in effect an embassy to the European Union. Members of the Committee carry out the detailed work on Commission proposals in advance of meetings of the Council of Ministers and will contribute to the briefing of their representative at the European Council.

Working Groups – representatives of national government departments and COREPER will hold preliminary negotiations on all proposals emanating from the Commission.

The Presidency of the Council is held by each state in turn for a period of 6 months. The UK last held the presidency between June and December 1992, and will hold it again in 1998.

Holding the presidency gives the member state concerned the opportunity (at least in part) to determine the Union agenda. However, it is held for only 6 months, and so any agenda must be a compromise between what has gone before and what is to come in the future, as well as the priorities of the holder.

2.2 The European Commission

The role of the Commission is to propose measures and to ensure their progression to legislation. In this sense it is both the executive body of the Union as well as its Civil Service. The President of the Commission (currently Jacques Santer of Luxembourg, previously Jacques Delors of France) holds a position of considerable influence and can do much to set the European agenda. The President is assisted by 19 other Commissioners who are nominated by the member states. The largest states send two Commissioners, the smaller only one. Each Commissioner is in charge of one of more policy-making divisions, called Directorates-General. These are responsible for developing policy and, once it is agreed, monitoring its implementation. Examples of the briefs held by Commissioners include Transport (Directorate General 16) and Social Policy (Directorate General 5). The British Commissioners are Sir Leon Brittan, who holds DG1 (External Trade Relations), and Neil Kinnock, who holds DG16 (Transport). Sir Leon has also been elected as one of the Vice-presidents of the Commission, Manuel Marin of Spain being the other.

Before any proposal put forward by a Commissioner can be adopted as Commission policy it must have the support of a simple majority of the 17 Commissioners.

2.3 The European Parliament

The European Parliament is the only European body directly elected by its citizens. Elections were most recently held in June 1994. Currently there are 567 members elected for a period of 5 years. The number of MEPs accorded to each nation is dependent upon population. So Germany, as the largest nation, has 99 members, the UK 87 and Ireland 15. The MEPs of Austria, Finland and Sweden are due to take their places later in 1996, bringing the total number to 626.

The Parliament has 20 specialist Committees. These examine in depth a whole range of issues. Essentially their role is one of scrutineer and critic. The Committees will report on the proposals put forward by the Commission. These reports are then debated at the Parliament's monthly plenary sessions. The report once debated and (if necessary) amended then becomes the official Parliamentary response to the Commission and its formal opinion.

Of all the European bodies the Parliament feels the most aggrieved. Although it is the only elected body, its powers are very limited. It is also treated with suspicion by (among others) the UK government. In recent years the Parliament has strove to carve a more creative and potent role for itself, usually without the full support of either the Commission or the Council, who both appreciate the benefits of maintaining the status quo.

2.4 The European Court of Justice

The Court will sit in ultimate judgement on disputes concerning European law and secondary legislation and is the final interpreter of the Treaties and Articles upon which the Union of Europe is based. Companies who have been fined by the Commission can appeal to the Court. The hearings of the court are in public but deliberations are undertaken in private. The Court produces its own reports containing the basic facts of the case, the summing up by an Advocate General and the judgement. The Court will also give preliminary rulings for the benefit of national courts. It may take proceedings against a member state if that state is not fulfilling its legal obligations. It reviews the legality of European Union Acts and it settles disputes.

Many of the routine cases are heard by the Court of First Instance, which is a subsidiary court. This is in order to reduce delay – notwithstanding which, the time taken to process and hear a case can be several years.

Each member state appoints a judge to serve for a 6-year period with the European Court. Additionally one extra judge is appointed by the large states in rotation, giving a total of 16. The judges are assisted by 6 Advocates General (one from each of the largest states, plus one appointed in rotation from the smaller states). The Advocates General deliver preliminary judgements on cases before they are put to the Court.

A judge can only be removed by the unanimous vote of colleagues. This effectively means that he or she is no longer considered fit to continue with his or her duties.

2.5 Other bodies

The Union has many other bodies and institutions with whom it will consult or to whom it will turn for advice when developing policy. The bodies include:

Specialist Technical Committees – these comprise experts from all member states who advise the Commission on technical issues. An example of such a committee would be the Health and Safety Advisory Panel.

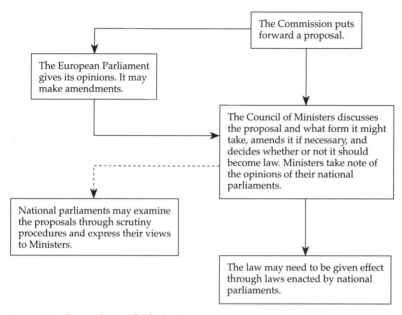

The Commission puts forward a proposal.

The European Parliament gives its opinions. It may make amendments.

The Council of Ministers discusses the proposal and what form it might take, amends it if necessary, and decides whether or not it should become law. Ministers take note of the opinions of their national parliaments.

National parliaments may examine the proposals through scrutiny procedures and express their views to Ministers.

The law may need to be given effect through laws enacted by national parliaments.

Source: Needham and Dransfield 1994.

Figure 19.1
Making European Union laws

The Economic and Social Committee – often shortened to ESC or ECOSOC, this committee must be consulted on all Commission proposals relating to economic and social affairs. Its membership includes representatives of consumers, trades unions and employers.

The Court of Auditors – responsible for auditing the Union budgets and the use of funds.

UNICE and ETUC – commonly referred to as 'The Social Partners' and comprising representatives of employer and union bodies from all member states. UNICE and ETUC are consulted on all matters relating to employment.

3. Decision-making in the EU

In essence the decision-making process for the Union is as follows: the Commission makes proposals, the proposals are debated and amended by the Parliament and are then adopted (or not) by the Council of Ministers (see figure 19.1).

The scope of the Union is limited by the Articles in the Treaty of Rome. That is to say, that the Union has no legitimate interest in areas that are not covered by the Treaty. The Treaty will also specify how all proposals should be processed. So, for example, proposals relating to employment rights are covered under Article 100 of the Treaty, while those relating to Health and Safety at Work are covered by Article 118A.

Under the process known as 'consultation' the proposal should receive one reading in the Parliament, and can only be adopted by the unanimous vote of the Council. Under the process of 'cooperation' two readings in Parliament are required and the measure can be adopted in the Council by qualified majority voting. Each Article of the Treaty of Rome will state how any proposals that fall within its scope should be actioned. Article 100 requires consultation, while Article 118A requires only cooperation.

Consultation requires unanimous agreement by the Council and therefore can be vetoed by any member. With cooperation (and what is known as qualified majority voting) votes are allocated to members roughly according to population. Therefore the larger countries (including the UK) have 10 votes each, while the smaller countries have fewer. For instance, Greece has 5, Denmark has 3 and Luxembourg only 2. A 'qualified majority' of the votes is achieved if 62 of the total 87 votes available are cast in favour of a proposal. Opposition from a minimum of 3 states is needed to block a proposal. Once the proposal is passed it should be implemented by all member states regardless of how they voted in the Council.

4. European Law

The laws of the European Union differ from the laws of the United Kingdom in several vital respects, but principally in that they are a body of statute law, paying scant regard to the common-law traditions of the UK. Essentially, European law is written down or codified. It is prescriptive in nature, detailing not only the principles of the law but also how it should be interpreted. In the UK there is a long tradition of not only having a less codified system of law but there are also the principles of common law – for example, reasonableness and equity – which can be used when there is no statute. Additionally, there is also a far stronger tradition of self-regulation in many industries, such as financial services.

The style of law adopted by the Union is that which was common among the original founders. It is based on Roman law and therefore follows a different tradition to English law. One of the practical implications for the UK is that the government is having to introduce statutory provision into areas in which such provision has not before existed, and that law is often in a form 'alien' to the British tradition – it is far more detailed and prescriptive.

European law comes in two main forms. The first form is from the Articles of the Treaty of Rome, many of which are directly applicable into national law. The other form of law is known as 'secondary' legislation, and this is based on an article of the treaty, but the form and substance of it will be negotiated and agreed by the member states before it is implemented, first into European law and then into national law. There are three forms of this secondary legislation:

Regulations: these apply directly and are binding on all member states.

Decisions: apply directly to the party or parties affected by them.

Directives: leave the method of implementation up to the member states, but are binding on all members. Generally, directives are incorporated into national law within a specified period, often two years.

The European Union also has a number of non-binding instruments. These tend to have a moral rather than a legal force, though they can be cited as evidence in court. They include Recommendations, Resolutions, Communications, Memoranda, Opinions and Declarations.

5. The Implications of European Law

- European Union law overrides national law.

- European law must be enforced by national courts.

- National courts can refer to the European Court of Justice, whose ruling will be binding on all member states.

- If a member state fails to implement European law complaints may be made (by individuals, companies, other states, pressure groups, etc.) to the Commission, who will investigate and may ask the member state for an explanation. If the infringement is not satisfactorily resolved or continues, the matter may be referred to the European Court of Justice, who may find against the state and pass a judgement ordering compliance. If individuals have been denied rights then compensation may be ordered.

- National law must be interpreted in line with any European law in that area.

6. Europe: The Social Dimension

It was never intended that the European Union would be merely a trading bloc. The founders always intended that it would also have a political and social dimension. The main instrument of social policy has been the Community Charter of the Fundamental Social Rights of Workers, which was adopted in 1989 by all members except the United Kingdom. The Charter, which has no legal force, is commonly known as the 'Social Charter'. It is a declaration by the Council and its aim was to highlight the significance that the majority of the members gave to social aspects of the community.

The Charter has as its objective the improvement of living and working conditions as well as ensuring a better and more effective use of human resources across the Community. The government of the UK did not sign up to the 12 principles enshrined in the Charter because it feared the result would be an increase in social and labour costs and a reduction in competitiveness. The Charter calls for a minimum level of basic employment rights across all member states with the aim of ensuring that:

a. The right of free movement within the Union is a reality.

b. Wages should be at a sufficient level to ensure that all workers enjoy a decent standard of living.

c. Workers have the right to join, or not to join, a trades union, to negotiate collectively and to take industrial action.

d. Workers have access to vocational training at all stages during their working lives.

e. The basic law on working time, employment of part-time and temporary workers, the provision of contracts of employment and redundancy is harmonized and improved.

f. All workers are protected by adequate social security provision.

g. Health and safety protection is improved.

h. Young workers are given access to training.

i. Information and consultation procedures are developed, taking into account national practices.

j. Policies and procedures are developed to ensure equal treatment and equal opportunities for men and women.

k. A sufficient income is guaranteed for the elderly.

l. Opportunities for the social and professional integration of people with learning disabilities are fully explored.

The Commission developed the Social Charter into the 1989 'Social Charter Action Programme'. From this the Commission developed many new proposals all based on Articles in the Treaty of Rome. If the proposals are approved by the Council then they will become part of European Union law (and will be applicable in the UK) despite the refusal of the UK government to sign the Social Charter.

7. The Maastricht Treaty

The 12 heads of the member states met in the town of Maastricht in 1991 at the end of the Dutch Presidency to discuss changes to the Treaty of Rome to provide for greater economic, monetary and political union.

Despite the wide varieties of opinion and interest present at the meeting, agreement was reached for most issues. The United Kingdom not only managed to negotiate an opt-out from the plan to introduce a single European currency by 1999, but also had many problems with the proposal to extend the Chapter on Social Policy to include more legal bases for Directives to harmonize employment law (instead of just Article 118A). This proposal was rejected by the UK government. It was not prepared to extend the remit of the European Union on social matters beyond the provisions of Articles 100 and 118A of the EEC Treaty. However, the other 11 members agreed to adopt the extensions to the Social Chapter as a separate agreement. This is contained in the Social Protocol, which is an attachment to the Treaty on European Union (the Maastricht Treaty).

The Social Protocol allows the original 11 (i.e. excluding Britain), and now the 14, to harmonize their employment laws using the Union's institutions and processes without being dependent upon the Articles of the original Treaty. The proposed harmonization can take place (via qualified majority voting – for this purpose a reduced 52 out of 77 votes) in the following areas:

Working conditions.

Information and consultation of workers.

Health and safety.

Equal opportunities and equal treatment for men and women.

The integration of people excluded from the labour market.

Harmonization of laws may also take place by unanimous vote in the following areas:

Social security and the protection of workers.

Protection of workers where contracts of employment are terminated.

Representation and collective defence of interests of employers and workers, this to include co-determination, conditions of employment for non-EU nationals currently resident in a member country, and financial contributions for job creation and the promotion of employment.

Although the UK did not sign up to the Social Protocol it is unlikely that it will be able to avoid entirely any proposals for change made under the areas listed above. The Commission has stated that it intends to (whenever possible) put forward its proposals via the original Treaty and, therefore, Articles 100 and 118A. It is only where opposition from the UK would stop such a proposal going through that the Social Protocol would be used as a basis for action.

8. An Expanding Union

The Union now has 15 members, with Austria, Finland and Sweden joining most recently in January 1995. Additionally, Iceland, Norway and Liechtenstein are members of the Single Market and as part of the European Economic Area Agreement are subject to all single market legislation and most employment legislation. They are not, however, full EU members.

The Commission is also looking at the applications of Cyprus, Malta, Poland and Hungary, who wish to join, and the Czech Republic, Slovakia, Bulgaria and Romania, who have also indicated their wish to join but have yet to make formal application.

The EU has formal trade agreements with Estonia, Latvia and Lithuania as well as Russia and the Ukraine.

There are three criteria for membership:

that the applying country is part of Europe;

that the country is democratic;

that the country is economically developed.

The implications of a larger Union are many, but include a greater strain on the institutions, on the composition of the Commission and on the voting systems within the Council, particularly the ability of any one member to veto many of the proposals that come before the Council. These will need to be reviewed as membership increases, but Britain has stated that it will veto any attempt to do away with the veto. Some see the opportunity to widen the Union as a chance to thwart the wishes of those who would see it deepened.

The UK exercised its opt-out from the Social Protocol of the Maastricht Treaty for the first time on 22 September 1994. The European Commission had put forward to the Council of Ministers a proposal to extend to parents the right to three months' unpaid paternity leave upon the birth of their offspring. A compromise proposal, put forward by the Commission's German President, to delay the implementation of the plan until the end of 1998, was also rejected by the UK's Employment Secretary, Michael Portillo. His refusal to give way on the proposals forced the other 11 European Union ministers to concede that they would have to bring in the new laws themselves. The proposal had been put forward under Article 100 of the Treaty of Rome which requires a unanimous vote of all members of the Council before implementation. The rejection by the UK means that the proposals will now only be implemented by the 11 member states who signed up to the Social Protocol of the Maastricht Treaty.

In defending his decision Mr Portillo stated that Britain could not accept a plan which would raise employers' costs and discourage them from taking on more workers at a time of high unemployment in Europe. He also claimed that Britain's maternity provisions were among the best in Europe, but said that the government was against extending statutory rights to parental leave to fathers. Many fathers, he said, were using holiday entitlement to take time off when their children were born. High labour costs, he claimed, were damaging European competitiveness, and governments had to be very careful about imposing extra burdens on business, however socially desirable the measure might be.

Mr Padraig Flynn, the Social Affairs Commissioner, said that he had hoped that Britain would accept the compromise put forward by Germany, but conceded that the proposal would now have to be brought forward under the Social Chapter.

Earlier in the day Mr Portillo had again used Britain's opt-out as the other 11 employment ministers voted to force multinational companies to set up works councils to inform and consult their employees. Mr Portillo said the laws were inflexible, bureaucratic and would slow down the decision-making process in companies forced to comply.

TASK
The British press mostly took the Commission's proposal to mean 'paternity' rights. Closer reading shows that it refers to no such thing. It instead offered <u>parents</u> the right to three months' unpaid leave from their jobs upon the birth of a child. The proposal was adopted by the other 11 member states. Consider the validity of Michael Portillo's arguments.

1. The Social Protocol agreement annexed to the Maastricht Treaty will provide all European Union member states, except the UK, with a new legal basis for harmonizing their employment regulations. Consider the advantages that the UK might have enjoyed had we signed up to the Social Protocol. What advantages do we enjoy by being outside of the Protocol and what implications might this have for our European partners?

2. There has been discussion that those countries who wish to press ahead with closer political and economic integration might form what has been called the 'core' of Europe, while those who are more reluctant might become more of a 'periphery'. What implications might this have for the UK? Can the UK continue to be sceptical about closer integration while still expressing a desire to 'remain at the heart of Europe'?

3. Europe and its institutions generally get a bad press in the UK. Why do you consider that this is so? Is the criticism justified, and what can be done to improve the image of 'Europe' in the eyes of the British public?

4. British business has consistently shown itself to be more enthusiastic about Europe, the single currency and the Social Chapter than has the British government. Why do you believe this to be so?

•REFERENCES•

Beardwell I & Holden L (1994)
HUMAN RESOURCE MANAGEMENT: A CONTEMPORARY PERSPECTIVE
London, Pitman.

Brewster C, Hegeswisch A, Holden L & Lockhart T (eds) (1992)
THE EUROPEAN HUMAN RESOURCE MANAGEMENT GUIDE
London, Academic Press.

Cecchini P (1988)
THE COST OF NON EUROPE
Brussels, The European Commission.

Cecchini P (1989)
THE BENEFITS OF THE SINGLE MARKET
London, Philip Allen.

Gibbs P (1992)
DOING BUSINESS IN THE EUROPEAN COMMUNITY
London, Kogan Page.

Institute of Personnel and Development (1995)
PERSONNEL IN EUROPE: EXECUTIVE BRIEF
London, IPD (Oct.).

KPMG Peat Marwick
EUROPE 1992: TRENDS, DEVELOPMENTS IN HUMAN RESOURCE MANAGEMENT
London, KPMG Peat Marwick.

Leighton P (1990)
EUROPEAN LAW AND ITS IMPACT ON UK EMPLOYERS
IMS, Sussex University.

Needham D & Dranesfield R (1994)
BUSINESS STUDIES
Cheltenham, Stanley Thorne.

Personnel Management and *Personnel Management Plus*
Published monthly by the Institute of Personnel and Development, both regularly contain 'Eurofile' columns.

Preston J (ed.) (1992)
CASES IN EUROPEAN BUSINESS
London, Pitman.

Society of Chief Personnel Officers in Local Government
THE SINGLE MARKET: PERSONNEL IMPLICATIONS
London, SCPOLG.

TREATIES ESTABLISHING THE EUROPEAN COMMUNITY TREATY ON EUROPEAN UNION
London, HMSO.

UK Department of Trade and Industry; various publications including:
THE SINGLE MARKET: THE FACTS
EUROPE OPEN FOR PROFESSIONS
GUIDE TO SOURCES OF ADVICE
TRADE WITH EUROPE
THE UNITED KINGDOM EXPORT SERVICE
London, DTI.

Welford R & Prescott K (1992)
EUROPEAN BUSINESS: AN ISSUES BASED APPROACH
London, Pitman.

Institute of Personnel Management / Income Data Services
1992: **PERSONNEL MANAGEMENT AND THE SINGLE EUROPEAN MARKET**
London, IPM / IDS.

Useful Sources of Information on the European Union

COMMISSION OF THE EUROPEAN COMMUNITIES

Provide free information on most aspects of Europe. Their free publications include:

The Week in Europe (general news bulletin)
Finance from Europe
Guide to the European Community Programmes
plus many guides / factsheets / reports, etc.

The Commission can be contacted on the following numbers:

Belfast	01232–240708
Cardiff	01222–371631
Dublin	(010)–353–1671–2244
Edinburgh	0131–225–2058
London	0171–973–1992

The Brussels office of the Commission is 010–295–235–5177, and has much additional information and many free guides. Its address is:

200 Rue de la Loi
B-1049 Brussels

THE EUROPEAN PARLIAMENT

Information about the European Parliament can be obtained from:

The European Parliament Information Office
2 Queen Anne's Gate
London SW1H 9AA
tel. 0171–222–0411

DTI BUSINESS IN EUROPE HOTLINE

tel. 01272–444888

Information on Centres for European Business Information, including the Small and Medium Enterprises Task Force, may be obtained from any of 26 regional offices around the country. These include:

London 0171–828–6201
Glasgow 0141–221–0999
Cardiff 01222–229525
Belfast 01232–491031
Dublin (010)–353–695011

For a comprehensive list of sources, services and contacts the DTI Single Market 'Guide to Sources of Advice' and 'Brussels Can You Hear Me' are very useful.

INDEX